Regulatory Capitalism

Regulatory Capitalism
How it Works, Ideas for Making it Work Better

John Braithwaite

Australian National University

With a Foreword by David Levi-Faur

Edward Elgar
Cheltenham, UK • Northampton, MA, USA

© John Braithwaite, 2008

All rights reserved. No part of this publication may be reproduced, stored in a retrieval system or transmitted in any form or by any means, electronic, mechanical or photocopying, recording, or otherwise without the prior permission of the publisher.

Published by
Edward Elgar Publishing Limited
Glensanda House
Montpellier Parade
Cheltenham
Glos GL50 1UA
UK

Edward Elgar Publishing, Inc.
William Pratt House
9 Dewey Court
Northampton
Massachusetts 01060
USA

A catalogue record for this book
is available from the British Library

ISBN 978 1 84720 002 0 (cased)

Printed and bound in Great Britain by MPG Books Ltd, Bodmin, Cornwall

Contents

Foreword by David Levi-Faur		vii
Preface		xi
1	Neoliberalism or regulatory capitalism?	1
2	The cyclical nature of the challenges of regulatory capitalism	32
3	Privatized enforcement and the promise of regulatory capitalism	64
4	The nodal governance critique of responsive regulation	87
5	Regulatory capitalism, business models and the knowledge economy *Janet Hope, Dianne Nicol and John Braithwaite*	109
6	Can regulatory ritualism be transcended?	140
7	Metagovernance of justice	157
8	Is regulatory capitalism a good thing?	197
References		208
Index		233

Foreword

The way capitalism is organized and governed is changing. A regulatory explosion – the proliferation of different mechanisms of control at both the national and global level – is balancing the effects of neoliberal reforms and is creating a new global order that is characterized in important ways by regulation, regulocrats, regulatory agencies and regulatory networks. The widespread expansion of regulation is rather striking and puzzling. In an era of liberalization, privatization and deregulation, the number, forms and sources of regulation were expected to be on the decline. Convergence on liberalization as a system *sans*-regulation was portrayed as the desired outcome by some and a horror scenario by others. The possibility that change will result with more regulation and that étatist forms of regulation will be mainly accompanied with international and voluntary forms of regulation was not on the agenda. By the early 1990s scholars had started to point out that deregulation was really a misnomer for the emerging reforms. Instead they had suggested that the notions of 'better regulation', '*re*regulation' and 'international regulation' best captured the change.

What we are learning to better appreciate nowadays is that the notion of 'regulatory explosion' captures and conveys better the nature and the implications of the changing political, social and economic environment in the age of governance. The evidence is only slowly accumulating through various indicators. My own attention and awareness of the phenomenon grew from a study of the restructuring of the modern bureaucracy and the rise of regulocracy as an alternative form of governing. In a study with Jacint Jordana of regulatory agencies across 16 different sectors in 49 countries from the 1920s through to 2002, we found that the number of regulatory agencies rose sharply in the 1990s (see Figures F.1 and F.2). Indeed, the rate of establishment increased dramatically: from fewer than five new autonomous agencies per year from the 1960s to the 1980s, to more than 20 per year from the 1990s to 2002 (peaking at almost 40 agencies per year between 1994 and 1996). By the end of 2002, we could identify an autonomous regulatory agency in about 60 per cent of the possible sector niches in the 49 countries. Probably more than anything else, it was the establishment of these agencies that made the regulatory state an attractive term for social scientists.

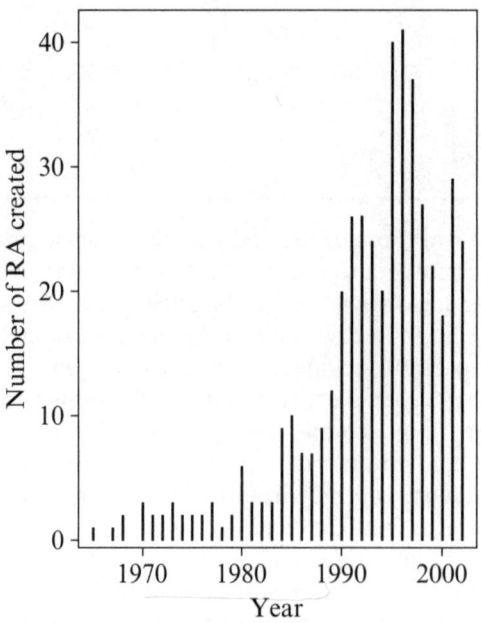

Figure F.1 Expansion of the number of regulatory agencies across 16 sectors of 49 nations, 1960–2002

Taken exclusively on its own, the widespread creation of regulatory agencies may indicate a restructuring of the state or even the rise of 'a regulatory state'. Yet, the explosion in the number of regulatory agencies is *only* part of a wider phenomena and the simultaneous expansion of the regulatory society and global regulations. As a matter of fact the co-expansion of voluntary as well as coercive regulation, national and global, civil and statist all testify to the shortcoming of a focus on the transformation of the state. The notion of 'regulatory capitalism' captures much better the changes around us than the notion of a 'regulatory state' which denotes a state-centred perspective. Regulatory capitalism is a political, economic and social order where regulation, rather than the direct provision of public and private services, is the expanding part of government. In this new order legal forms of domination are increasingly conditioned by functional rather than territorial considerations, and power is allocated and regulated along functional demarcation lines. The distribution of power, and the corresponding form of interest intermediation in each arena, are therefore shaped by the particular interaction of civil and state forms of regulation and may result with varying degrees of social, economic and political effectiveness and legitimacy.

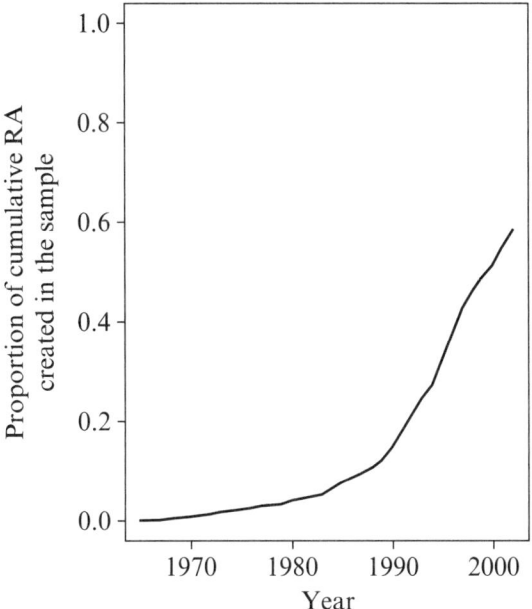

Figure F.2 Increase in the proportion of regulatory agency niches filled for 16 sectors across 49 nations, 1960–2002

On this background it is not surprising that the study of regulation and governance, once fragmented across disciplines and subject areas, has emerged at the cutting edge of paradigmatic change in the social sciences. Regulation, especially in its soft decentred and fragmented forms, becomes a major issue on the agenda of disciplines that deal with international relations, international political economy, global governance, international relations and international law, institutional economics, public administration, public policy and comparative politics. Scholars from disciplines with well-established interest in regulation such as Law and Society, Law and Economics, Criminology and American political development are increasingly finding themselves interacting with a legion of scholars from other disciplines.

Some of the interest in the study and effects of regulation can be safely ascribed to the rise of regulation and rule making as a major form of governance. Much of the rest is due to the contribution and inspiration of John Braithwaite's scholarship and his personal qualities. John's work, which does not respect disciplinary boundaries, places regulation both as a core concept, and as a major puzzle for the social sciences. The success of this project may affect not only the study of regulation but also the scientific standing of the social sciences more generally. This book suggests that we can be cautiously optimistic about our ability to overcome the challenges ahead of us.

David Levi-Faur
The Hebrew University,
Jerusalem

Preface

In the 1990s people started recognizing that while the state was running fewer things, it was regulating more of them, and spending ever higher proportions of its budget on regulation. So some analysts (including me) started talking about the state as a regulatory state. Then it was recognized that many other organizational actors beyond the state were also doing a lot more regulating of other organizations than in the past, so some analysts (including me) spoke of a regulatory society. Along came David Levi-Faur and Jacint Jordana to point out that capitalist markets had become more vibrant at the same time as regulation of markets had become more earnest.

Not only did they coin a term, 'regulatory capitalism', that better captured the realities than the 'regulatory state' or 'regulatory society', they also produced a large body of cross-national data on the global expansion of privatized markets and regulatory institutions. David's foreword to this book gives the flavour of these data. At the Australian National University (ANU) we established a Regulatory Institutions Network to study this phenomenon. David Levi-Faur joined us as a Faculty member for a period, Jacint Jordana as a Visiting Fellow. They proved delightful and stimulating members of our intellectual community. David proposed that we start a new journal called *Regulation & Governance*, which we set up with Cary Coglianese as a Co-editor and Jacint Jordana as a member of the Editorial Board.

We said in the promotional blurb for the new journal: 'Research on regulation and governance, once fragmented across various disciplines and subject areas, has emerged at the cutting edge of paradigmatic change in the social sciences.' The notion that the kind of globalizations that had evolved by 1980, the kind of societies we now live in, are regulatory capitalist, rather than neoliberal or welfare states, is an example of the kind of reframing of social science agendas this new field is stimulating. The long journey of Western history of the past millennium is from feudalism to regulatory capitalism (so far), with liberalism, neoliberalism, the welfare state, fascism and communism all re-theorized herein as significant sidetracks of modest duration within that long history of the West.

With the exception of three decades of Chinese communism, these are Western sidetracks that the South and East have not followed in long or large ways. Levi-Faur and Jordana's work shows graphically (for example, Figures F.1 and F.2) that regulatory capitalism in contrast is something that in its first three decades has expanded remarkably rapidly beyond the West. Chapter 2, for example, discusses how waves of scandal and reform on Wall Street create large ripples of regulatory reform in China. Obversely, while Asian financial crises do not ripple much reform back to the West, in the regulatory capitalist era, unlike previous eras, they do at least ripple regulatory reform right across Asia. Most villages in Africa and New Guinea may be almost totally cut off from this globalizing phenomenon as sites of production, but not of consumption and trade. Hence, Africans and New Guineans have potentially much more to gain than Europeans from the globalization of open-source biotechnology as considered in Chapter 5 because their health and productive systems are the most vulnerable to decimation by the globalization of disease in forms such as HIV-AIDS.

While the globalization of business regulation has a long history (Braithwaite and Drahos 2000), in domains that are central to the constitution of networked knowledge capitalism, such as competition policy and intellectual property regulation, most of the globalization has occurred since 1990. The majority of the world's states have only begun to take the enforcement of competition law and intellectual property law as institutional priorities since 1990. *Global Business Regulation* (Braithwaite and Drahos 2000) was a book that attempted to explain *how* what we now call regulatory capitalism globalized through a variety of mechanisms such as modelling. This book does not return to that full story; rather, it seeks to identify some patterns in regulatory capitalism and what they imply for how we might struggle to make it work better.

The traditional social science disciplines are not well prepared to come to grips with globalizing networking because of their preoccupations only with geographically bounded national societies, or political systems, or economies, legal systems, business systems, philosophical systems, cultures and identities, macro-international relations, micro-individual action or individual psyches. We must draw on all of these and more to understand regulatory capitalism. It has an ecology of patterned niches. It has an evolutionary history, codes and architectures, including micro-codes that may not be molecular, rather values and motivational postures that are recurrently patterned in response to regulatory institutions (Braithwaite 2008). Integration of knowledge at this level is not the way of the social sciences, yet it is the way the organization of scholarly communities in the biological sciences has accomplished huge strides in recent decades.

Regulation has certainly proved a rewarding field of research for me. It has attracted many inspiring PhD students and postdoctoral fellows. My passion for the subject must be pathological, as I notice that of the small number of really close friends I have, the majority are my co-authors of books on regulation! I have enjoyed so much learning and love from them. Now I have decided to get a life and instead dedicate myself to fieldwork and books on peace-building (albeit that draw on regulatory theory!). Twenty-five years ago I wrote in the preface to a book that this would be my last book on regulation or crime. I moved away from the world of research and teaching to take a position in the Australian consumer movement, which I found most rewarding. But Valerie Braithwaite, who always seems to have a better understanding of where I am heading than I do myself, insisted on the deletion of this last book reference. This time Val has not censored the Preface, so it really will be the case that any future books will be on peace-building. I therefore have used this book to pull a lot of my work together as a small contribution to the rich conversation on regulation that now abounds in the universities of the world.

Some pages and bits of pages have been taken here and there from previous work. There is an amount of self-reference at which more humble scholars would shudder in shame. The works I have most drawn upon are:

Braithwaite, J. (1984), *Corporate Crime in the Pharmaceutical Industry*, London: Routledge & Kegan Paul.
Braithwaite, J. (2002), *Restorative Justice and Responsive Regulation*, New York: Oxford University Press.
Braithwaite, J. (2004), 'Methods of power for development: weapons of the weak, weapons of the strong', *Michigan Journal of International Law*, **26**(1), 298–330.
Braithwaite, J. (2005), *Markets in Vice, Markets in Virtue*, New York and Sydney: Oxford and Federation Press.
Braithwaite, J. (2006), 'The regulatory state'? in R. Rhodes (ed.), *Handbook of Political Institutions*, Oxford: Blackwell.
Braithwaite J. (2006), 'Responsive regulation and developing economies', *World Development*, **34**(5), 884–98.
Braithwaite, J. (2007), 'Contestatory citizenship; deliberative denizenship', in G. Brennan, R. Goodin and M. Smith (eds), *Common Minds: Essays in Honour of Philip Pettit*, Oxford: Oxford University Press.
Braithwaite, J., T. Makkai and V. Braithwaite (2007), *Regulating Aged Care: Ritualism and the New Pyramid*, Cheltenham: Edward Elgar.

But this is not just, not mainly, a book that synthesizes an old body of research in a new way. No chapter has been previously published and every one of them is mostly a fresh contribution to the new theme of regulatory capitalism. I really am grateful to David and Jacint for how I have been stimulated and energized by their way of seeing contemporary globalization as on a trajectory towards regulatory capitalism. Indeed, I am grateful for the stimulus from the whole wonderful community of scholars who have passed through ANU over the past few decades. That community has been strewn with fine human beings and fine minds. In specific chapters, I acknowledge individual appreciation that is due to many of them. Special thanks to Leah, Celeste, Brian, Val and the family for their day-to-day kindness, tolerance and support, to Peter and Jean for being so careful with the references and indexing, and to Edward Elgar and all of his helpful and professional staff, particularly Caroline Cornish and Alexandra O'Connell. Without the Australian Research Council, the work would not have been possible. Without my University of Tasmania colleague Dianne Nicol, and my RegNet colleague Janet Hope, Chapter 5 would never have happened.

John Braithwaite
Canberra

1. Neoliberalism or regulatory capitalism?[1]

REGULATION AND NETWORKED GOVERNANCE

States can be thought of as providing, distributing and regulating.[2] They bake cakes, slice them, and proffer pieces as inducements to steer events. Regulation is conceived as that large subset of governance that is about steering the flow of events, as opposed to providing and distributing.[3] Of course, when regulators regulate, they often steer the providing and distributing that regulated actors supply. We build on Jacint Jordana and David Levi-Faur's (2003; 2004) systematic evidence that, since 1980, states have become rather more preoccupied with the regulation part of governance and less with providing.[4] Yet non-state regulation has grown even more rapidly, so it is not best to conceive of the era in which we live as one of the regulatory state, but of regulatory capitalism (Levi-Faur 2005a). This involves expansion of the scope, arenas, instruments and depth of regulation (Levi-Faur et al. 2005). Levi-Faur (2005a) identifies transitions from laissez-faire capitalism (1800s–1930s) to welfare capitalism (1930s–1970s) to regulatory capitalism (1970s on). This chapter seeks to refine somewhat the transitions from feudalism to more welfarist and regulatory capitalisms.

Governance is a wider set of control activities than government. Students of the state noticed that government has shifted from 'government of a unitary state to governance in and by networks' (Bevir and Rhodes 2003: 1; Rhodes 1997). But because the informal authority of networks in civil society not only supplements but also supplants the formal authority of government, Bevir, Rhodes and others in the networked governance tradition (notably Castells 1996) see it as important to study networked governance for its own sake, rather than as simply a supplement to government. Lazer (2005) has theorized regulatory capitalism as a networked order where diffusion mechanisms account for spread in the scope and depth of regulation (see also Busch et al. 2005; Gilardi 2005; Meseguer 2005; Post 2005; Way 2005; Ramsay 2006).

Corporations have also been transformed into networks. Top-down design of strategy invites failure in the face of diverse market dynamics in different parts of the globe. Information technology now allows the decentralized

1

retrieval of information about market dynamics from different points in space and time and the integration of this information into flexible systems of strategy-making and flexible production systems. Small and medium businesses increasingly link across borders with large corporations to form endlessly adapting networks. 'Thus, the actual operating unit becomes the business project, enacted by a network, rather than individual companies or formal groupings of companies' (Castells 1996: 117). Companies that fail to adapt to these new possibilities in the networked economy cease to dominate global markets. So the information age is one where we find a lot of hollowed-out corporations: 'lean' businesses that specialize in intermediation between financing, production and sales on the back of an established brand. Similarly we see growing numbers of hollowed non-governmental organizations (NGOs) that have shifted their energies from being influential through building a large membership to influence mediated by nimble networking (Skocpol 2003). States that fail to adapt to the possibilities for networked governance fail to dominate global governance. Dorf and Sabel (1998) use the way the Pentagon creates competing collaborations of private and public partners at different levels of a project (for example, weapon, targeting information technology [IT], delivery vehicle) so that in the end the best set of private–public collaborations for each segment of the project might be integrated into the best whole-of-project integration.

Warfare is one of many governance functions that became increasingly networked during the era of regulatory capitalism. If the enemy is better able than you to integrate a diaspora of local factions and warlords onto their side of the struggle, then you are likely to lose, as the Soviet Union found in Afghanistan. As Chapter 5 explores, and 'as Microsoft has found, there is no good monopolistic solution to a mature open-source effort' (Robb 2005: A35). In a networked society, the soft power of networks can move around hard monopolies of power. John Robb (2005) characterizes radical Islam's insurgency against the West as an open-source war. This is what is making it difficult for superpower monopoly of ultimate force to defeat it. It would be easier to defeat Al Qaeda were it organized hierarchically like Cosa Nostra families whose minions would fall away when all the leadership group were captured or killed. Instead, violent jihadists operate by putting on the Internet 'source code' on how to make bombs, how to infiltrate mosques, how to commit suicide in a way that gives you access to countless virgins, and how to educate others on why it is virtuous to do these things. Unknown readers of these 5000-odd websites (Packer 2006) are encouraged to innovate in how and where to find new recruits unknown to Western intelligence, to innovate in how they execute their own fundraising and their own attacks, and to pass on their innovative idea so that, for example, it might be used in simultaneous attacks before targets are hardened against the innovation. Dominant states face a challenge in learning how to complement their monopoly of superior firepower with open-source warfare capabilities if they are to defeat violent jihadists.[5]

Networked governance means a shift in both the private and public sector from Fordist control of a systematically specialized, broken-down production system to post-Fordist steering of more volatile systems that are partially contracted out and partly contracted in to shifting collaborative groups that compete for growth with outsiders and insiders. According to Dorf and Sabel (1998), this competition is part of the error-detection system; work groups watch for flaws in the work of competing groups so they can show how their output can surpass the benchmarks set by these competitors. Excellence is grounded in collaboration, detection of poor performance in competition. Everyone is learning how to continuously improve by monitoring everyone else. Monitoring and steering are therefore not only top-down. Twenty-first-century production methods institutionalize more participatory and complex forms of self-regulation of production of public goods as well as private ones.

At the time of his germinal writings Frederick von Hayek (1944) may well have been wrong that central state planning could not work because states would never have satisfactory local knowledge of what was needed. A large Westphalian state, Hayek believed, lacks contextual wisdom in its top-down planning, is incapable of the synoptic wisdom to understand how the economy works. So he prescribed spontaneous ordering through the price signals of the market as a better institutional design than state planning. In conditions of Fordist production, it is doubtful whether Hayek was right. In the capitalist world, coordinated market economies seem to do better in certain market niches than liberal market economies (and vice versa) (Hall and Soskice 2001). As the World Bank's (1993) East Asian Miracle report documented, the late industrializing states of Asia did so through a developmental state model, as Japan did after the Meiji Restoration in the nineteenth century, that involved quite a heavy hand of state planning. The Soviet economy seemed to grow faster than the West for most of its existence up to the 1970s (Castells 2000: 5–67). German national socialism also seemed a formidable production machine in the mid-twentieth century. The German and Russian war production capabilities seemed so formidable during the heyday of industrial capitalism that, had they been turned against the Franco–Anglo–American capitalist axis, instead of turned against each other on the Russian front, it would have been the economies with the greater centralized planning capabilities that would have prevailed against the more liberal economies.

According to Castells, the Soviet economy and the Soviet war machine finally fell behind the West not because it could not manage industrialism but because it could not manage an information economy. Just as on Clegg's (1989: 248) analysis late medieval towns were nodes that prised open cracks in feudal circuits of power, so dot.com companies might be conceived as nodes of private governance that had the unintended effect of splitting open the industrial and military power of the Soviet bloc. An information economy cannot be centrally planned; it can only be centrally facilitated and coordinated. Indeed, as Chapter 5 suggests, it might do better with an open-source design, with a management system closer to wikipedia than the *Encyclopaedia Britannica*. The ideas, the networked connections, the new directions, come more from below.

PLAN OF THE CHAPTER

The first section of the chapter argues that regulatory capitalism is not about neoliberalism. Those who think we are in an era of neoliberalism are mistaken. The historical forces that have produced regulatory capitalism are then sketched as a police economy that evolved from various feudal economies, the supplanting of police with an unregulable nineteenth-century liberal economy, then the state provider economy (rather than the 'welfare state') that gives way to regulatory capitalism. In the era of regulatory capitalism, more of the governance that shapes the daily lives of most citizens is corporate governance than state governance. The corporatization of the world is both a product of regulation and the key driver of regulatory growth, indeed of state growth more generally. The big conclusion of the chapter is that the reciprocal relationship between corporatization and regulation creates a world in which there is more governance of all kinds. 1984 did arrive. The interesting normative question then becomes whether this growth in hybrid governance contracts freedom, or expands positive liberty through an architecture of separated powers that check and balance state and corporate dominations. The chapter sets up this quandary of our time, it does not answer it. In the final chapter of the book we take some small steps towards an answer.

THE NEOLIBERAL FAIRYTALE

A widely believed chronology, on the left and the right, is that from the end of the 1970s neoliberalism conquered the world (Chomsky 1999). 'What is neoliberalism?' asks Bourdieu (1998: 2), 'A programme for destroying collective structures which may impede the pure market logic.' In the Foucauldian tradition, the methodological prescription is to study neoliberalism as a programme rather than as a reality. Of course it is possible, indeed likely, that neoliberalism as a programme has all sorts of real, unintended effects on the world without actually creating a neoliberal world. My interest in this section, however, is limited to whether neoliberalism has become an institutional reality. Institutionally, neoliberalism means privatization, deregulation, including a deregulated international trade regime, and a diminished public sphere. During the 1970s, according to one conventional chronology, the Keynesian welfare state that we had known since the New Deal died. Hayek, a scorned intellectual for most of his life, replaced Keynes as the ascendant inspiration of political economy (Peters 1999). Not only had Keynes been sidelined, the dominant intellectual alternative to him in the academy – Marx – was also about to wither away. The fairytale continues that decisive political moments for this tumultuous change in the world of ideas were the election of Margaret Thatcher in the UK in 1979 and Ronald Reagan in the US in 1980. The Hayekian prescriptions of these leaders were for small government, privatization and deregulation. The revolution quickly seemed complete when Labor governments in Australia and New Zealand in the early 1980s bought in to policies of privatization and deregulation as then did many European states. Indeed, New Zealand took these to greater heights than seen in Thatcher's Britain, just as Ireland later took her low corporate tax policies to deeper lows. The lessons of Labor in the Antipodes were not lost at the Metropoles. It was necessary for Blair and Clinton to be New Labour, New Democrats, not 'tax and spend' social democrats. The leadership was English-speaking; it was not until the late 1990s that the German social democrats seized power after they learnt to be 'New'.

The 'Chicago boys'[6] were sending missionaries to places like Latin America as well. The leadership of the likes of Carlos Menem in Argentina was lionized by the International Monetary Fund (IMF) as demonstrating the neoliberal path out of underdevelopment. Short-lived improvements in the performance of countries such as Argentina and New Zealand, which had been the developed economies that had performed worst during the provider state era, were not interpreted by neoliberal missionaries as regression to the mean, but as fundamentally effective transformations. When they started performing worse than more regulated economies, the IMF, oblivious, continued to tout their virtues. Some thought this showed that Keynes was right after all – that there was nothing so influential as the ideas of a dead economy.[7]

Ignoring the fact that the Soviet economy had outperformed the US and UK for most of the industrial capitalist era from the First World War to 1970 (Castells 2000: 10–19), Reagan and Thatcher believed that their military and economic strength so persuaded Gorbachev that socialist economies could never work that, well, he just gave up and ultimately handed over the keys of the Soviet economy to the Margaret Thatcher Foundation and other Anglo-Saxon neoliberal missionaries.[8] This was the 'End of history' (Fukuyama 1989). Neoliberalism was now the 'Washington consensus'. Once the entire Second World had signed up to the Washington consensus, one by one Third World nations fell into line, pushed by the IMF to hire consultants from New Zealand to explain how they had seen the light.

China was a minor exception! But Tiananmen Square in 1989 showed that it was only a matter of time before China realized that neoliberalism would fix its economic malaise, just as it was fixing Russia. Confucian capitalism in China and crony capitalism in Indonesia were just steps along a path to neoliberalism. Diehard Keynesians pointed feebly to dragon economies in Asia like Korea and Singapore as achieving sustained economic growth at a level that was consistently outpacing all the neoliberal economies. The Washington consensus explained it was a myth that these were strong states with dirigiste industrial policies and comparatively egalitarian distributions of wealth. Actually they were just complicated examples of neoliberalism working in more mysteriously oriental ways. When the tigers hit the Asian financial crisis of 1997, there was a sigh of relief as this interpretation shifted. These were not neoliberal economies after all. The IMF needed to go in and demand that they learn all the lessons of the Washington consensus, not just pick and choose from its reform menu.

The twisting and turning in Asia was the end of the fairytale, the last gasp of neoliberalism as a coherent ideology that pretended to rule the world. Not only did Asia recover quickly to higher growth than the First and Second Worlds, Joseph Stiglitz (2002) convinced growing numbers of economists that the economies that recovered quickest were those, like Malaysia and South Korea, that most aggressively rejected the advice of the IMF. The Washington consensus finally collapsed under the brute fact that Asia was, after all, not a minor exception, but half the world, and the half that was performing best economically. If there is a widely shared economic orthodoxy in the current decade, in Asia it is becoming more a soft power 'Beijing consensus' (Ramo 2004) than a hard Washington one. Keynes was alive and well in the hands of regulatory economists like Nobel laureate Joseph Stiglitz – who shaped Washington thinking during the 1990s as Chair of the Clinton Council of Economic Advisors and as James Wolfensohn's Chief Economist at the World Bank. Stiglitz is to regulatory capitalism what Milton Friedman and the Chicago school were to neoliberalism.

Just as a New Zealand Labor government in the 1980s could be more neoliberal than Reaganites and Thatcherites, so in the current decade the

Bush administration turned out to be more Keynesian than the New Democrats it supplanted. Gone was the fiscal rectitude of the Clinton years. The Bush administration managed the 2001–02 recession with an expansionary Keynesian fix. John Howard's conservative Australian government likewise out-Keynesed the new social democrats it supplanted, though not by racking up the huge deficits of the Bush administration. It did so with an unparalleled tax and spend binge, funded by more than a decade of corporate tax collection growth to 2007 at three times the rate of gross domestic product (GDP) growth (Braithwaite 2005: ch. 2). This was accomplished through improved regulatory technologies while reducing the corporate tax rate, so Howard looked like Thatcher while acting like Keynes. A government that collects more tax through reducing profit-shifting by multinationals and slowing the movement of the cash of wealthy individuals into tax havens, as the Howard government has done, can boost domestic demand without racking up a deficit. Howard's big government regulatory capitalism delivered strong growth compared to other Western economies and to Australia's own past performance.

The Asian financial crisis aftermath was but a last gasp of neoliberalism. It had already been dealt a fatal blow by its triumph in the Second World. The privatization that the IMF and the likes of the Margaret Thatcher Foundation insisted upon in Russia was a disaster. By the rouble crisis of 1998, Russian GDP had fallen to almost half what it had been at the end of Communism (Stiglitz 2003). It has been growing vigorously since, on the back of surging prices for its oil and gas exports, now back under state control. Some former Soviet states fared even worse negative growth in their first post-Communist decade. The Washington consensus adapted to the 'Washington consensus plus'. The 'plus' was 'good governance' and the 'rule of law'. In fact the ideology of the Washington consensus plus was getting close to what Levi-Faur (2005a) describes as regulatory capitalism. For neoliberals, regulation remained a dirty word. 'Good governance' and 'rule of law' was a way for them 'not to talk about the war' they had lost for the hearts and minds of the world's policy-makers.

This is not to deny that the Chicago assault permanently insinuated market values into what had been the public sphere. Yet Jody Freeman (2003) points out that in addition to the privatization of the public, we have seen considerable publicization of the private – progressively more potent infiltration of public law values like transparency into what is expected of public companies. Government by contract, the new public contracting, is one of the mechanisms that produces this effect (Vincent-Jones 2006). There is no point speculating whether it is the privatization of the public or the publicization of the private which is the more important development, as they are incommensurable. Both have been important. There are few people at the top of large American corporations today persuaded by Milton Friedman's prescription that it is wrong to use shareholders' funds for any purpose other than maximizing profits. Commitment in corporate America to having a sound triple bottom line – financial, environmental, social – is now widespread. Green and public values have permeated what Grabosky (1994) calls 'Green markets', wherein market imperatives to be green are more potent than state regulatory imperatives. Green markets are mediated by the interventions of private/NGO regulators such as Forest Stewardship Council certifications of the sustainability of the practices that deliver furniture to the stores of European retailers (Meidinger 2006). Eco- and social-labelling are about harnessing the market choices of consumers to regulatory projects of green, labour and human rights social movements. Part of what regulatory capitalism means is using markets as regulatory mechanisms, as opposed to the neoliberal schema of markets as the antithesis of regulation (Cashore et al. 2004). The state increasingly experiments in creating markets for tradable pollution permits with the objective of creating more cost-effective pollution control, carbon taxes or carbon trading to internalize externalities of markets, and more. The neoliberal programme Bourdieu (1998: 2) characterized as 'destroying collective structures which may impede the pure market logic' has retreated in the face of a regulatory capitalist reality of hybridity between the privatization of the public and publicization of the private.

THE MYTH OF DEREGULATION

It had been the case from the early 1980s that there had been, except perhaps in New Zealand, a wide gulf between what the Anglo-Saxon neoliberals said and what they did. The Washington consensus, Stiglitz (2004: 23) alleges, was never what its executors believed was good for Washington; it was never what Washington did; it was what Washington believed was good for other countries to do because it would benefit American business operating in those other countries. Washington econocrats knew a collapse of business regulation was bad for America, but it was mostly good for American multinationals when other countries eschewed regulatory burdens upon American investments/exports. 'The medicine we dispensed abroad was, in important respects, not really the same stuff we drank at home' (Stiglitz 2004: 23).

Actually, this is not quite right. In the first two Reagan years there was genuine deregulatory zealotry. But by the end of the first Reagan term, business regulatory agencies had resumed the long-run growth in the size of their budgets, the numbers of their staff, the toughness of their enforcement and the numbers of pages of regulatory laws foisted upon business (Ayres and Braithwaite 1992: 7–12). Overall, real business regulatory spending increased 10 per cent during the Reagan years (Tramontozzi and Chilton 1989). Environmental deregulation proved so unpopular as to drive from office by early 1983 a deregulatory zealot like Anne Gorsuch, to whom Reagan had handed stewardship of the Environmental Protection Agency. Later in the Reagan administration financial deregulation came unstuck with a savings and loans debacle that cost American taxpayers over $200 billion (Rosoff et al. 2002: 255). In this domain, the Reagan and Thatcher governments actually reversed direction globally as well as nationally. The Federal Reserve (US) and Bank of England led the world down to financial deregulation in the early 1980s, then led global prudential standards back up through the G-10 after the banking crises of the mid-1980s for fear of the knock-on effects foreign bank collapses could have on American business (Braithwaite and Drahos 2000: 4). By the end of the Reagan administration, the enfeeblement of the regulation of Wall Street in the early 1980s was being ridiculed even in Hollywood by Michael Douglas's portrayal of the insider trader who believed that 'greed is good'. By then New York Republican prosecutor, Rudolf Giuliani, was building a big political reputation by slapping handcuffs on Wall Street icons like Michael Milkin, inventor of the junk bond. The Republican administration of the current decade presided over a 42 per cent increase in regulatory staffing levels from 2001 to 2005 of 242 473 full-time equivalents. Admittedly 56 000 of the increase were airport screening agents in the Transportation Security Agency (Dudley and Warren 2005: 1).

In Britain, privatization proliferated in a way that created a need for new regulatory agencies. When British telecommunications was deregulated in 1984, OFTEL was created to regulate it; OFGAS with the regulation of a privatized gas industry in 1986, OFFER with electricity in 1989, OFWAT with water in 1990, and the Office of the Rail Regulator (mercifully not OFRAILS!) in 1993 (Baldwin et al. 1998: 14–21). When the Thatcher government radically shifted the provision of nursing-home beds from the public to the private sector (Day and Klein 1987), 200 little nursing-home inspectorates were set up in district health authorities to upgrade the previously cursory regulatory oversight of the industry, later consolidated by the Blair government into a Social Care Inspectorate of 2600 inspectors. This led Patricia Day and Rudolf Klein as early as the mid-1980s to speak of the rise of a new regulatory state in the health and welfare sector. Privatization combined with new regulatory institutions is the classic instantiation of Osborne and Gaebler's (1992) prescription for reinventing government to steer rather than row. Jordana and Levi-Faur (2003; 2004) show that the tendency for state regulation to grow with privatization is a global one. As privatization spreads, they find new regulatory agencies spread even faster, and they show how the diffusion of regulatory agencies moved from the West to take off in Latin America in the 1990s.

Francis Fukuyama (2004), the same who told us that the end of history had arrived with a Washington consensus that was the 'end point of mankind's ideological evolution' and the 'final form of human government' (Fukuyama 1989), now agrees that Russian privatization was a disaster because 'privatization inevitably creates huge information asymmetries, and it is the job of governments to correct them' (Fukuyama 2004: 18). Moreover, he reports Milton Friedman saying that in the early 1990s he had three words for countries making the transition from socialism: 'privatize, privatize, privatize'. 'But I was wrong,' Friedman continues. 'it turns out that the rule of law is probably more basic than privatization' (Fukuyama 2004: 19). Fukuyama (2004: 18) also attributes the financial crises experienced by Thailand and South Korea to 'premature capital account liberalization in the absence of adequate regulatory institutions'. Finally, he interprets the strong correlation between per capita GDP and the percentage of GDP extracted by governments as evidence that a strong state is vital for long-term economic growth.

In summary, while the neoliberal policy package of smaller government, privatization and deregulation was never an accurate way of describing what was happening in the US or the UK, it at least was a description of what the Chicago boys and the IMF thought should be happening. And it was something global corporations saw themselves as having an interest in promoting in the Second and Third Worlds, even if the business agents of the ideology did not really see it as sound economics. Today there is scant sign of ideological consensus on anything like this neoliberal package. Yet big policy changes in many countries were justified by the rhetoric of neoliberalism.

At a certain level there *is* more consensus than during the Cold War. Neither Marx nor Milton Friedman are the ideological forces they once were. The consensus is not liberal. Guantanamo Bay, the profiling and detention of citizens generally, the burgeoning punitive-police apparatus of the crime control industry (Christie 1993), revealed the Bush administration of the 2000s and the American judicial branch to be anything but liberal in its limitation of state power over individuals. Neoconservative perhaps, neoliberal hardly. The consensus shared by the policy communities around both Bush and Clinton was quite a confined one in favour of strong markets and a strong state. But there is dissensus on how those strong markets should be regulated, how its fruits should be distributed and to what ends the regulatory power of the state should be directed.

If neoliberalism is neither the end of history nor even a useful way of describing what was happening during a passing moment, what is an analytically insightful way of describing recent institutional history? I used to describe the key transition as one from the liberal nightwatchman state, to the Keynesian welfare state, to the new regulatory state (after 1980, or during the 1970s) and a regulatory society (see also Majone 1994; Loughlin and Scott 1997; Parker 1999; Jayasuriya 2001; Midwinter and McGarvey 2001; Muller 2002; Moran 2003; Amann and Baer 2006). The nub of the regulatory state idea is power is deployed 'through a regulatory framework, rather than through the monopolization of violence or the provision of welfare' (Walby 1999: 123). Now I prefer Levi-Faur's (2005b) adaptation of the regulatory state idea into regulatory capitalism. According to Levi-Faur, we have seen since 1980 not only what Vogel (1996) found empirically to be *Freer Markets, More Rules*, but also 'more capitalism, more regulation'. Privatization is part of Levi-Faur's characterization of regulatory capitalism. But it sits alongside proliferation of new technologies of regulation and metaregulation (Parker 2002), or metagovernance (Jessop 1998; Sorensen 2006), or control of control (Power 1997), increased delegation to business and professional self-regulation and to civil society, to intranational and international networks of regulatory experts, and increased regulation of the state by the state, much of it regulation through and for competition.[9] The regulatory capitalism framework theorizes the new public management post-1980 as a conscious separation of provider and regulator functions within the state, where sometimes the provider functions were privatized and regulated, and sometimes they were not privatized but nevertheless subjugated to the 'audit society' and government by (audited) contract (Power 1997).

The Keynesian welfare state now seems a poor description of the institutional package that dominated until 1980. One reason is that Keynes is alive and well not only in the political economy of new social democrats like Tony Blair, Gordon Brown, Kevin Rudd and Helen Clark but in neoconservatives like George W. Bush and John Howard. Second, it is not true that the state has hollowed out – Bush and Howard are by far the most profligate spenders their nations have seen. Nor has the welfare state atrophied. Welfare-state spending by rich nations has not declined (Castles 2004; Guillen 2001). Finally, the state provider economy was not just about providing welfare; it was about states providing transport, industrial infrastructure, utilities and much more beyond welfare, a deal of which was privatized in the transition to regulatory capitalism.

Even the idea of the nightwatchman state of the nineteenth century needs qualification. The prehistory of the institutional change summarized in this chapter could be described as a transition from various feudalisms to a police economy. The sequence I describe is a transition then from that police economy to the unregulable economy tending to laissez-faire after the collapse of police, to the state provider economy (rather than the welfare state) to regulatory capitalism (rather than the regulatory state).

THE POLICE ECONOMY

What does Tomlins (1993: 37–8) mean when he says that writing a history of the American state without a reference to the genealogy of police is 'akin to writing a history of the American economy without discussing capitalism'? In the white-settler societies it is easier to see with clarity the police economy because it did not have to struggle to supplant the old economy of monopolies granted by the king to guilds, market towns and trading companies like the Hudson Bay Company (even though the New World was partly constituted by the latter). That economy of monopoly domination granted by the king was not only an earlier development in the transition from feudalism to capitalism that was subsequently (de)regulated by police, it was also a development largely restricted to cities which were significant nodes of manufactures and long-distance trade.[10] Tiny agricultural communities that did not have a guild or a chartered corporation had a constable. The early modern idea of police differs from the contemporary notion of an organization devoted to fighting crime (Garland 2001). Police from the sixteenth to the nineteenth centuries in continental Europe meant institutions for the creation of an orderly environment, especially for trade and commerce. The historical origins of the term through German back to French is derived from the Greek notion of 'policy' or 'politics' in Aristotle (Smith 1762 [1978]: 486; Neocleous 1998). It referred to all the institutions and processes of ordering that gave rise to prosperity, progress and happiness, most notably the constitution of markets. Actually, it referred to that subset of governance herein conceived as regulation.

Police certainly included the regulation of theft and violence, preventive security, regulation of labour, vagrancy and the poor, but also of weights and measures and other forms of consumer protection, liquor licensing, health and safety, building, fire safety, road and traffic regulation, and early forms of environmental regulation. The institution was rather privatized, subject to considerable local control, relying mostly on volunteer constables and watches for implementation, heavily oriented to self-regulation and infrequent (even if sometimes draconian) in its recourse to punishment. The lieutenant de police (a post established in Paris in 1667) came to have jurisdiction over the stock exchange, food supplies and standards, the regulation of prostitutes and other markets in vice and virtue. Police and the 'science of police' that in eighteenth-century German universities prefigured contemporary regulatory studies[11] sought to establish a new source of order to replace the foundation laid by the estates in the feudal order that had broken down.

English country parishes and small market towns, as on the Continent, had constables and local watches under a Tudor system that for centuries beyond the Tudors regulated the post-feudal economic and social order. Yet there was an English aversion to conceptualizing this as police in the French, German and Russian fashion. The office of the constable had initially been implanted into British common law and institutions by the Norman invasion of 1066. The office was in turn transplanted by the British to New England, with some New England communities then even requiring native American villages to appoint constables. Eighteenth-century English, but not American,[12] political instincts were to view continental political theory of police as a threat to liberty and to seek a more confined role for the constable. Admittedly, Blackstone in his fourth volume of *Commentaries on the Laws of England* (1769 [1966]) adopts the continental conception of police, and Adam Smith applauds it in his *Lectures on Jurisprudence* (1762). But Neocleous (1998) detects a shift from the Smith of the *Lectures* to the *Wealth of Nations*, both of which discuss police and the pin factory. The shift is from seeing 'police power contributing to the wealth-producing capacities of a *politically constituted* social order to being a site of autonomous social relations – the independent factory employing independent wage-labourers within a *laissez faire* economy'.

Polanyi (1957: 66) quotes Montesquieu (1989) as sharing the early Smithian view of English police as constitutive of capitalism, when he says in the *Spirit of Laws* that 'The English constrain the merchant, but it is in favor of commerce.' Even as institutions of eighteenth-century police are to a considerable degree in place in the nations that become the cutting edge of capitalism (this is also true of the extremely effective policing of the Dutch Republic (Israel 1995: 677–84)), the leading interpreters of capitalism's success move from an interpretation of markets constituted by police to laissez-faire markets.

Peel's creation of the Metropolitan Police in London in 1829 and the subsequent creation of an even more internationally influential colonial model in Dublin were watersheds. Uniformed paramilitary police, preoccupied with the punitive regulation of the poor to the almost total exclusion of any interest in the constitution of markets and the just regulation of commerce, became one of the most universal of globalized regulatory models. So what happened to the business regulation? From the mid-nineteenth century, factories inspectorates, mines inspectorates, liquor licensing boards, weights and measures inspectorates, health and sanitation, food inspectorates and countless others were created to begin to fill the vacuum left by constables now concentrating only on crime. Business regulation became variegated into many different specialist regulatory branches. The nineteenth-century regulatory growth is more in the number of branches than in their size and power. Laissez-faire ideology underpinned this regulatory weakness. The regulators' feeble resourcing compared with that of the paramilitary police, and the comparative wealth of those they were regulating, made the early business regulators even more vulnerable to capture and corruption than the police, as we see with poorly resourced business regulators in developing economies today.

THE UNREGULABLE LIBERAL ECONOMY

Where problems were concentrated in space, nineteenth-century regulation secured some major successes. Coal mines became much safer from the later years of the nineteenth century, as did large factories in cities (Braithwaite 1985), regulatory transitions that are yet to occur in China that today accounts for most of the world's coal-mine fatalities. Rail travel was causing thousands of deaths annually in the US late in the nineteenth century (McCraw 1984: 26); by the twentieth century it had become a very safe way to travel (Bradbury 2002). Regulation rendered ships safer and more humane transporters of exploited labour (slaves, convicts, indentured workers, refugees from the Irish famine) to corners of empire suffering labour shortages (Macdonagh 1961). The paramilitary police were also successful in assisting cities like London, Stockholm and Sydney to become much safer from crimes against persons and property for a century and a half from 1820 (Gurr et al. 1977). But it was only problems like these that were spatially concentrated where nineteenth-century regulation worked. In most domains it worked rather less effectively than eighteenth-century police. This was acceptable to political elites, who were mainly concerned to make protective regulation work where the dangerous classes might congregate to threaten the social order – in cities, convict ships and factories.[13]

In addition to the general under-resourcing of nineteenth-century regulatory inspectorates, the failure to reach beyond large cities,[14] the capture and corruption, there was the fact that the inspectorates were only beginning to invent their regulatory technologies for the first time. They were still learning. The final and largest limitation that made their challenge impossible was that in the nineteenth century almost all commerce was small business. It is harder for an inspector to check ten workplaces employing six people than one with 60 workers. This remains true today. We will see that the regulatory reach of contemporary capitalism would be impossible without the lumpiness of a commerce populated by big businesses that can be enrolled to regulate smaller businesses. Prior to the nineteenth century, it was possible to lever the self-regulatory capabilities of guilds in ways not dissimilar to twentieth-century capabilities to enrol industry associations and big business to regulate small business. But the well-ordered world of guilds had been one of the very things destroyed by the chaotic emergence of laissez-faire capitalism outside the control of such pre-modern institutions. Where guilds did retain control, capitalism did not flourish, because the guilds restricted competition.

While the nineteenth-century state was therefore mostly a laissez-faire state with very limited reach of its capacity to regulate, it was a state learning to regulate. While the early nineteenth-century tension was Smith's between the decentralized police economy and laissez-faire liberalism, the late nineteenth-century tension was between laissez-faire and the growth of an administrative state of office blocks in large cities. The late nineteenth century was both more disciplined by the market and more disciplined by growing state capacity to govern.

THE UNREGULABLE LIBERAL ECONOMY CREATES THE PROVIDER STATE

A simple solution to the problem of private rail companies charging monopoly prices, bypassing poorer towns, failing to serve strategic national development objectives and flouting safety standards, was to nationalize them. A remedy to unsanitary private hospitals was a public hospital system that would make it unnecessary for patients to resort to unsafe private providers. The challenge of coordinating national regulation of mail services with international regulation through the Universal Postal Union (established 1863) rendered a state postal monopoly the simplest solution to coordination otherwise beyond the unregulable nineteenth-century liberal economy. The spread of socialist ideas during the nineteenth century gave an ideological impetus to the provider state solution. Progressively until the beginning of the second half of the twentieth century, the provider state model proliferated, especially in Europe, with airlines, steel, coal, nuclear power, urban public transport, electricity, water, gas, health insurance, retirement insurance, maternal and child welfare, firefighting, sewerage and countless other things being provided by state monopolies.

Bismarck consciously pursued welfare state provision as a strategy for thwarting the growing popularity of the idea of a socialist revolution to replace capitalism entirely with a state that provided everything. Lloyd-George was impressed by Bismarck's diagnosis and the British Liberal Party also embraced the development of the welfare state, only to be supplanted by a Labour Party that outbid the Liberals with the state provision it was willing to provide workers who now had votes and political organization.

While many of these state takeovers also occurred in the United States during the century and a half that preceded Jordana and Levi-Faur's arrival of regulatory capitalism, the scope of what was nationalized was much narrower there. One reason was that trade unions and the parties and socialist ideologies they spawned were much weaker in the US during the twentieth century. There were periods up to the first decade of the twentieth century when trade unions in the United States were actually numerically and politically stronger than in Europe. The big businesses that grew earlier in the United States used their legal and political capabilities to crush American unionism in the late nineteenth and early twentieth centuries, frequently through murder of union officials and threats of violence (Braithwaite and Drahos 2000: 229). American big business could simply organize more effectively against the growth of trade unions and the provider state ideologies they sponsored than could the smaller family firms that predominated in Europe.

A paradox of the fact that American business culture moderated the growth of the provider state was that the regulatory state grew more vigorously in the US, especially during the progressive era (1890–1913) (which saw the creation of the Federal Trade Commission, Food and Drug Administration, and Interstate Commerce Commission, among other agencies) and the New Deal (1930s) (which saw the creation of the Securities and Exchange Commission, the National Recovery Administration, the Federal Communications Commission, the Civil Aeronautics Board, among others) (McCraw 1984). Building paradox upon paradox, the growth in the sophistication of regulatory technologies in the US showed that there were credible alternatives to the problems the provider state set out to solve. The New Deal also supplied an economic management rationale to an expansive state. Keynes's general theory was partly about increasing public spending to stimulate an economy when it was in recession, as it was at the time of the New Deal.

REGULATION CREATES BIG BUSINESS

Braithwaite and Drahos (2000) have described the corporatization and securitization of the world as among its most fundamental transformations of the past three centuries.[15] I summarize here how this was enabled by regulation, but then how corporatization in turn enabled regulatory capitalism to replace the provider state economy. Corporations existed for more than a millennium before securities. For our purposes, a security is a transferable instrument evidencing ownership or creditorship, as a stock or bond. The legal invention of the security in the seventeenth century was the most transformative moment in the history of corporations. It enabled the replacement of family firms with very large corporations based on pooled contributions of capital from thousands of shareholders and bondholders. These in turn enabled the great technological projects of eighteenth- and nineteenthth-century capitalism – the railroads, the canals, the mines.

When it was first invented, however, the historical importance of the security had nothing to do with the corporatization of the world. Rather, it transformed state finances through bonds that created long-term national debts.[16] While the idea of dividing the national debt into bonds was invented in Naples in the seventeenth century, it was England that managed by the eighteenth century to use the idea in a financial revolution that helped it gain an upper hand over its principal rival, France (Dickson 1993). England became an early provider state in a particularly strategic way by seizing full national control of public finance: formerly private tax and customs collecting were nationalized in the seventeenth century, a Treasury Board was established in the eighteenth and, finally, the Bank of England was given national regulatory functions. The Treasury Board realized that the national debt could be made, in effect, self-liquidating and long term, protecting the realm from extortionate interest rates at times of war and the kind of vulnerability that had brought the Spanish empire down when short-term loans had to be fully repaid after protracted war. Instead of making England hostage to continental bankers, the national debt was divided into thousands of bonds, with new bond issues placed on the market to pay for old bonds that were due to be paid.

Securitization paid for the warships that allowed Britannia to rule the waves, to trade and colonize – to be a state provider of imperial administration and national as opposed to feudal security on a scale not imagined before. Today national debts no longer can be used to rule the world because they are regulated by other states through the Paris Club and the IMF. The key thing here is that the early providers of state control of public finance in the process also induced a private bond market. This created the profession of stockbroking and the institution of the stock exchange. For most of the periods when Amsterdam and London were the leading stock exchanges in the world, they were predominantly trading securities in the debts of nations. Gradually this created a market in private stocks and bonds. These enabled the English to create the Massachusetts Bay Company, the Hudson Bay Company, the British South Africa Company, the East India Company and others that conquered the world, and the Dutch to create an even more powerful East India Company and the

United New Netherland Company that built a New Amsterdam which was to succeed London as the next capital of the world.

State creation of a London market in the broking of securities fomented other kinds of securities exchanges as well, the most important of which was Lloyd's of London. Britannia's merchant fleet ruled the waves once an efficient market in spreading the lumpy risk of ships sinking with valuable cargoes was created from a base in Lloyd's Coffee Shop. Lloyd's in turn became an important inventor of regulatory technologies that made regulatory capitalism possible in advance of the supplanting of the provider state with regulatory capitalism. For example, in building a global reinsurance market it invented the Plimsoll line that allowed insurers to check by simple observation at ports whether ships arrived overloaded.

But by far the most important impact of securitization was that it began a process, which only took off quite late in the nineteenth century, of replacing a capitalism of family firms with one of professional managers of securities put in their trust by thousands of shareholders. Even in New York, where the corporatization of the world was most advanced, it was not until the third decade of the twentieth century that the majority of litigants in appellate courts were corporations rather than individual persons, and the majority of actors described on the front page of the *New York Times* were corporate rather than individual actors (Coleman 1982: 11).

ANTITRUST GLOBALIZES AMERICAN MEGA-CORPORATE CAPITALISM

In the 1880s, predominantly agrarian America became deeply troubled by the new threat to what they saw as their Jeffersonian agrarian republic from concentrations of corporate power that they called trusts. Farmers were especially concerned about the 'robber barons' of railroads that transported their produce across the continent. But oil, steel and other corporate concentrations of power in the Northeast were also of concern. Because Jeffersonian republicanism also feared concentrations of state power in the Northeast, the American solution was not to nationalize rail, oil and steel. It was to break up the trusts. By 1890 at least ten US states had passed antitrust laws, at which point the Sherman Act was passed by a virtually unanimous vote of the US Congress.

The effect of enforcement of the Sherman Act by American courts was not exactly as intended by the progressive era social movement against the railroad, oil, steel and tobacco trusts. Alfred Chandler Jr noted that 'after 1899 lawyers were advising their corporate clients to abandon all agreements or alliances carried out through cartels or trade associations and to consolidate into single, legally defined enterprises' (Chandler 1977: 333–4). US antitrust laws thus actually encouraged mergers instead of inhibiting them because they 'tolerated that path to monopoly power while they more effectively outlawed the alternative pathway via cartels and restrictive practices' (Hannah 1991: 8). The Americans found that there were organizational efficiencies in managerially centralized, big corporations that made what Chandler called a three-pronged investment: (1) 'an investment in production facilities large enough to exploit a technology's potential economies of scale or scope'; (2) 'an investment in a national and international marketing and distribution network, so that the volume of sales might keep pace with the new volume of production'; (3) 'to benefit fully from these two kinds of investment the entrepreneurs also had to invest in management' (Chandler 1990: 8).

According to Freyer's (1992) study in the Chandler tradition, the turn-of-century merger wave fostered by the Sherman Act thrust US long-term organization for economic efficiency ahead of Britain's for the next half century, until Britain acquired its Monopolies Act 1948 and Restrictive Trade Practices Act 1956. Until the 1960s the British economy continued to be dominated by family companies that did not mobilize Chandler's three-pronged investment. Non-existent antitrust enforcement in Britain for the first half of the twentieth century also left new small business entrepreneurs more at the mercy of the restrictive business practices of old money than in the US. British commitment to freedom of contract was an inferior industrial policy to both the visible hand of American lawmakers' rule of reason and the administrative guidance of the German Cartel Courts. For the era of managerial capitalism, liberal deregulation of state monopolies formerly granted to Indies Companies and guilds was not enough. Simple-minded Smithean invocation of laissez-faire missed the point. A special kind of regulation for deregulation of restrictive business practices was needed which tolerated bigness.

Ultimately, Braithwaite and Drahos (2000) show that this American model of competitive mega-corporate capitalism globalized under four influences: (1) extension of the model throughout Europe after the Second World War under the leadership of the German anti-cartel authority, the Bundeskartelamt, a creation of the American occupation (Freyer 2006);[17] (2) cycles of mergers and acquisition (M&A) mania in Europe catalysed in part by M&A missionaries from American law firms; (3) extension of the model to the dynamic Asian economies in the 1980s and 90s, partly under pressure from bilateral trade negotiations with the US and Europe (who demanded breaking the restrictive practices of Korean chaebol, for example); and (4) extension of the model to developing countries with technical assistance from organizations like the United Nations Conference on

Trade and Development (UNCTAD), prodded by the IMF good governance agenda that succeeded the Washington consensus. This history of regulation that promoted competition among large corporations from the 1880s (in the US) is very recent in other states. Most of the world's competition regulators have been created since 1990. There were barely 20 in the 1980s; today there are about 100.[18]

MEGA-CORPORATE CAPITALISM CREATES REGULATORY CAPITALISM

This story is one of reciprocal causation. The regulatory state creates mega-corporations, but large corporations also enable regulatory states. We have seen that antitrust regulation is the primary driver of the first side of this reciprocal relationship. Yet other forms of regulation also prove impossible for small business to satisfy. In many industry sectors, regulation drives small firms that cannot meet regulatory demands into bankruptcy, enabling large corporates to take over their customers (see, for example, Braithwaite et al.'s 2007 account of how tougher regulation drove the 'mom and pops' out of the US nursing-home industry in favour of corporate chains). For this reason, large corporations often use their political clout to lobby for regulations they know they will easily satisfy, but that small competitors will not be able to manage. They also lobby for ratcheting up regulation that benefits them directly (for example, longer patent monopolies) but that are mainly a cost for small business (Braithwaite and Drahos 2000: 56–87).

To understand the second side of the reciprocal relationship more clearly – mega-corporates create regulatory capitalism – consider the minor example of the regulation of the prison industry (Harding 1997). It is minor because most countries have not taken the path of privatizing prisons, though in the US, where prisons house more than 2 million inmates and employ about the same number, it is not such a minor business. In the 1990s many private prisons were created in Australia, a number of them owned by the largest American prison corporations. A question that immediately arose was how was the state to ensure that American corporations met Australia's national and international human rights obligations. When the state was the monopoly provider of prison places, it simply, if ineffectively, told its civil servants that they would lose their jobs if they did not fulfil their duty in respect of such standards. This requirement was put into contracts with the private prisons. But then the state has little choice but to invest in a new regulatory agency to monitor contract compliance.

As soon as it puts this in place, prisoner rights advocates point out that in some respects the old state-run prisons are more abusive than the new private providers, so the prison inspectorate should monitor the public prisons. Moreover, it should make public its reports on the public prisons so that transparency is as real there as with private prisons (Harding 1997). Of course, the private corporations lobby for this as well to create a 'level playing field' in their competition with the state. Hence, the corporatization of the prison industry creates not only a demand for the independent, publicly transparent regulation of the corporates, but also creates a potent political demand for regulation of the state itself. This is central to understanding why the regulatory state is not the correct descriptor of contemporary transformations; regulatory capitalism involves heightened regulation of the state as well as growth in regulation by the state (Hood et al. 1999). We have seen this in many other domains including the privatization of British nursing-home provision described earlier leading to inspection of public nursing homes.

Security generally has been a major domain of privatization. Most developed economies today have a ratio of more than three private police to one public police officer (Johnston and Shearing 2003). But the highest per capita numbers of private security are in poor nations recovering from armed conflict; by far the two largest private employers in Timor Leste are private security firms. Under provider capitalism it was public police officers who would provide security at football stadiums, shopping complexes, universities, airports. Today as we move from airport to shops to leisure activity to work, we move from one bubble of private security to another (Johnston and Shearing 2003; Shearing and Wood 2003). If our purse is stolen at the shopping mall, it is a private security officer who will come to our aid, or who will detain us if we are caught shoplifting. The public police mostly cover us only as we move in public space between bubbles of private security. As with prisons, public demand for regulation of the private security industry arises when high-profile incidents occur, such as the recent death of one of Australia's most talented cricketers after a bouncer's punch outside a nightclub.

International security has also privatized. Some of those allegedly leading the abuses at Abu Ghraib in Iraq were private security contractors. Many of these contractors carry automatic weapons, dress like soldiers and are killed as soldiers by insurgents. In developing countries, particularly in Africa, military corporations have been hired to be the strike infantry against adversaries in civil wars. An estimated 70 per cent of the former KGB found employment in this industry (Singer 2002). This has led the British government to produce a White Paper on the need to regulate private military organizations and to the quip that the regulator be dubbed OFKILL!

So the accumulation of political power into the hands of large private corporations creates public demand for regulation. Moreover, we have seen that the largest corporations often demand this themselves. In addition, the regulatory processes and (partly resultant) competitive imperatives that increase the scope and scale of corporations made what was unregulable in the nineteenth century, regulable in the twentieth. The chemicals/ pharmaceuticals industry, for example, creates huge public demand for regulation. Incidents like Bhopal with the manufacture of agricultural chemicals and thalidomide with pharmaceuticals, that kill thousands, galvanize mass concern. The nineteenth-century regulatory state could only respond to public outrage by scapegoating someone in the chemical firm and throwing them in prison. It was incapable of putting a regulatory regime in place that might prevent reoccurrence by addressing the root causes of disasters. There were too many little chemical producers for state inspectors to monitor and it was impossible for them to keep up with technological change that constantly created new risks.

After the Bhopal disaster, which ultimately caused the demise of Union Carbide, the remaining large chemical producers put in place a global self-regulatory regime called Responsible Care, with the objective of averting another such disaster that might cause a multinational to go under leaving a stain on the reputation of the entire industry (Moffet et al. 2004). That is all very well, the regulatory cynic notes, but it still remains the case today that most chemical risks are posed by small, local firms with poor self-regulatory standards, not by the multinationals. Yet the fact of mega-corporate capitalism that has evolved over the past century is that almost all small chemical firms are linked upstream or downstream to one multinational or another. They buy or sell chemical ingredients to or from the large corporates. This fact creates a mass tort risk for the multinationals. The multinationals are the ones with the deep pockets, the high public profile and brand reputation, so they are more vulnerable to the irresponsibility of small chemical firms linked to them than are those firms themselves. So Responsible Care requires large firms to sustain a chain of stewardship for their chemicals upsteam and downstream. This has the effect of making large corporations the principal regulators of small chemical firms, not the state. This is especially so in developing countries where the temptations of state laissez-faire can make the headquarters risks potentially most catastrophic.

State regulation and private regulation through tort create larger chemical corporations. We see this especially in pharmaceuticals where the costs of testing new drugs now run to hundreds of millions of dollars. Global scandals that lead to demand for still tougher regulation creates a community of shared fate among large firms in the industry (note Rees's 1994 study of how the Three Mile Island disaster created a community of fate in the nuclear industry, a belief that another Three Mile Island could cripple it).

Big business responds to finding itself in a community of fate in a risk society (Beck 1992) by industry-wide risk management. This implies managing upstream and downstream risks. Again we see that regulatory capitalism is not only about the regulatory state, though this is a big part of the chemicals, pharmaceuticals and nuclear stories. It is also about regulation by industry associations of their large members and regulation of small producers by large producers who share the same chain of stewardship for a risk. It is not only states (with technical assistance from international organizations like the World Health Organization and the Organisation for Economic Co-operation and Development – OECD) doing the regulating, it is global and national industry associations and large multinational firms. Not only does this ease some of the logistical burdens on the regulatory state in monitoring a galaxy of small firms, it also eases some of the information problems that made chemicals unregulable in the nineteenth century. As partners in regulatory capitalism, state regulators can lean on Responsible Care, the OECD and large multinationals that may know more than them about where new chemical risks are emerging. Of course, there is debate about how well these private–public partnerships of regulatory capitalism actually work (Gunningham and Grabosky 1998).

Braithwaite and Drahos (2000) revealed the importance of yet other actors who are important as non-state regulators. Ratings agencies like Moody's and Standards and Poors, having witnessed the bankrupting of imprudent chemical producers, downgrade the credit rating of firms with a record of sloppy risk management. This makes money more expensive for them to borrow. Reinsurers like Lloyd's also make their risks more expensive to reinsure. The cost and availability of lending and insurance also regulates small firms. Care homes (including nursing homes) frequently go bankrupt in the UK; these bankruptcies are often connected to the delivery of poor-quality care. Reports of British government care home inspections are on the Internet. When homes approach banks for loans, it is good banking practice today to do an Internet check to see if the home has any looming quality of care problems. If it does, banks sometimes refuse loans until these problems are addressed. Banks have thus become important regulators of little and large British care home firms.

CORPORATIZATION, TAX AND THE CONSTITUTION OF PROVIDER AND REGULATORY CAPITALISM

One effect of the corporatization of capitalism in the twentieth century was that it made it easier for the state to collect tax. This revenue made it possible to fund both the provider state and the regulatory state. State provision of things like welfare and transport and state regulation are expensive activities. So tax-paying becoming regulable was decisive to the subsequent emergence of the provider state and regulatory capitalism. In most developing societies, tax-paying remains unregulable and this has closed the door on credible state provision and state regulation.

Of course it is more cost-effective to collect tax from one large corporation than ten small ones; most corporate tax is collected from the largest 1 per cent of corporations in wealthy nations.[19] But this is not the main reason that corporatization created a wealthy state. More fundamentally, corporatization assisted the collectability of other taxes (see Braithwaite and Drahos 2000: ch. 9). As retailing organizations became larger corporates, as opposed to family-owned corner stores, the collection of indirect tax became more cost-effective. When most of the Australian working class was rural, itinerantly shearing sheep for pastoralists, cutting cane or picking fruit, collecting taxes from them was difficult and costly. But as the working class became progressively more urban – in the employ of city-based corporations – income tax collections from workers became a goldmine, especially after the innovation of Pay As You Earn (withholding of tax from pay packets by employers, which started after the New Deal or the Second World War in most countries). The final contribution of mega-corporatization was financial institutions becoming more concentrated and computerized, making withholding on interest and dividends feasible. So tax on salary income, corporate tax, sales taxes and tax on income from interest and dividends all became more collectable. The result was that, contrary to the fairytale of neoliberalism, the state grew and grew into a regulatory capitalism where the state both retained many of its provider functions and added many new regulatory ones.

Pay As You Earn (PAYE) was an innovative regulatory technology of wider relevance. Pay-As-You-Earn taxpayers cannot cheat because it is not them but their employers who hand over the money. Theoretically, of course, the employer can cheat. But they have no incentive to do so, since only their employee benefits from the cheating, and the cheating is visible in the accounts. The regulatory strategy of general import here is to impose regulatory obligations on keepers of a gate that controls the flow of the regulated activity, where the gatekeepers do not benefit personally from opening and closing the gate. This not only separates the power from the incentive to cheat, it also economizes on surveillance. It is not necessary to monitor all the regulated actors at all times. The regulator must only monitor the gatekeeper at those points when gates can be unlocked.

THE REGULATED STATE

For 90 per cent of the world's states there are large numbers of corporations with annual sales that exceed the state's GDP. The chief executives of the largest corporations typically are better networked into other fonts of power than the presidents of medium-sized states. Consequently, large corporations do a lot of regulating of states. There are also some smaller global corporations like Moody's and Standards and Poors that have specialized regulatory functions over states – setting their credit ratings. More generally, finance capital holds sway over states. This is exercised through capital movements, but also through lobbying global institutions like the IMF, the Basle Committee, World Trade Organization Panels and the World Bank, who might have more direct control over a specific sphere of state activity. The most formidable regulator of debtor states is the IMF, as a result of its frequently used power to impose regulatory conditions upon debt repayment.

While states have formidable regulatory leverage over airlines, for example, airlines can enrol the International Civil Aviation Organization to regulate landing rights to and from states that fail to meet their obligations to the orderly conduct of international transport. While states regulate telecommunications, they must submit to regulation by the International Telecommunication Union (ITU) if they want interconnectivity with telecommunications in other states, and powerful corporations invest heavily in lobbying the ITU and in having their executives chair its technical committees.

Many states simply forfeit domains of regulation to global corporations that have superior technical capability and greater numbers of technically competent people on the ground. For example, in many developing nations the Big Four accounting firms effectively set national accounting standards. States are also regulated by international organizations (and bilaterally) to comply with legal obligations under treaties they have signed. Sanctions range from armed force down to air and sea blockades, suspension of voting rights on international organizations, trade sanctions, and 'smart sanctions' such as seizure of foreign assets and denial of visas to members of the regime and their families. Regional organizations such as the European Union and the African Union also, of course, have a degree of regulatory leverage over member states. Leverage tends to be greatest when states are applying for membership of an international club such as the World Trade Organization or EU from which they believe they would benefit.

One of the defining features of regulatory capitalism is that parts of states are set up with independent capacities to regulate other parts of the state. We have seen that even Milton Friedman now believes that having an independent judiciary with a real capability to enforce the law against the executive government is a top priority for economic development and a central plank of the World Bank and IMF good governance agenda. But we have also seen since 1980 the globalization of the Swedish institution of the ombudsman, a proliferation of audit offices to the point where some describe what Levi-Faur calls regulatory capitalism as *The Audit Society* (Power 1997). Finally, there is the development mentioned earlier of independent inspectors of privatized industries moving their oversight back to public provision.

Of course, the idea of a separation of powers where one branch of governance regulates another so that neither executive, judiciary nor legislature can dominate governance is an old one, dating at least from the Spartan constitution and Montesquieu (Braithwaite 1997). But practice has become more varied, especially in Asian constitutions such as those of Thailand and Taiwan, which conceive of themselves as having more than three branches of governance, with branches such as the Election Commission, Ombudsman, Human Rights Commission, Counter Corruption Commission, Audit Offices, Control Yuan and Examination Yuan enjoying constitutionally separated powers from the legislative, executive and judicial branches. The theory as well as the practice of the doctrine of separation of powers under regulatory capitalism has also moved forward on how innovative separations of powers can deter abuse of power (see Braithwaite 1997). To the extent that there are richer, more plural separations within and between private and public powers in a polity, there is a prospect of moving towards a polity where no single power can dominate all the others and each power can exercise its regulatory functions semi-autonomously even against the most powerful branch of state or corporate power. As Durkheim began to see, the art of government 'consists largely in coordinating the functions of the various self-regulating bodies in different spheres of the economy' (Schepel 2005: ch. 1; see also Durkheim 1930: 1901 preface; Cotterrell 1999).

Weiss (2005) calls this governed interdependence. What constrains the ability to dominate does not necessarily weaken governance: the state's capacity to govern is actually extended by capabilities to enlist through negotiation the governance capabilities of other actors. As global regulatory regimes expand, state regulatory capabilities are not necessarily contracted. Indeed, capable states learn how to increase their capabilities by governing through and with global institutions (Levi-Faur 2005a; Weiss 2005).

CONCLUSION

Those who believe we are in an era of neoliberalism – where this means hollowing out of the state, privatization and deregulation – are mistaken. The transitions since feudal structures of governance fell to incipient capitalist institutions have been from a police economy, to an unregulable nineteenth-century liberal economy (that oscillated between laissez-faire, dismantling the decentralized police economy and laying the bricks and mortar of an initially weak urban administrative state), to the provider state economy, to regulatory capitalism. Across all of these transitions, markets in fits and starts have tended to become progressively more vigorous, as has investment in the regulation of market externalities. Not only have markets, states, and state regulation become more formidable, so has non-state regulation by civil society, business, business associations, professions and international organizations. Separations of powers within polities have become more varied, with more private–public hybridity. This means political science, conceived narrowly as a discipline specialized in the study of public governance to the exclusion of corporate governance, NGO governance and the governance of transnational networks, makes less sense than it once did. If we have entered an era of regulatory capitalism, regulation may be, in contrast, a fruitful topic around which to build intellectual communities and social science theory.

In seeing the separations among the periods posited in this chapter, it is also important to grasp the posited continuities. Both markets and the state become stronger, enlarged in scope and transaction density, at every stage. The amount of governance in the world also continuously grows, because non-state forms of governance by firms, industry associations, NGOs and global institutions expand alongside growth in state governance capability. Elements of eigthteenth-century police are retained in the creation of nineteenth-century paramilitary police and other specialized regulators. Post-1980 regulatory capitalism learns from and builds upon the weaknesses (and the strengths) of nineteenth- and early twentieth-centuries regulation – from private security corporations learning from Peel's Metropolitan Police and the KGB, to state shipping regulators and the International Maritime Organization learning from regulatory technologies crafted in Lloyd's Coffee Shop. While many problems solved by state provision prior to 1980 are thence solved by privatization into contested, regulated markets, most of the state provision of the era of the provider state persists under regulatory capitalism. Even some re-nationalization of poorly conceived privatization has begun.

While less welfare is state administered today and more is provided through contracted-out, contested, regulated markets for welfare provision, state spending on welfare has not fallen. The rumours of the death of Keynes, and of Hayek's immortality, at the 'end of history' were both exaggerated. Keynesian demand management is more complicated in the global economy, but remains a central preoccupation of regulatory capitalism.

Hayek's insistence that central states lack sufficient local knowledge to plan investment underpins both the attraction of markets in regulatory capitalism and the attraction to devolved regulatory technologies that harness local knowledge (Shearing and Wood 2003).

Most developing countries are in a process of more rapid transition towards regulatory capitalism than rich nations experienced over the past two centuries. Their states are in a process of filling out rather than hollowing out. Commenting on Vanuatu, Forsyth (2007) says its problem is not the hollowing out of the state, but the hollowing out of village governance. Perhaps in the West as well, it is local neighbourhood governance that has weakened, even as it has been substituted with different kinds of communities based on workplace, profession, recreation and geographically dispersed extended families.

A fair criticism of this chapter would be that its attack on the analytic value of neoliberalism as a package of privatization, deregulation and rolling back the state assails a straw (wo)man. Milton Friedman agrees that privatization is and should be combined with at least some kinds of regulation. No one implements the more radical prescriptions of the old Chicago school for abolishing antitrust. Those who point to the hollowing out of the state today mostly do so in a governance frame that notes its capacity to get things done through proliferating interdependencies, or in a Foucauldian frame that notes capacities to 'govern at a distance' (Rose and Miller 1992). Across all points of the political spectrum, there now seems as much concern about state failure as market failure, and about their interdependence. Perhaps that suggests there is some consensus around what Levi-Faur and Jordana label regulatory capitalism. Yet we have seen that it is very limited. It follows that interesting agendas are Levi Faur's (2006) of documenting and comparatively dissecting the 'Varieties of regulatory capitalism', the Hall and Soskice (2001), Stiglitz (2002), Sachs (2005) and Rodrik (2004) agendas of diagnosing the institutional mixes that make capitalism buzz and collapse in the context of specific states, the Dorf and Sabel (1998) agenda of evidence-based 'democratic experimentalism', and the Campbell Collaboration and behavioural economics agendas for real policy experiments on the impacts of regulatory interventions (www.campbellcollaboration.org).

A contribution of this chapter has been to suggest that regulation, particularly antitrust and securitization of national debt, enabled the growth of both provider and regulatory states. Regulation did this through pushing the spread of large corporations that made Chandler's (1977; 1990) three-pronged investment. The corporatization of the world increased the efficacy of tax enforcement, funding provider and regulatory state growth. The corporatization of the world drove a globalization wherein many different kinds of actors became important national, regional and global regulators: transnational networks, industry associations, professions, international organizations, NGOs, NGO/retailer hybrids like the Forest Stewardship Council, and most importantly corporations themselves (especially, but not limited to, stock exchanges, ratings agencies, the Big Four accounting firms, multinationals that specialize in doing states' regulation for them like Société Général de Surveillance,[20] and large corporates that regulate small upstream and downstream firms in the same industry). This was a very different capitalism and a very different world of governance than existed in the early twentieth-century industrial capitalism of family firms. Hence the power of Jordana and Levi-Faur's conceptualization of regulatory capitalism. While states are 'decentred' under regulatory capitalism, the wealth capitalism generates means that states have more capacity both to provide and to regulate than ever before.

NOTES

1. My thanks to Rod Rhodes, Peter Grabosky, Jennifer Woods, Susanne Karstedt, Adam Crawford, Clifford Shearing, Christine Parker and Peter Drahos for helpful comments on drafts of this chapter.
2. Sen (1992), Nussbaum (1995) and March and Olsen (1995: 91–139) argue that developing capabilities is a central and distinctive role of the state. While I agree, I am happy to conceive this as a particularly strategic kind of provision, as by developing capabilities through state provision of education, training, science funding and opportunities for political deliberation, among other public goods.
3. There is merit in Julia Black's (2002) view that for some analytic purposes narrower conceptualizations of regulation as steering through state rules or law can have more use, while for others broader conceptualizations that do not require the purposiveness of steering, that allow in Foucauldian governmentalities for example, can have more analytic use.
4. They may have become less preoccupied with distributing as well, but here there is not so clear a body of empirical evidence on trends, so this is not an issue addressed in this chapter.
5. For one account of how this might be done see David Kilcullen's (2005) ideas on how Western governments might flood the Internet with persuasively youthful anti-jihadist websites that are decidedly not pro-American and do not leave American fingerprints, recruit local elders by solving local problems in the mosques, villages and *madrasahs* of Afghanistan, Pakistan and across the Islamic diaspora. His idea is that because the US monopolizes the most potent forms of centralized hard power, that does not preclude it from relying mostly on soft power deployed through diffuse networks (see Packer 2006).
6. Hayek moved to the University of Chicago in 1950, where he joined his influential disciple, Milton Friedman.
7. Indeed, the New Zealand economy has been performing outstandingly under the more Keynesian policies of the current Prime Minister, Helen Clark.
8. Of course, Gorbachev really did believe in glasnost and perestroika, really did believe that a continuing arms race with the US was not in the economic interests of his people or the security interests of the world, and did have the vision to see that Soviet economic planning that had worked quite productively during the heyday of Fordist industrialism, would never flourish under the post-Fordist production imperatives of the information age (see Castells 2000: 2–67).

30   *Regulatory capitalism*

9. Hood et al. (1999) count 135 separate regulators of British government within British government, employing 14 000 staff.
10. France was an exception that made guilds state organs and spread their regulatory authority out from towns across the entire countryside (Polanyi 1957: 66).
11. Pasquino (1991: 112) reports a 1937 bibliography for German-speaking areas that lists 3215 publications from 1600 to 1800 under the listing, 'science of police in the strict sense'.
12. The emerging American republics gave a republican interpretation to police, as did many European intellectuals of the science of administration and police. Police was partly about restraining the power of the king. It denoted both the condition of a just and free social order and the means for securing that order – local governance that steers a polity toward republican freedom (Tomlins 1993: 35–59). The Delaware Declaration of Rights of 1776 stated 'that the people of this State have the sole exclusive and inherent Right of governing and regulating the internal Police of the same'. Pennsylvania, Maryland, North Carolina and Georgia adopted the same formulation, or a similar one, over the next year (Tomlins 1993: 57). Many a history book says that when Jefferson was elected to the Board of Visitors of the College of William and Mary in 1779, his advocacy pioneered the first chair of Law in North America at a time when the only other in the world was the Vinerian Chair at Oxford. Of course, there were a number of chairs of the science of police on the Continent at this time. And actually the title Jefferson chose for the William and Mary Chair was 'Law and Police'. Jefferson believed in the guidance of the economy not only by a rule of national law, but much more fundamentally by a governance of local, participatory police.
13. In the village or the rural sweatshop the centralized regulatory agencies offered little protection. To a considerable extent that is still true today. If you live in an Australian outback town, you put up with a lot of crime and there is not much you can do if the butcher sells you underweight meat or if the two petrol stations in town collude to charge an outrageous price. In the city you could complain to a consumer protection regulator who would check out the complaint. In the outback the metropolitan offices of the regulator are too far away for that to be feasible. A radical solution would be to deputize and train police in the bush as delegates of consumer protection, fire safety, nursing home, food safety and other regulators. The only way for rural communities to get their fair share of the regulatory state may be to go back to the eighteenth-century constable. Clifford Shearing has been an advocate of giving remote and marginal people a claim to their share of a policing budget (as opposed to a police force budget) to reinstate a form of Jeffersonian police for an era of regulatory capitalism (Shearing and Wood 2003). The bush also lost out to the city with the move away from the provider state after 1980. When the Post-Master General provided the telephone service, country folk could at least get their local member to do something about poor service. Police and weights and measures inspectorates worked, up to a point, in the nineteenth-century city. But they left the hinterland unregulable, plundered by highwaymen and commercial crooks. The far West of Australia's Eastern states remain wild in a way akin to the Wild West that President Jefferson opened up to a liberal nineteenth-century economy he would have been disappointed to see. Contemporary Australian outback towns today are likewise afflicted with high levels of violence, buildings that are fire traps, and occupational health and safety practices that are scandalous. Such places have lost many of the virtues of agrarian republicanism without gaining many of the civilizing influences the provider state and the regulatory state supplied to cities.
14. For example see Clarke's (1986) characterization of British club governance as regulating the city. And see Moran (2003) for the most influential discussion of British club governance. The paramilitary crime police, as we have already implied, also succeeded only in regulating large cities in the nineteenth century.
15. Corporatization and securitization are themselves part of a deeper historical process of propertization in which assets both tangible and intangible become subject to regulation by formal property rights that enable these assets to be traded (Drahos 2002).
16. Today as well, some of the most important securitization involves a transformation of banking and finance that does not involve the creation of new corporations. An example

17. is mortgage-backed securities – securities backed by bundles of loans on real estate, automobiles or credit cards issued by banks.
17. Freyer (2006) shows that the model that globalized was not Chicago school antitrust, which in most nations enjoyed rather short periods as a paradigm of major policy significance.
18. I am indebted to Professor Eleanor Fox of New York University in helping me with various sources to reach these figures.
19. In the US in 1997, 9017 of the 4.71 million corporations had $250 million or more in assets. This group of less than half a per cent of the corporations paid 78 per cent of the corporate tax collected (Yin 2001: 228). In Australia, the skew is similar but not so extreme: 75 per cent of company tax collections are from 'large' companies with total income over A$10 million (Wickerson et al. 2001: 265).
20. This is a large Swiss multinational that provides all manner of regulatory services for states from environmental inspection to collecting nations' customs duties for them in innovative ways (Braithwaite and Drahos 2000: 492–3).

2. The cyclical nature of the challenges of regulatory capitalism

Chapter 1 made reference to watersheds in regulatory growth such as the New Deal. Yet it could be read as suggesting a continuous growth of regulation that took off at an accelerating rate after 1970 as the era of regulatory capitalism dawned. While it is true that overall there was growth of regulatory institutions throughout the nineteenth and twentieth centuries that accelerated after 1970, different domains of regulation grew in different periods of the past 200 years and they grew unevenly, in spurts. Much of my writing about regulation has been about how scandal has produced such spurts (in nursing-home regulation (Braithwaite et al. 2007), coal mine safety (Braithwaite 1985), pharmaceuticals (Braithwaite 1984) and the regulation of corruption (Fisse and Braithwaite 1993, for example)). Non-governmental organizations that are regulatory model mongers actively promote regulatory growth by keeping a list of regulatory development projects in their back drawer until the right disaster comes along (Braithwaite and Drahos 2000: ch. 25). The fire safety reformer waits for a disastrous fire to promote new building regulations for more resistant materials. The environmentalist waits for the tanker to run aground to promote new laws to control oil spills at sea. To this extent the cyclical nature of regulatory capitalism is a purposive creation of reformers who decide for long periods to keep their reform projects in their back drawer until the ripe moment arrives.

The topic-selectiveness of cycles of regulatory growth is a result of an issue-attention cycle (Downes 1972) in which public attention is a scarce resource, as is the capacity of legislatures to digest new law. The policy change agenda would be too crowded for politicians, the media and the bureaucracy to absorb if all cycles of regulatory growth had the same upswing. So our analysis is of punctuated equilibria where pro- and anti-regulation interest groups are in stalemate for long periods where the regulatory landscape changes only minimally. Then a disaster or crisis brings a certain kind of regulation out of the top drawer for NGOs; the issue basks in the media's issue-attention lens for a moment of reform. Because new mine safety, nursing-home or pharmaceuticals legislation is triggered by things like a mine explosion, elder abuse, or a thalidomide disaster in which large numbers of deformed babies are born, most regulatory cycles are quite independent of the business cycle. On the other hand, at least two large domains of regulation are cyclical in response to business cycles. When stock markets enjoy long periods of upswing, capital market regulation tends to be ignored. Booms create regulatory quiescence, busts produce bursts of regulatory reform. In the next section, we consider the important special case of capital markets and then the latter part of the chapter partially generalizes the argument to financial forms of regulation, illustrated with aggressive tax planning.

BOOM, BUST AND REGULATION

The metaphor of a stock market boom producing a speculative frenzy, a bubble of overconfidence that expands until it bursts, is an attractive one for network theorists. As the bubble expands, networks of misplaced trust struggle to hold the molecules of the bubble together until finally they stretch beyond their limits. Bubbles burst when the trusted managements of prominent corporations like Enron and WorldCom are exposed as crooks. Many scholars have documented a boom–bubble–bust–regulate cycle in capital markets across several centuries (Banner 1997; Partnoy 2000; Grundfest 2002; Ribstein 2003; Clarke 2004; Black 2005; Skeel 2005; Coffee 2006; and Yeager, forthcoming, on the increasing frequency and intensity of business crime waves). This phenomenon is best documented in the command economies of the UK, then the US Banner (1997: 850) argues that 'All of the 18th-century English regulation, and even all of the 18th-century proposed regulation, came immediately after sustained price declines'. He found that prices dropped in 1720, 1733–34, 1746–48, 1753–56, 1758–62 and the early 1770s, while Parliament considered new regulation in the early 1720s, 1733–34, 1746, 1756, 1771 and 1773.

Then the newly independent US in 1792 passed in New York its first significant securities regulation after the big crash of 1792, though it was not until the crash of 1929 that federal laws arrived. In between, an 1873 railroad fraud and collapse triggered the '1873 Panic' in which many kinds of companies collapsed. A wave of railroad and corporate law reforms followed, reinvigorating reforms from crashes earlier in the century, particularly concerning self-dealing and public investment in railroads purchased with free stock for legislators (Skeel 2005: 43–53). A populist pro-regulation (especially of railroads) movement called the Grange or Granger movement became a major political force, especially in rural America, in the mid to late nineteenth century. At the beginning of the twentieth century Progressivism became a counterpart to Populism in more well-heeled circles in the Northeast. Progressive era regulatory reform touched many areas of regulation beyond capital markets, including the establishment of the Food and Drug Administration, the Federal Trade Commission and Theodore Roosevelt's reforms prohibiting corporations from making contributions directly to political candidates in 1907, the year of another stock market panic.

By the 1950s Marver Bernstein (1955) was documenting a tendency for the phalanx of federal regulatory agencies created in the two big waves of the Progressive era and the New Deal of the 1930s to go through a life cycle of gestation, youth, maturity (devitalization) and old age (debility and decline). Bearing in mind Bernstein's analysis, once core regulatory infrastructure is in place, the most consequential waves of regulatory reform can be those that reinvigorate enforcement more than law reform. This was the case following the stock market crash of 1987. The Reagan era was romanticized as one of deregulation (even if as we saw in the last chapter, the reality was of regulatory growth); the ideology was as immortalized by Michael Douglas in the Hollywood interpretation of Wall Street, 'greed is good'. Both the 1987 and 2001–02 market collapses ushered in a new kind of American hero, the prosecutor/politician with the handcuffs out on Wall Street in a mission to toughen corporate law enforcement – Rudolf Guiliani in 1987, Eliot Spitzer in 2001 (O'Brien 2007). Their leadership was important to US capital market regulation becoming by far the most punitive in the world (Coffee 2007). Spitzer also ratcheted up corporate self-regulation (a term he hates) in the finance sector through settlements between regulators and leading investment banks, starting with the watershed case of Merrill Lynch (O'Brien 2004; 2005; 2006; 2007). Both eras also produced consequential growth in regulatory law – new regulation of the savings and loans (S&L) industry in 1987 (albeit limited to that industry (Black 2005; Calavita et al. 1997)) and more general Sarbanes–Oxley corporate law reform after 2001.

As capital markets became progressively more global, crashes in the US are more predictably followed by collapses in most other markets. Even if Enron and WorldCom are not traded on the Australian Stock Exchange, even if all the misconduct that triggered sagging share prices occurred in the US, the collapse of confidence also ripples out as far as Australia. But the bursting of the Australian bubble exposes indigenous Australian frauds; the big ones in 2001–02 Australia were HIH – the largest insurance company collapse in Australian history – and One-Tel, a telecommunications collapse that embroiled Australia's two wealthiest families – the Murdochs and the Packers. Part of the global collapse of confidence as it worked through to Australia did have a tangible US connection, however. Arthur Andersen, which audited Enron and WorldCom and was bankrupted after criminal indictments were lodged against it, audited both HIH and One-Tel. Arthur Andersen should have been prosecuted for proffering magnificent service to the most famous criminal of the S&L debacle, Charles Keating, in deceiving regulators about his fraudulent junk bond underwriting (Black 2005: 250, 265; for a different view, see Coffee 2006: 27). The CLERP 9 corporate law reform debate that began in 2002 in Australia addressed many of the same issues as the US Sarbanes–Oxley Act of 2002, though in different and in some respects less interventionist ways (for example, in Australia the new requirement for provision of non-audit services by the audit company was limited to disclosure) (Clarke 2004: 160). But of course the rest of the world not only catches a cold when the US sneezes; it has homegrown crises as well. Even when these are huge – like the Asian financial crisis of 1997–98 – mostly the effects on the US market are quite modest, engendering regulatory reform in the markets where they occur, but not in the US.

INTEREST GROUP EQUILIBRIA AND CYCLICAL FINANCIAL REGULATION

Once a bust produces a wave of regulatory reform, during the long period of expansion that mostly follows in developed economies, companies and investors again become more interested in wealth creation than in regulation that secures retention of wealth (and the legal use of it). Everyone is happy to make money without enquiring too deeply into how they are making it. Actors who benefit from tighter regulation include reformers like Guiliani and Spitzer who acquire national reputations from it. Peddlars of regulatory ideas also benefit, as do regulators themselves, and firms with superior compliance system capabilities that are better equipped to cope with new regulation.

> In normal and boom times, new regulation would not help any distinct group enough to motivate the group to push for it. Regulated entities therefore have enough clout to defeat significant increases in liability or regulation. Those who might shift the balance, such as consumers or investors, do not see a need for new regulation while they are riding a rising market. (Ribstein 2003: 79)

Larry Ribstein argues that crashes destabilize this interest group equilibrium. Start-ups and marginal firms that profited from the boom no longer have the financial and political strength to resist regulation; reformers can enrol business interests who see that they can benefit from renewed 'investor confidence' inspired by new regulation, and can draw on populism and envy of the rich that abates only during those periods 'when the rich generate significant wealth for the rest of us' (Ribstein 2003: 79). The issue-attention cycle gives reformers only a brief window of opportunity to make their mark; then they do better to put their market reform agenda on the back burner while they become mayor of New York, for example, during the ensuing boom.

HOW CAPITALISM LURCHED OUT OF CONTROL

Berle and Means (1932) were important policy entrepreneurs in the brains trust of the New Deal. Their research revealed for the first time that a managerial revolution had occurred in American capitalism. The owners of capital were no longer in charge; managers were. Often the managers acted in the interests of managerial aggrandizement rather than wealth creation for shareholders. Then in the 1990s we see that managers lost control. One solution to the problem of managers not acting for owners that took hold in the US during the 1990s was to reward first top managers, then managers and traders at less lofty levels of financial organizations, with stock options. It was rare to reward top management with stock options in the 1980s; after 1997 most remuneration of chief executive officers (CEOs) of industrial companies was delivered in equity rather than cash; in 2001 cash remuneration fell to less than one-third of US CEO pay. The theory was that when managers were given options to buy their own company's stock at a given price, when they succeeded in getting it above that price they would get rich. This would concentrate their attention on returns to shareholders.

It was a dumb theory. Managers and traders certainly acquired an interest in pushing prices up. But there was no pain when the price went down; only shareholders felt that. Hence, managers and traders acting on behalf of financial organizations were given an interest in high-risk strategies, one of which was fraud, that pumped up stock prices stupendously. Denis et al. (2005) show that the greater a corporation's reliance on compensation with stock options, the greater the likelihood of securities fraud allegations and fraud charges against the corporation. Peng and Roell (2004) show a positive association between option-related compensation and private securities litigation, and several studies have shown top management compensation by stock options is related to a need to restate the company's financial statements and financial misrepresentation (discussed by Coffee 2006: 62–4, 75).

The answer to the seeming paradox of why managers, who were supposed to be in control according to the theory of managerial capitalism, allowed shareholders to seize back control by paying managers in stock options, is that the shareholders did not seize back control. From a managerial perspective, another reason stock options were great was because they steered around another regulator – the Internal Revenue Service (IRS). Well-crafted stock option remuneration packages left top managers in the 1990s with much higher incomes on which they paid much less tax than they did in the 1980s. If shareholder interests thought they were putting top managers back in their box, they were making a mess of it.

In financial organizations top managers with everything to gain from rolling the dice, and less to lose, can have an interest in hiring traders who also err on the side of high-risk strategies when they buy and sell financial products on behalf of the organization. So they pay the traders huge bonuses when they produce stellar short-term returns. Now you might say a trader who gets rich from sending his or her company's shares sky high nevertheless suffers a reputational loss when they collapse and his or her reckless rolling of the dice is revealed as the reason. Yes, but trading on a frenetic 24-hour global market is often viewed as an invigorating pastime when traders are young and can thrive on caffeine at 3 a.m. As they get older, many become attracted to the idea of making $10 million or $100 million through their bonuses (which many do in the New York market) and then get out to invest their capital in a more staid small business. They might buy a chain of funeral parlours for the investors who commit suicide after the trader's old firm collapses!

I said above that in the 1990s managers lost control in the New York financial market. They lost control to traders who invented ever more incomprehensible derivative products. Derivatives are financial instruments derived from some other asset rather than from trade in the asset itself. A derivative has a value derived from the price of something else. For example, a grain futures contract is a simple derivative with a value derived from the price of grain at a specified future date. A plain vanilla interest-rate swap is a derivative that allows you to swap a variable interest loan with a fixed interest loan. So bank A that is worried about having too many floating interest loans, and bank B that worries about too many fixed interest loans, in effect agree to swap some. When derivatives are traded prudently, they reduce the risks a company faces, as in the simple example of currency derivatives that hedge the company against radical fluctuations in the value of a currency in which they do a lot of their sales. A bank can have bets placed against both big rises and big falls in interest rates and currency values, leaving it solvent whatever happens. Trading in credit derivatives by banks is much more important than state prudential regulation in accomplishing dramatically reduced risks of system-wide banking collapses in sophisticated markets. They replace public with private regulation of systemic risk to banking systems. Yet we will see trading in derivatives itself needs regulation. For example, banks use derivatives to pass on credit risks to insurance firms and industrial companies that are not regulated as providers of credit in the way banks are.

Trading in derivatives is a game where traders make money at one another's expense. This is one explanation for engineering of new derivative products that are better understood by the inventor than other traders who buy and sell them. It conduces competition in the complexity and incomprehensibility of derivatives. As a consequence, managers routinely, even in sophisticated firms, do not understand the derivatives the traders working for them are selling. Frank Partnoy (2003) quotes one CEO who did not understand what his traders were doing as saying to one of them: 'my biggest trade was hiring you'. In such a world it can make sense for CEOs to roll the dice of hiring a few traders who in turn roll the dice for that big upside, partially oblivious to the downside. Trouble is the system did get so out of the control of managers. Traders could rip off other traders working for the same CEO when that CEO did not understand the nature of the trades. More importantly, traders could cheat shareholders by hiding losses until they got out with their upside bonuses. If the CEO could no more see those losses than the shareholders, which was often the case, CEOs could be duped too. And, of course, because prudential and securities regulators and those in the IRS and the Federal Bureau of Investigation (FBI) did not understand derivatives, were timid about making fools of themselves when confronted with their complexity, derivatives could help game-players avoid or cheat on tax and befuddle all manner of state regulators.

In the 1990s the best way to make a fortune was through avoiding regulation. Enron is a well-known example. This was not only true of capital markets but also of markets for tax shelters, as we discuss later in this chapter. Wall Street became a world in the 1990s where, in numerous of the most successful firms, as many assets and liabilities were off balance sheet as on. Their reported earnings were a fiction. Frank Partnoy (1997; 2003) says this happened because financial engineering was used to massage earnings and avert regulation. Control and ownership moved further apart as 'even sophisticated investors could not monitor senior managers, and even diligent senior managers could not monitor increasingly aggressive employees' (Partnoy 2003: 4). There was a daisy chain of lost control that allowed wild and lucrative risk-taking for those who knew enough about what they were doing to exit the casino before it caught fire: 'In just a few years, regulators had lost what limited control they had over market intermediaries [for example, auditors, analysts], market intermediaries had lost what limited control they had over corporate managers, and corporate managers had lost what limited control they had over employees' (Partnoy 2003: 4).

A central purpose of derivatives in the era of regulatory capitalism is to avoid private and public regulation of tax, accounting standards, investment restrictions, government subsidies, and more (Partnoy 1997: 228–35). This can take the highly principled form of the bank that pleads for relief from prudential regulatory intervention because it is doing a superior job of hedging its risks through derivative trades. The difficulties Qantas encountered in keeping its foreign shareholdings within prescribed limits post-privatization motivated Macquarie Bank to tailor-make QanMac: 'an innovative security which had the characteristics of a Qantas share, in terms of price and yield, but which was not subject to the same regulatory restrictions, since it was not considered to give foreign investors a direct shareholding in Qantas' (Sackman and Coltman 1996: 28). This was a less principled gaming of a democratic decision to preserve the considerable benefits of Qantas ownership for the Australian citizens who had paid to create Qantas through their taxes. Japanese companies used derivatives to subvert regulations capping their exposure to foreign-currency denominated securities (Partnoy 1997: 233; 2003). 'As long as "securities" were regulated, but similar "derivatives" were not, derivatives would be the dark place where regulated parties did their dirty deeds' (Partnoy 2003: 406). Derivatives are not only used to steer around state regulation, but also the private regulation of credit rating agencies, for example. When Moodys was punishing investments in the Thai Baht after the Asian financial crisis, this was circumvented by swaps denominated in US dollars.

Trade in financial instruments derived from assets mostly does not have to be declared in financial statements in the way trade in actual assets must be. Hence it becomes possible for managerial gamblers with larger interests in the upside than the downside to take risks the shareholders would not like if they knew about them. For example, a manager may see a large upside in taking a gamble on the direction interest rates will move through interest rate swaps. Because the swaps are not disclosed in the financial statement delivered to the board as well as the shareholders, the control of the board over the CEO is also eroded. Finally, as we saw earlier, the rocket scientists of financial organizations can engineer new financial products that have risks that are seen by them or by traders who specialize in winning bonuses by trading them, but not by their CEO.

In Chapter 1 we saw that a feature of regulatory capitalism is that not only is state provision privatized, so is a lot of regulation. Not only does state regulation grow in the era of regulatory capitalism, so does regulation of corporations by other corporations (for example, downstream chemical companies by upstream chemicals' suppliers), regulation of corporations by ratings agencies and stock exchanges that are themselves traded corporations, regulation of corporations by their own compliance groups and by external financial and non-financial auditors, regulation by audit committees of outside directors and regulation by NGOs who in some countries even get to exercise this through board membership. Derivatives are the quintessential counter-regulatory instruments in such a world of regulatory capitalism. We have seen that derivatives are used to steer around: (1) national and international rules; (2) regulation by ratings agencies; (3) self-regulation by boards; (4) 'regulation by markets' through the agency of shareholders and analysts on which shareholders rely; (5) regulation by auditors; (6) regulation of traders by top management and other supervisory employees. As a result, says Partnoy (2003: 394), markets have become like 'Swiss cheese, with the holes – the unregulated places – getting bigger every year, as parties transacting around legal rules eat away at the regulatory system from within' (for a discussion of how a Swiss cheese can be privately and publicly regulated, see Chapter 6).

We have regulatory capitalism because capitalism is out of control. One reason regulation has expanded, within the regulatory capitalist paradigm of simultaneous growth in private and public regulation since 1990, is because derivatives were engineered to free those who trade in them from regulatory controls. Earlier, Berle and Means (1932) were among the architects of the New Deal because the managerial revolution had removed mega-corporations from the control of shareholders and market forces. Critics of a broad conceptualization of regulation that encompasses private and public steering of the flow of events say that this is analytically useless because almost everything becomes regulation. It is true that many phenomena, though not all, have regulatory dimensions, just as they may also have dimensions of governance through provision of goods and services and distribution of these. But the point such critics miss is that you cannot understand the contemporary state without seeing it as both a regulator and a regulatee. You cannot understand the contemporary corporation without seeing it as a regulator of the state as well as its regulatee. We can understand a lot about derivatives by seeing them as instruments designed to produce and redistribute wealth. But we will never really begin to understand them without also seeing derivatives as instruments to steer the flow of events, particularly to steer around the attempts of other public and private actors to control the corporation.

We have regulatory capitalism because capitalism is out of control. One reason enforcement is so much tougher in US capital markets regulation than in any other national market (Coffee 2007) is that capitalism is more out of control in the US. Law enforcement needs to be most muscular where markets are most vibrant, thereby generating the most cutting-edge financial engineering. The paradox is that this tough enforcement then helps reduce the cost of capital in the US market, engendering a kind of virtuous circle between capitalism and tough regulation of it. Coffee (2007) shows that non-US firms that cross-list on a US exchange benefit from a considerable listing premium. Dodge et al.'s (2004) study, 'Why are foreign listed firms in the US worth more?', found the valuation premium for foreign firms cross-listing on one of the three major US exchanges to be a remarkable 37 per cent on average. Coffee (2007) explains the pattern of cross-listing premiums – premiums firms do not get by cross-listing in London for example – in terms of firms signalling that they are willing to subject themselves to the extra risk of enforcement and scrutiny uniquely available when the listing is in New York. Coffee (2007) questions the influential 'law matters' conclusion of La Porta et al. (1998; 2006). While La Porta et al. conclude that there are 'law in the books' reasons for more rapid financial development of countries with common law origins than those with civil law origins, Coffee (2007) concludes this may be more to do with the 'law in action'. He shows that the USA is the toughest capital markets enforcer in the world by far, both in terms of state and private enforcement, and that common law countries in general are tougher than civil law countries in securities and financial regulation.

FIGHTING THE LAST WAR

Unfortunately, the boom–bubble–bust–regulate cycle produces rushed reform. The imperative is not so much to get the reform right but to 'do something' to restore investor confidence (O'Brien 2007). A root-cause analysis of complex phenomena like bankruptcies that may or may not have been caused by fraud, and a resultant market collapse, takes time. Something that does not abound in a bust that follows a boom is patience and attention to analytic detail. Typically, reform is locked in before the learnings from the crash are fully digested. Often populist demands for punishment make for good media copy, and overwhelm demands for effective future prevention. There have been many corporate scandals where the window of reform opportunity was so effectively monopolized by a gripping narrative of punishment in which a scapegoat or two were pilloried, that interest groups pushing a return to business as usual without fixing the problem 'hunker down' to win the day (Fisse and Braithwaite 1983; 1993).

Rushed reform can conduce to over-regulation just as easily as the under-regulation in the scenario of the last sentence. With hurried policy deliberation in which populist soft-heads want something 'tough' and old-money hard-heads want something that will reignite investor confidence, crucifying a symbol of the excesses of new money might do. Tough new controls that are easy for established business to put in place, but onerous for start-ups, equally might do. A solution that works to simultaneously placate these two constituencies is likely, ritualistically (Chapter 6), to create the appearance of a firm response rather than the reality of a solution. Where over-regulation that does not work is the upshot, the most hospitable conditions are created for a new generation of financial engineering to game the new law. That is, there is more economic incentive to do so, the more extreme and costly the over-regulation; there is more moral legitimacy in doing so when everyone on Wall Street knows the new rules are a political sop that fixes nothing.

Simultaneously placating populist punitivists and establishment business confidence-restorers is likely to require a solution that is backward-looking to the dirty deeds done dirt cheap during the boom. This means the reforms fall prey to the generals' curse of fighting the last war, that is, training their soldiers with scenarios from the last war instead of possible future scenarios of the next.

Is there a solution to this problem? In a global economy, yes. As we will see more acutely with the problem of the regulation of aggressive tax planning in the next section, Sydney and even Paris lag behind New York. New York, and to a much lesser extent London, is the incubus of the latest and greatest in the new financial engineering. It is the place where the returns to the highest-risk financial innovation are most splendid, the crashes most spectacular, the kudos most politically gratifying for prosecutors who get the right notches on their gun, the scripts most worthy of Hollywood. While Nick Leeson gets a B-grade movie for bankrupting the London establishment of Barings Bank, Michael Milkin warrants a global blockbuster.

Comparatively sleepy Sydney's financial crooks do not rate any kind of movie. They lag a generation behind New York in the financial sophistication of their thievery. Many of the crashes that occur in capitalism's periphery occur after a boom–scandal–crash in New York triggers a boom–crash–scandal in their B-grade market. That is, while the crash in New York is triggered by a US scandal, the crash in Hong Kong is triggered by the cash in New York and then subsequently exposes Hong Kong scandals (Gunningham 1990). This means the Hong Kong policy community has more notice that a wave of regulatory reform is coming. They may be poring over policy papers analysing what New York might do to address the US scandal at the moment their lookalike Hong Kong scandal breaks. Or they may not have a Hong Kong scandal at all, just a Hong Kong crash consequent on the New York crash and an opportunity to reflect on whether any of the reforms the Americans put in place should be considered to pre-empt such a future scandal in Hong Kong. That is, they may be able to do their policy work with both the benefit of American experience and without the distraction of local hounds baying for quick blood. If they are really lucky, their financial rocket scientists might be one whole generation behind New York – as Sydney and Melbourne have been with aggressive tax planning (Braithwaite 2005). This means their current boom–bust–regulate cycle is populated by a genre of malfeasance that was the problem in the last New York cycle. Then they have the very great luxury of analysing what is known about how the US reforms in response to it worked or backfired. Commercial regulators from second-tier economies need to be more assiduous in sending their intelligence units regularly to New York and London to consolidate the regulatory competitiveness advantage they can reap to compensate for the inferior financial innovation in their economies. Such regulatory intelligence units must pay particular attention to how US legal game-players engineer around American regulatory reforms and what compliance systems the most financially sophisticated firms put in place in response to consent agreements (learning not just from American regulation but from American metaregulation – from regulated self-regulation – Parker 2002).

My argument therefore is that markets that lag somewhat in sophistication and innovation behind New York benefit from considerably more deliberative, less rushed, more evidence-based, and sometimes more experientially mature enquiries conducted with a policy humility that befits B-grade economies. And there are smart things such economies can do to reap even more of those benefits. It follows that New York can learn a lot from what they come up with. *Markets in Vice, Markets in Virtue* (Braithwaite 2005) is in a sense an extended case study of this policy opportunity. It argues that Australian aggressive tax planning lags a generation behind New York and that Australian responses to their tax shelters have been mostly more effective than American responses. Hence, I argue, America needs to swallow its policy pride and learn the regulatory lessons of less financially sophisticated economies. While the United States has the best universities, the most creative financial engineering expertise, the most theoretically fertile policy debates that are productively imbued with the American pragmatist and experimentalist traditions (Dorf and Sabel 1998) that are so lacking in Europe, America's comparativist tradition of policy analysis is impoverished. It is easy to understand why. America is such a big pond; knowing all the things going on in the US is challenge enough without also knowing what is happening in France.

Yet impetus for change does not have to come from the US. It can come from non-American universities. Scholars from small national ponds can seek to show Americans the benefits of scholarship that compares how they have responded to regulatory crises with how other nations have responded. Let us not worry too much if the Americans take no notice; they are only a small proportion of the world's population; their most important role is to be the laboratory from which India and China and Brazil and Indonesia and many other places can learn. The role of good regulatory scholars outside the US is to pay attention in their research to the glorious experiment that is New York with comparativist, forward-looking wisdom.

One of the ironies in all this is that a key to understanding why American capitalism started to catch up with the leading world economy two and a half centuries ago, and passed it a century ago, is that the mistakes of corporate over- and under-regulation the US made were not as great as those of Britain from the eighteenth century to the mid-twentieth century. The previous chapter discussed the key role of an American antitrust that averted the regulatory excess of outright prohibition of largeness while rejecting British under-regulation of corporate abuse of monopoly power. Early in the eighteenth century, British regulation had an extreme overreaction to the bursting of the South Sea bubble that may have put back the development of its economy for over a century (Ribstein 2003: 94–7). The South Sea Bubble resulted from scandalous stock manipulation by a company formed to trade African slaves to Spanish America, the South Sea Company. The resultant South Sea Bubble Act 1720 overreacted by flatly prohibiting the formation of new joint-stock companies. More important perhaps than the law itself was an attitude of the British Crown that persisted well into the nineteenth century, after the Bubble Act was superseded, that entrepreneurs were dangerous people. Hence their requests for corporate charters should be responded to warily. This was a scandal where old money networked with the royal court was able to harness populist and parliamentary outrage to crush new money entrepreneurship. In America the hand of the Crown in the eighteenth and nineteenth centuries did not weigh so heavily against new incorporations. Today, all the dynamics are reversed, with the lead economy in the US regulating securities more intrusively than in the UK. Today it is American entrepreneurs who are worried that some significant securities business has shifted from Wall Street to the City of London during the 2000s. It is probably too early to judge whether the Paulson Report (2006) is right in concluding that as a result of Sarbanes–Oxley 'the United States is losing its leading competitive position as compared to stock markets and financial centers abroad'. My point is simply that foreign regulators can learn from sitting back and following the debate in New York.

AGGRESSIVE TAX PLANNING CYCLES

Frank Partnoy (2003: 4) quotes James Grant as saying 'People are not instrinsically greedy. They are only cyclically greedy.' My study of aggressive tax planning in Australia and the United States also finds this and attempts an account of why (Braithwaite 2005). What Australians refer to as the market for aggressive tax planning, Americans call the market for tax shelters. The Australian usage is more communicative of what is actually involved. Aggressive tax planning can mean engineering transactions that generate tax losses, exclude income from taxation, defer recognition of income into a later year, or convert income into a different, lower-taxed form. Contrivance is used to 'shelter' income, wealth or capital gain from being taxed. Most aggressive tax planning involves the asymmetric treatment of losses and profits across two or more taxable entities. Funds are shuffled between entities so that the losses will be held where they generate a maximum tax loss and the profits flow to where they are untaxed (or less taxed). Because aggressive tax planning is characterized by innovation in finding new ways of getting around the intended effects of laws, a definition with too much specificity risks capturing the tax shelters we currently know about without netting newly emerging tax products. So I opt for the broad definition of aggressive tax planning as a scheme or arrangement put in place with the dominant purpose of avoiding tax.

The history of aggressive tax planning in the United States and Australia manifests an almost perfect cyclical harmonization between what was happening in the US and Australia. Both countries' Treasuries fought off a major wave of tax schemes targeted at individual taxpayers of above average wealth from the mid-1970s and early 1980s, and both suffered another boom in tax schemes between 1995 and 2000. On the surface it appears that Australia and the US are locked into the same cycle of aggressive tax planning crises that get out of hand for a few years, then dampen down till two decades after the last crisis began – following a credible response from the tax authority and the courts. As discussed above, both Australia and the US also had a 'greed is good' boom in stock market fraud during the same period in advance of the 1987 crash (the Bonds and Skases in Australia, the Levines and Milkins in the US). In both countries, corporate crime enforcement was greatly strengthened in the late 1980s and early 1990s. But in the long boom that ended in 2001, greed once again became good in both nations. Arthur Anderson being a common factor between both the worst Australian and American bankruptcies of 2001 must cause us to consider the possibility that globalization is delivering a harmonization of white-collar crime cycles between nations. Braithwaite (2005) concluded from extensive interviews with leaders of the tax shelter business in New York, Sydney and Melbourne that cycles of aggressive tax planning are supply driven by the promotion of crooked schemes by global organizations like Arthur Andersen.

At the same time, the data suggested that the US and Australia do not have the harmonized aggressive tax planning cycles that seem apparent on the surface. Rather, it was found that the US is at present one cycle ahead of the Australian aggressive tax planning cycle. Australia can therefore look to the tax avoidance crisis the US faced at the very end of the twentieth century to see some important features of Australia's future problems. Second, the correspondence with cycles of corporate fraud in capital markets is not perfect. Boom conditions where profits are high create conditions for an aggressive tax planning wave precisely because it gives companies and wealthy individuals growing interest in hiding profits from tax authorities. As with securities fraud, there is as the boom progresses a warm glow that everyone is raking in more money, including the tax collector. But as the cycle of aggressive tax planning gets out of hand (see Figure 2.1 on p. 49), this either ceases being true or tax officials come to the conclusion that the problem is getting so out of hand that tax receipts will soon drop. So aggressive tax planning tends to expand progressively during a boom until it reaches a take-off point late in the boom. Enforcement countermeasures and then public scandal tends to end it before the stock market bubble bursts. Whereas securities fraud cycles are boom–bust–scandal–regulate, aggressive tax planning is boom–regulate–scandal–bust. All four cycles of Australian and American aggressive tax planning in the Braithwaite (2005) study correspond to this pattern – while they correspond to upswings in corporate fraud and its regulation, the tax shelter booms all peak years before the stock market and corporate profits take a large fall.

Contagion was an important aspect of all four US and Australian booms in aggressive tax planning. The literature on contagion suggests that, at a private level, in a considerable variety of circumstances where one's personal knowledge of a phenomenon is truncated, it can be rational to follow the herd (Bikhchandani and Sharma 2000). Information can be too costly for investors who are not insiders, so each investor might benefit from looking at the market reaction to a tax scheme. With aggressive tax planning contagions, in those circumstances where there is economic rationality in following the herd, often the benefits are greatest for those who follow early, before ending the contagion becomes a policy priority. Contagion also becomes rational when the use of a tax arrangement becomes too big to stop. The losers then are those who fail to jump onto an unstoppable bandwagon. A contagion is typically started by promoter entrepreneurship to seize structural opportunities, with the herd instinct being a secondary factor.

A way of describing the history of the late 1990s Australian tax scheme boom is of a tax advice industry that since the previous boom of aggression ended in the early 1980s had lived in fear of aggressive enforcement of Australia's General Anti-Avoidance provision against them. After more than a decade of non-aggressive use of the provision by the Australian Tax

Office (ATO) and the courts, doubts arose that it was effective. Aggressive promoters of schemes first narrowcast their promotion to individual taxpayers with a taste for risk. When they got away with it, this attracted more aggressive opinion-writing from barristers on the legality of schemes and in some cases favourable rulings from one regional office or another of the ATO. Then broadcasting of schemes became more common, combined often with broadening the aggression of schemes beyond what had received a tick from the lawyers. A trickle of hundreds of investors in aggressive schemes became a stampede of tens of thousands of mostly high-income individuals. As ordinary people became more aware of acquaintances who had been getting away with such scheme investments for years, who asserted that they had a copy of a letter from a respected lawyer to assure them that the scheme was legal, more risk-averse taxpayers began to ask their accountants whether they should get involved. What started as a supply-driven phenomenon became more demand driven.

In highly complex systems of law such as Australian and US tax, 'hundreds of loopholes exist, of which only a small portion has been exploited' (Keinan 2001: 3). For example, of PricewaterhouseCoopers' database of 1000 mass-marketed tax planning ideas, only 30 were actually marketing in the peak year of the US shelter boom, 1998 (Keinan 2001: 5). My interviews identified four new structural causes of the late 1990s boom in corporate tax shelters that was led from New York:

1. Deregulation in the professions and the finance sector drove greater competition on the *supply* side in the promotion of shelters – competition in letters of comfort, promotion and insurance; and competition among law firms, investment banks, accounting firms and boutique financial advisers. Opinion shopping and tax planning rewarded by success fees of a proportion of the tax obligations eliminated were particularly critical drivers of more risk-free use of corporate tax shelters.
2. On the *demand* side, competition in more aggressive management of costs resulted in tax being no longer seen as inevitable. The tax department became a profit centre rather than a manager of public obligations.
3. Globalization expanded opportunities for international arbitrage. Global linkages among and within firms enhanced capability for exploiting these opportunities.
4. Financial engineering of derivatives and other new financial instruments created a new generation of shelter products.

These structural drivers were mutually reinforcing. More competitive and creative supply was important to enabling more aggressive demand for shelters. What Vito Tanzi (2000) called the 'fiscal termites' of globalization, such as the growth of tax havens, international arbitrage and global marketing of derivatives that liquidate tax, in turn engender 'moral termites'. As more people seize structural opportunities to cheat, tax morality erodes. Contagion becomes part of the problem here. There is empirical evidence in tax compliance research that when one believes that everyone is cheating, one is more likely to believe it is all right to cheat oneself (Scholz 1998).

Figure 2.1 attempts to model the drivers of shelter cycles from US experience in recent decades. The aggressive tax planning wave begins with the growth of 'deregulation of the professions and the finance sector', 'new financial engineering' (derivatives) and 'globalization enabling international arbitrage'. Three fiscal termites on the supply side drive gaming of the law and more aggressive supply of tax shelters. When followed by swamping and both detection failure and enforcement failure, these cause a shelter contagion to begin. Yet the recent empirical experience of four shelter booms in Australia and the USA shows that following of the herd into shelters can be reversed. The integrity of the law can be reasserted by either the legislature or the courts or both. If there are General Anti-Avoidance principles in play, enforcement might even be renewed without renewing the law – for example, by the announcement effect of the tax authority declaring it will attack the shelter under the General Anti-Avoidance principles. Either way, we have seen that shelter contagions can be thrown into reverse. Announcements by the Australian or US Commissioner of an intent to attack a scheme can result in an overnight stampede away from that scheme. Figure 2.1 summarizes the Braithwaite (2005) empirical conclusions.

My interviews revealed in the aftermath of such reverse contagions much holier-than-thou pontificating by practitioners who may have been involved in other equally egregious schemes. Participants in the aggressively competitive market for tax advice would ruthlessly seize upon opportunities to sully the reputations of competitors who put their clients into schemes that were struck down. But there were also so many people in business who simply preferred their company to pay their fair share of tax, many tax professionals who hated the pressure to put people into schemes or write favourable opinions on the legality of doubtful schemes. This was not just a matter of the personal integrity at work that most of us like to think of ourselves as having; it was also about nurturing a culture of integrity for everyone in our workplace. One of Bankman's (1999: 1785) senior business executives said: 'If you cheat, your employees will notice that, and they'll cheat you.' This executive is applying a general principle about how cultures of white-collar criminality, which start out for the benefit of a large organization, come back to bite the organization. We have

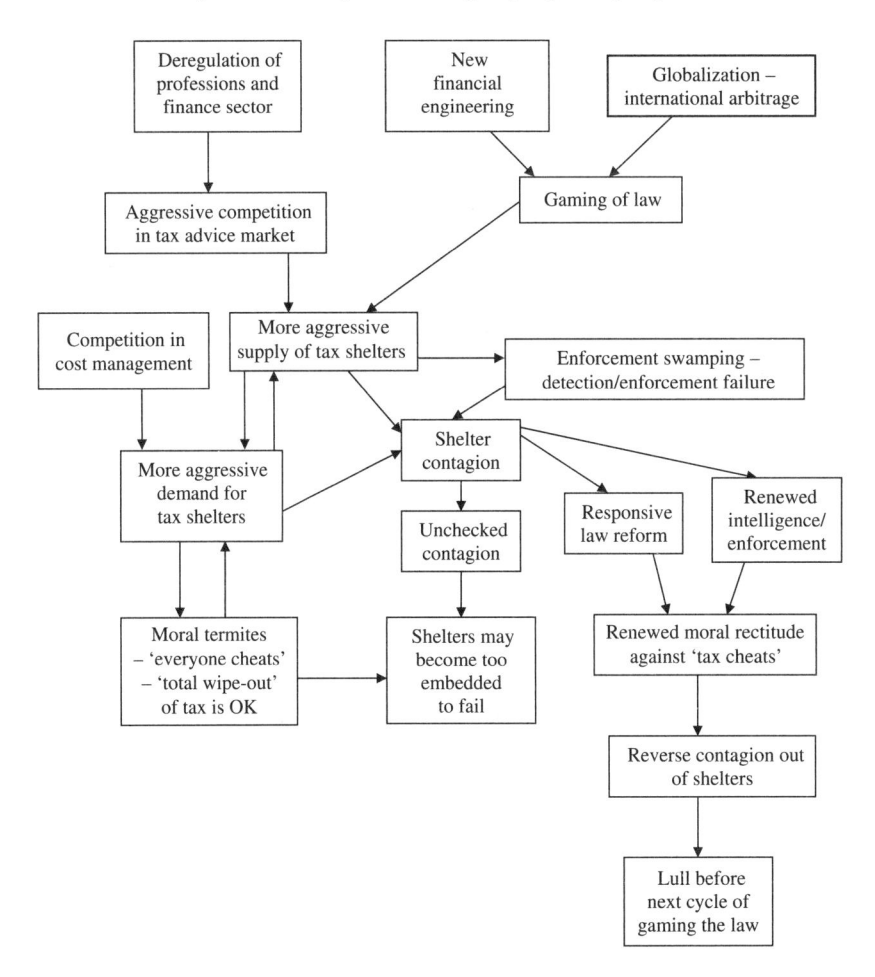

The cyclical nature of the challenges of regulatory capitalism   49

Figure 2.1 Empirically derived model of drivers of the aggressive tax planning market: fiscal and moral termites

seen this with bribery, financial fraud, market manipulation and scientific fraud (Fisse and Braithwaite 1983; Braithwaite 1984).

Hence, just as the drivers of the emerging global market for tax advice conduce to shelter contagion, they also allow reverse contagion out of shelters. On the other hand, excessive delay in detecting or moving against shelters can allow a shelter to become so embedded in deals of large corporations as to make it politically infeasible for the aggressive tax planning to be attacked. The enforcement challenge is to flip shelter contagions into reverse contagions before they pass that political point of no return.

The dynamics of Figure 2.1 apply to Sydney and Melbourne as much as to New York. But what the rest of the world can see more sharply from studying New York is the sophistication and depth that the three drivers at the top of Figure 2.1 can run to. Australian competition policy has increased competition between accounting firms, investment banks, law firms and other players in the finance sector. But it never reached the extent of the Big Four touting total tax wipeouts to large corporations in return for a fee of a third of the tax avoided, as I found in New York. It has not attained a market for insurance against unfavourable tax decisions that can eliminate uncertainty for a wide range of aggressive plays. '[The shelter] will work. But if you don't believe me, or if you just want to sleep better, I can put you in touch with an insurer who will cover you against the risk of the IRS striking it down.' Australian financial product engineering is in the process of catching up to New York. Australia has increasingly aggressive shopping for lawyers' opinions.

So my conclusion was that the fundamental dynamics in both countries are of contagion with the same drivers, as listed in Figure 2.1. But New York is a generation, a cycle, ahead in the sophistication with which those dynamics have been played out. Many of my New York informants felt exactly the same was true of Europe; this was one reason they found US–Europe arbitrage a game of choice, just as they did US–Australia arbitrage.

FLIPPING MARKETS IN VICE TO MARKETS IN VIRTUE

Responsive regulatory strategies can be more successful than in the past for flipping stampedes into aggressive tax planning to reverse stampedes out of shelters. This is because stampeding herds of tax avoiders are mostly led by a few dozen promoters. Moreover, New York helps us to see that changes in the technology of tax planning and its increasingly global nature means that it is the Big Four that have ever-widening competitive advantages over other players in this market, even as they collaborate with elite law firms and others in the New York tax planning community. It follows that a sophisticated regulatory strategy aimed at the compliance cultures of the big players can have knock-on effects with large ramifications for tax system integrity. When KPMG is motivated to self-regulate to become more virtuous, as arguably it has been by the publicity over its shelter practices and other vices, the whole world becomes more virtuous.

Competition policy has been a good thing for the wealth of the world. Yet we have seen it has its downside. Just as competition can deliver improvements in things we regard as virtuous, competition in vice is also a reality. The very idea of the corporate tax department being a profit centre rather than a cost centre is that it is a department that competitively pursues goods, rather than one that controls bads. Enron's tax department was so much a profit centre that it was set annual revenue targets (Johnston, 2003: 297). Ed Kleinbard (1999) may be right that the growth in corporate tax shelter activity is an integral part of competition for efficiency in corporate management – corporate tax liabilities are treated, along with other business liabilities, as costs that respond to aggressive management techniques to turn them into benefits. One New York lawyer put it poetically:

> In Arcadia, tax lawyers would discuss with each other what was a fair interpretation confident that the IRS would be looking for that fair interpretation and that the courts would be looking for it as well. The worm in the apple was progressively more ruthless competition for tax business that was not under the control of any single set of professional norms, certainly not those of tax lawyers alone. Accounting firms, investment banks, financial advisers, all with in-house lawyers compete with law firms for advice.

Arcadia crumbled under deregulated markets that progressively broke down professional monopolies. Investment banks like Merrill Lynch seem to have played an important role in setting new standards of aggression in the New York shelter market of the mid-1990s only to back away from it by the end of the 1990s when their aggression threatened the reputational capital so important for them to flourish in other domains like stockbroking and investment banking. So this corporate ethical transformation occurred years before Merrill Lynch's consent agreement with Eliot Spitzer transformed the ethics of its investment advice business. By the time the most aggressive investment banks were becoming more conservative in the corporate shelter market, the Big Five accounting firms had fought back to compete ruthlessly with one another for the lion's share of that market. Regulatory capitalism cannot take us back to an Arcadia of professional virtue grounded in professional monopoly; what it can do, and what I will do in the next few pages, is proffer strategic regulatory interventions that flip markets in professional vice to reputational competition in virtue.

Australian factor analytic research on preferred types of tax advisers by Yuka Sakurai and Valerie Braithwaite (2003) found the most popular cluster of tax agent characteristics defined 'honest, low fuss' advisers followed by 'cautious minimising with conflict avoidance' advisers, with the least preferred being the 'creative accounting, aggressive tax planning' type. There is a demand for preparers who keep taxpayers out of trouble. This is what makes it rational for most tax advisers to be virtuous agents of the law. And the evidence is that mostly they are. Klepper and Nagin (1989) and

Klepper et al. (1991) found that using a tax preparer discourages non-compliance on legally unambiguous income sources but encourages non-compliance on ambiguous sources. At least where the law is clear, tax professionals do a lot of the tax authority's work in educating taxpayers on what the law requires. Even in ambiguous regions of the law, such as transfer pricing by multinationals, sophisticated tax administration can flip advisers into being agents of compliance. One ATO official said of the interest of large accounting firms in its Transfer Pricing Record Review and Improvement Project: 'they have an interest in sending the message that unless you employ us to get your method in order you'll be audited'. Both creating business among those who want to cheat and business among those who wish to avert cheating are possible market niches for the tax adviser. The trick of institutions of taxation is to cause advisers to move from the first to the second niche. Braithwaite (2005) identified nine of the simpler strategies for flipping markets in vice to markets in tax virtue:

1. *Heavy promoter penalties*. Promoters are going to find the honest taxpayer market niche more attractive when promoter penalties are heavy in aggressive tax planning cases. As a result, promoters will create less demand for vice (see Figure 2.1), because like other vices – from problem gambling to tobacco to illicit drugs – excess in indulgence of the vice is initially created by sophisticated promotion (Braithwaite and Drahos 2002). So heavy promoter penalties is a general strategy – if the vice is people smuggling, we can shift the most severe punishment onto the promoter who organizes the people smuggling and away from its emphasis on those who are smuggled, from sex workers to promoters of the sex trade.
2. *Restorative justice*. When investors in illicit schemes face bankruptcy, divorce and suicidal depression, as we found happened to a troubling degree in Australia when the tax scheme boom collapsed, the public interests at stake are wider than the integrity of the tax system. Rituals of healing are needed after such terrible life events. There is now a lot of experience in helping people move on with their lives from restorative justice practice. There is evidence that doing so builds perceptions of procedural fairness and commitment to comply in future (Braithwaite 2002). The other kind of case where the social damage at risk justifies a large investment in restorative justice is with the Arthur Andersens of aggressive tax planning. Arthur Andersen was in trouble with multiple regulators in both the 1980s and the 1990s. In Australia it managed this with appeals to regulators to view their dirty work as that of a 'rogue partner'. A restorative justice conference with supporters of the rogue partner and the firm's leadership would have

revealed that the rogue partner was indeed following the ethics he or she was taught in Arthur Andersen. Here the public interest is flipping this year's ethical laggards into next year's ethical leader who pulls the advice industry to a new level of best practice as their only way out of deep trouble with regulators. First, we need heavy promoter penalties to motivate the next Arthur Andersen or the next Merrill Lynch to sit in the restorative justice circle out of fear of those penalties and indeed of corporate capital punishment at the peak of the enforcement pyramid – losing their licence for tax practice. Likewise with the mum and dad scheme investor who are about to lose their home, draconian promoter penalties need to be hanging over the head of their promoter and their tax adviser. Then the promoter and the adviser will come to the conference and more readily agree to pay a share of the investor's penalty tax and interest as an alternative to promoter penalties and being struck off as a tax preparer. Again restorative justice is a strategy of general import. Chapter 7 argues that its relevance is general because our deepest disputes over injustice consistently tend to have disturbing relational meanings to disputants. If it is the case that there are human relationships that stakeholders would like to see healed and identities under threat that they would like to be vindicated, restorative justice may have relevance.

3. *Targeting the clients of 'A' lists of promoters.* Enforcement swamping is a risk once a contagion of aggressive tax planning has taken off. Like heroin addiction or problem gambling or child pornography, however, once we have made the mistake of allowing the aggressive marketing of vice to fester undeterred, we then have a demand-driven problem on our hands that is harder to manage. Even in markets as sophisticated as New York, contagion is a powerful force. People rationalize following where they think the herd is charging: 'I've got a good opinion on this. I can see others doing it. How bad can it be?'

Not all promoters can be tackled at once when there is an enforcement swamping crisis. But if the clients of an A-list of promoters are attacked, clients will learn that they had better not end up in the clutches of an A-list adviser. Demand will shift further to the 'honest, no fuss' advisers. With less business going to aggressive advisers, they in turn create less demand through their promotion of aggression (see Figure 2.1). And 'honest, no fuss' advisers will act as agents of the state to pull aggressive clients back to prudent compliance lest they tarnish their reputational appeal in the market in virtue as someone whose clients the tax office is less likely to target. Because enforcement swamping is a general problem with markets in vice, targeting A-lists of recruiters into vice, targeting the most criminogenic gatekeepers

(Kraakman 1986; Gunningham and Grabosky 1998) to virtue or vice, as opposed to the perpetrators of vice, is a general strategy.

4. *Ban professional fees contingent on the magnitude of legal liabilities avoided*. It is inconceivable that promoter penalties could ever be heavy enough to deter the rewards of contingency fees as high as 40 per cent of tax saved on corporate shelters that can be worth hundreds of millions of dollars. My interviews revealed the phenomenon of promoters retiring on the investment income from millions they made from just one scheme in a short period of months. In the first instance we might look to professional associations to enforce ethical codes that address this moral termite of professional ethics within regulatory capitalism.

5. *Strict liability*. A surprising feature of the response of the elite tax practitioners of the New York State Bar Association (1999) to Treasury's original 1999 proposals to confront the tax shelter problem was their support for 'a strict-liability regime' with respect to lawyers' opinions whereby 'reliance on professional tax opinions would no longer have the effect of eliminating the penalty imposed on corporate taxpayers with respect to corporate tax shelter transactions'. One reason they favoured this was concern that: 'We suspect that many others of us, whether we would acknowledge it to ourselves or not, feel subtle pressures to give favourable opinions to be "at the table", to continue to be involved with our clients' transactions, and ultimately to generate our fair share of revenues for our firms' (New York State Bar Association 1999: 893). The market of shopping for 'more likely than not' tax opinion letters in both New York and Australia is a classic market in professional vice. A compromise option here that was also floated by the US Treasury in 1999 is to forbid taxpayers from relying on letters of comfort from lawyers to avoid penalties unless they disclose such a letter at the time of lodging their tax return. This would force taxpayers to choose between alerting the IRS to the latest shelter they have moved into and abandoning shopping for letters of comfort. This compromise seems appropriately less oppressive for individual investors who are sometimes plain naive. The strict liability standard to counter shopping for letters of comfort could be limited to corporations above a certain size. It is difficult to say whether this is a strategy with more general import beyond aggressive tax planning because it is a rather extreme reaction that might only be justified when markets in vice have become as virulent a threat as they became to tax system integrity in New York. The more general strategy could be formulated as ensuring that responsibility is imposed on all who are responsible (Fisse and Braithwaite 1993). This means not allowing principals to slide away from responsibility by blaming their advisers, not allowing

impunity for some who bear part of the responsibility for any vice – be it mistreatment of prisoners of war or insider trading – simply because a scapegoat has been found.
6. *Shelter disclosure and book-tax disclosure for corporations.* US shelter registration and disclosure requirements need a lot of fine-tuning before they will work well. The same would be true of the Canellos and Kleinbard (2002: 2) proposal for both tax auditors and stock investors to have access to a public book-tax reconciliation schedule which we consider further in the next chapter. Nevertheless, here the US debate is showing nations like Australia with less pernicious corporate shelter problems a productive direction to head in future. This is another strategy that is rather specific to tax. But of course disclosure and transparency is a more general strategy; sunlight disinfects many different vices. And the Canellos and Kleinbard proposal is about disclosure with a view to harnessing a form of private market in the virtue of detecting cheating, a general strategy developed in Chapter 3.
7. *Integrating the private and public markets for tax advice.* Braithwaite (2005: ch. 12) argued that tax authorities should compete on price to buy the best professionals from the private sector. One reason is that this would undercut 'narrow perfectionism' (Martin 2003) and encourage entrepreneurship in virtue in the public sector. However, it would also have some effect in reducing the incentives for the worst excesses of entrepreneurship in vice in the private sector. This would happen because excess in vice would render a professional unemployable with the biggest employer in the market – the tax authority. Perhaps more fundamentally, late career service to the tax authority would be a way to complete a work life of virtuous practice mainly in the private market.
8. *Educate investors to the risks.* Educating investors to the risks is precisely what virtuous tax professionals do in competing with aggressive advisers. The fact is that many advisers who are aggressive in ripping off the revenue also aggressively rip off clients. Tragic stories of lives ruined by investments in tax shelters are worth repeating in the educative work of both the tax authority and responsible tax professionals. A large proportion of the 1990s Australian shelter investments were commercially irrational. Individual taxpayers in particular need to be educated to be suspicious of advisers with a taste for risk because they are getting a commission for putting their client into the scheme. Both recent waves of aggressive tax planning in Australia were fundamentally commission-driven. It follows that consumers need to be educated to be commission-suspicious and get second opinions when they smell risk motivated by fat commissions. Consumer protection law for

commission disclosure is also important here. An Australian Securities and Investments Commission (ASIC) study found that 28 of 92 offer documents for primary production tax schemes did not meet legal standards on the disclosure of commissions (ASIC 2003: 12). When more consumers have a nose that smells commission-suspicion, the market in professional virtue will become more lucrative than the market in professional vice. This is a strategy of the most general relevance to any market in vice. The 1970s disclosures of multinational markets in the vice of bribery to sell products from aircraft to pharmaceuticals (Fisse and Braithwaite 1983; Braithwaite 1984) showed that slush funds and accounting practices to enable bribe payments supposedly in the interests of shareholders were also widely used by management and bribe-paying intermediaries like Adnan Khashoggi in the Lockheed case (Fisse and Braithwaite 1983: 148) to cheat investors. There were many who suffered in those scandals from being duped by shady characters into believing that they would be beneficiaries of the riches that would flow from paying the bribes, when in fact they were counted among the victims.

9. *Corporate certification of continuous improvement in tax integrity.* The idea of 'continuous improvement' has been crucial to ratcheting up standards in regulatory domains like environmental protection, occupational health and safety and Equal Employment Opportunity (Braithwaite and Drahos 2000: ch. 26; Parker 2002). This involves a shift away from the notion that regulation is about lifting everyone above the floor defined by a legal standard. What would be required to enforce it would be for a voluntary standards association like Standards Australia to draft collaboratively a Tax Integrity Continuous Improvement Standard. It would include protocols on specific issues like transfer pricing (as in the Transfer Pricing Record Improvement Review (Braithwaite 2005: 85–100), evidence of the board being active in demanding data that triangulate on adherence to the principles in the law, that the firm steers away from shelters that might be struck down by the courts, a proactive Board Audit Committee that encourages whistle-blowing on tax integrity problems and deals effectively with the issues brought to it, continuous improvement in the software, sampling and variety of checks performed by internal audit, continuous improvement in staff training on tax integrity issues, effective prompt cooperation with external auditors and the tax authority, open sharing of concerns as soon as an issue is detected (not holding findings until strategically advantageous), and so on. External auditors would certify each year whether there had been an improvement over the previous year's performance in the terms laid down in the standard. The hope is

this would, year by year, company by company, ratchet up integrity standards. When the tax authority undertook a full audit of the company's accounts, it would also meta-audit the outside auditor's review of compliance with the Tax Integrity Continuous Improvement Standard. The Commissioner could publish in her Annual Report the names of companies and accounting firms whose Tax Integrity Continuous Improvement Certifications the authority's audit were unable to verify.

Why would corporations spend money on a process like this? What would be in it for them? Sometimes it would rectify tax overpayments as well as underpayments. If meeting the standard succeeded in improving integrity, it would show up as a preventive factor[1] (as opposed to a risk factor) in tax office multivariate analyses that predict returns from audits. If indeed returns were less from audits of firms who were certified as continuously improving in most recent years, then these firms would not be targeted for audit. Relieving such firms of the burdens of audit would also make sense for the tax authority as a strategy to encourage lead firms to innovate with new software that increases transparency and other technologies that hold out the prospect of lead firms pulling tax integrity standards up through existing ceilings. If the firm did make a mistake that put it at risk of heavy tax penalties in the courts, its certification would be a mitigating factor when the level of penalty was set. All this would make its insurance premiums against adverse tax decisions and professional indemnity cheaper. Finally, as someone who sat on the Reputex Ratings Committee that rated the corporate social responsibility of the top 100 firms in Australia on a variety of criteria, including financial ones, that committee would have loved access to a list of companies that had met a credible Tax Integrity Continuous Improvement Standard. Reputex and like ratings matter to companies first for the positive and negative direct media exposure received by the companies who come out top and bottom. Second, they matter for the way they drive the now substantial investments of ethical investment funds. Third, in extremis, they can affect judgments of ratings agencies like Standards and Poors that decide how much interest firms pay for money they borrow. This final strategy for flipping markets in vice to markets in virtue – corporate certification of continuous improvement – has already been advanced as one that drivers like Reputex might give more relevance in domains like environmental stewardship, affirmative action and occupational health and safety where firms have a more profound interest in taking the virtue of their performance up through ceilings. We return to this idea throughout the rest of the book.

WEBS OF CONTROL

None of the strategies above has any prospect on its own of flipping markets in vice to markets in virtue. While promoter penalties are extremely important, in markets where killings to retire on can be made in a few months before a scheme goes bad, it is implausible that odds of early detection and severe penalties could ever do the job on their own. While each strand in a web of influences to create markets in professional virtue might be weak, together they might weave a fabric that effectively restrains vice. Crucial to that accomplishment is the way the strands are tied together each to reinforce the other. So, for example, we have seen that credible penalties are needed to motivate people to sit in the restorative justice circle about their tax affairs. Equally, of course, procedural justice is needed to motivate sitting in the circle. Business people and tax practitioners will participate in a restorative justice conversation with tax authorities because in the words of one Sydney practitioner: 'Our most valuable asset is our reputation with the tax office . . .'

Restorative justice circles might work at strategic junctures (like Merrill Lynch after the shelter it crafted for Colgate-Palmolive failed) in securing commitment to future tax compliance. This is possible because individual citizens who work in such organizations actually do feel ashamed of some of the things their organization does and do believe in the virtue of a high integrity tax system. As Joseph Bankman put it, some of them would not want 'their momma to know' what they had been up to. Faced with the spectre of heavy penalties in the aftermath of a crisis, many will grab the opportunity restorative justice holds out to flip the organizational dynamic from the pursuit of vice to the pursuit of virtue. Many will not. But one advantage of a regulator with the club of heavy penalties behind their back is that they can respond to an executive who is a hard target by adjourning the restorative justice circle and then reconvening it with his boss in the circle. If the boss turns out to be an even tougher nut, the circle can be widened again until a soft target who can be deterred by shame or by a simple appeal to their integrity becomes the senior corporate player in the circle. It is naive to respond to the empirical evidence from tax compliance research that shame and ethical obligations to comply with the law predict compliance better than the severity of sanctions (Schwartz and Orleans 1967; Scott and Grasmick 1981; Grasmick and Scott 1982; Grasmick and Bursik 1990; Ahmed et al. 2001) by thinking that penalties do not matter. Penalties mostly matter because of the way they interact with informal social control. John Scholz's programme of research suggests that, in spite of low penalties, most people irrationally comply with tax laws because they think it is the right thing to do. However, this ceases being true if they

The cyclical nature of the challenges of regulatory capitalism 59

believe that dishonest taxpayers are getting away with cheating without any punitive consequences (Scholz 1998). Strong penalties and moral reasoning reinforce each other when tied together in a web of influence for flipping vice to virtue. Braithwaite (2005) discussed a variety of these strands beyond the above list of nine strategies for flipping markets in vice to markets in virtue.

That book also tried to draw some wider lessons on how to flip markets in other kinds of vice into markets in virtue. In conditions of regulatory capitalism, markets in professional services, where success depends on reputations for professional ethics, are the most important markets in virtue. As regulatory capitalism renders professional intermediation in markets more common, and the widening scope of competition policy invigorates both more markets in goods and more markets in bads, thinking about how to flip markets in vice to markets in virtue becomes more strategic. Braithwaite's (2005) wider lessons are reordered and recrafted below as hypotheses of more general import about how to flip vice to virtue:

- Do not place too much reliance in any single strand of a web of controls; work the web as a fabric that is tied together at a variety of nodes (a theme developed in Chapter 4).
- Regulate in a collaborative and conversational way; the conversations at nodes of governance pull together intelligence about the vice (connect the dots) and build up a story book of successes and failures that constitutes shared sensibilities, that makes for systemic wisdom about a web of controls, that explores errors as interesting challenges to be corrected (opportunities to learn how to solve problems).
- Organize controls into a responsive regulatory pyramid that encompasses a consideration of the elements below.
- Organize regulatory tools in response to problems (Sparrow 2000) rather than problems around tools from a standard tool-kit (discursively creative regulation as opposed to procedures manual regulation).
- Enact laws based on principles that technically untrained people can understand.
- Connect laws to natural systems people use in their business and social lives as opposed to artificial systems contrived to be convenient for the administrative purposes of the state.
- Experiment with meta regulation (Parker 2002) – regulated self-regulation, to discover where it works.
- Enact heavy penalties for promoters of vice, as opposed to perpetrators of vice. Target on the clients of A-lists of promoters of vice (in response to the enforcement swamping and system capacity

theses, target to increase demand in the market for virtue and reduce demand in the market for vice).
- Pay bounties to private detectors of corporate vice; mandate more fulsome disclosure of the affairs of large corporations (such as shelter disclosure and book-tax disclosure) to create the market for bounty-hunting (see Chapter 3).
- Educate consumers and investors for commission suspicion; market the stories of intermediaries who promise to make consumers the beneficiaries of a vice and end up making them victims of it.
- Experiment with restorative justice near the base of enforcement pyramids that elicit responsibility from all who are responsible without necessarily imposing punishment for that responsibility. This goes, for example, to preventing taxpayers from denying responsibility by simply saying they relied on bad professional advice. It goes to preventing impunity based on scapegoating.
- Redesign competition policy to protect and strengthen standards of professional ethics that strike down structural inducements to profit from the vice of one's clients (for example, contingency fees on taxes avoided).
- Certifiy large private and public sector organizations for continuous improvement in reducing vice and promoting virtue of specified kinds; pulling virtue through ceilings as a strategy for pushing vice above a floor (see Chapter 5).

These are no more than a menu of sensible options to be considered for the task of crafting a contextually attuned integrated strategy for flipping specific markets in vice into markets in virtue. Tax policy, especially Australian enforcement against aggressive tax planning, does illustrate that it can be an instructive policy menu. But it is no recipe. Every market in vice will have its own contextual distinctiveness. We have used cyclical problems of tax cheating to show that a web of control strategies can always be discerned and woven together to make the next surge in a cyclical market in vice less severe than the last.

As with tax, so in other domains as we consider the bullet points above for application to disparate vices, technical competence needs to be mobilized at nodes of governance that tie together stands in a web of controls (see Chapter 3). As with tax, nodes of governance are crafted by and with citizen groups who care about the vice. Governance that works more decently and effectively, in the conditions of an information economy, networks the above influences through collaborations of governments, businesses and NGOs (Castells 2000; Shearing and Wood 2003; Wood and Shearing 2007). The most important reason for this is that what is vice and what is virtue, and how to respond to it, must be deeply contested and contextually contested in a democracy.

It is because virtue is diffused through community networks as well as professional networks that webs of controls that include many informal strands are critical to flipping markets in vice to markets in virtue. That is also why stories, principles, education and natural systems are more important for the business of flipping markets than rules about state-constructed systems; people in civil society think and act on stories and principles more than on technical rules.

Normative scholarship on what should be regarded as a vice or a virtue is of great import. But the interest here is in the analytic point that if markets enable the more efficient production of goods, this also applies to the more efficient production of bads (however defined). The interest is in the sociological point that if vice is perceived by large sections of the community, advocacy of virtue will be a reaction that in a market society will run to a market in virtue. The interest is in the economic point that these counter-currents mean that markets in perceived vice will be more cyclical and more prone to herding than other markets. Being more cyclical, norms of virtue do take hold during the virtuous period of the cycle. We saw this in the hearings in the US Senate at the end of the last US wave of aggressive tax planning, where one major accounting firm after another appeared to condemn their own conduct during their period of vice in the late 1990s. We saw the same phenomenon with business speeches post-Enron, just as we did when the 'greed is good' cycle of the 1980s on Wall Street collapsed.

Rather than be cynical about this normative flip-flop, it can be seen as a resource for working at strategies that more deeply embed norms of virtue and evidence-based compliance policies that are effective – that help the upswing last longer against the drivers of the next downswing into vice. Because virtue, and compliance innovations, flourish during the reaction against the period of vice, regulated self-regulation makes more sense than with non-cyclical problems. Self-regulation can work well during the period of upswing into virtue; its failure during the descent into vice becomes an opportunity for responsive escalation to tough enforcement that sets new benchmarks for the next upswing. When this works, we get a higher and smarter ceiling through which the lead producers ascend, setting new expectations for the ethical laggards.

CONCLUSION

We have seen that the best way to make a fortune fast in the era of regulatory capitalism is to game the rules of financial and other markets. Each cycle of regulatory innovation and financial engineering around that innovation is progressively more innovative. Derivatives in the 1990s became the quintessential tool of the game-player's trade, and financial engineering the paragon of markets both in vice and in regulatory capitalist virtue. Derivatives markets were used virtuously to steady some firms during storms just as they recklessly sailed other firms into storms they would never survive.

Since Marver Bernstein's (1955) classic, we have known that regulation is patterned in a life cycle that moves from vigilance to venality. Vibrant civil society and professional communities are needed to seize the opportunities that cyclical scandals offer to expose the collapse of regulation into ineptitude. Regulation is hard to do well – politically hard, technically hard, legally hard to adduce evidence that sticks, and hard to resource even basic forms of monitoring. Hence it is the inevitability of cyclical ineptitude and regulatory capture that produces the inevitability of cyclical scandals. We have seen that in some central arenas – in capital markets and markets for tax advice – waves of regulation follow the flows of the business cycles. But business cycles simply add momentum to cycles of (financial–securities–tax) regulation that are a phenomenon of more general import about the nature of regulatory capitalism beyond finance.

Regulatory capitalism conduces to commercialization of virtue and commercialization of vice. Because competition policy is so institutionally important in conditions of regulatory capitalism (Freyer 2006), professions that were once more autonomous from both markets and the state are levered by the state to be its agents through market demands for professional virtue and professional reputation (Coffee 2006). This market dynamic also professionalizes advocacy in civil society. For example, unwashed environmental advocates are transformed into besuited environmental compliance consultants in a market whose design principle from the environmental regulator's and the competition regulator's point of view should be as a market in the virtue of improving corporate environmental stewardship. From the corporation's point of view, what is wanted is competition that provides them the advice that protects their environmental reputation from being besmirched. They want a market in greenwash that bribes former unwashed greenies to launder their ethics as well as their clothes. Pro-environmental regulatory strategy then becomes crucially about seizing those cyclical opportunities to press the reset button on the regulatory life cycle, to flip markets in greenwash to markets in environmental stewardship.

The essentially cyclical nature of the historical saga of regulation creates a challenge for good governance. Regulatory reform is crafted in a rush and in an atmosphere of crisis that tends to ratchet regulation ever upwards. This very cycle produces the growth in regulation that is constitutive of regulatory capitalism. The worry is that polities cycle between obverse ineptitudes, between regulatory capture and inept over-regulation. A responsive regulatory attitude is a remedy to this challenge, an attitude where all sides in the regulatory debate come to see it as desirable to play the game at as low a level of their regulatory pyramid as they can manage (see further, Chapter 6). This means business, government, NGOs and professions all see it as smart to be open to ideas from the other players that simultaneously reduce regulatory burdens and produce better outcomes on the matter of regulatory concern. Responsiveness is the most fundamental virtue of the era of regulatory capitalism (Selznick 1992; see further, Chapter 7).

We have seen that another important virtue is for the scholarly communities of regulatory capitalism to learn to be better comparativists of democratic experimentalism (Dorf and Sabel 1998). The great population centres of the world can learn by sitting back and watching the mistakes the little community at the southern tip of Manhattan makes, and it can learn from what less rushed national policy communities have made of Wall Street's mistakes. Both Wall Street and its victims have a lot to gain from an attitude of responsiveness combined with an attitude of evidence-based comparativism. That implies a big change. For now Wall Street is herd based rather than evidence based, insular in spite of its global character. The ethos of the street during its moments of crisis is sacrificial, scapegoating, symbolic and ritualistic more than restorative and responsive. Other nations can instruct it in how to transcend crisis through supplanting a blame culture with a learning culture (see Chapter 6). So can non-financial domains of regulation, as I illustrate with comparative nursing-home regulation in subsequent chapters. The dispensation of global regulatory capitalism is of less financially innovative economies and domains that can learn from their cyclical lags to craft more cost-effective regulation, closing some of the competitive gap between them and Wall Street. The world would do well to love New York for the way it radiates market virtues and vices more profligately than anywhere else, love follower economies for the way they frequently radiate more thoughtful regulatory solutions.

NOTE

1. The terminology of preventive factors versus risk factors comes from public health. A risk factor increases the chance of disease, a preventive factor reduces it.

3. Privatized enforcement and the promise of regulatory capitalism

The first two chapters were about the form of regulatory capitalism: its cyclical nature in Chapter 2, its fundamentally different character from neoliberalism in Chapter 1. It showed how regulatory capitalism resulted from securitization, corporatization and the rise of networked governance. This chapter shifts attention to how such a reconfigured capitalism creates opportunities for reconfigured regulation. It argues that the large, strong states that securitization of the national debt enabled, the growth of megacorporations, metagovernance and NGOs that are private regulators creates the possibility of a new era of hybrid private–public enforcement. Qui tam suits under the False Claims Act in the United States are seen as a harbinger of this possibility. The next section considers the history of qui tam and why it is a strategy with new promise in the era of regulatory capitalism. Then we consider the potential role of NGOs in qui tam enforcement, using the examples of trade unions enforcing breaches of labour laws and environmental groups demanding compliance with pollution standards. Then we consider the new possibilities for interplay between the financial complexity of regulatory capitalism and networking information technology with private enforcers. Finally, we consider how weak states and strong NGOs might interact to create new hybrids of privatized regulation appropriate to the crony capitalism of many developing economies.

WHY PRIVATE LITIGATION MOSTLY ADDS LITTLE VALUE TO SECURING REGULATORY OBJECTIVES

Pamela Bucy (2002a) has surveyed the diversity of ways that private law enforcement has been enabled in US regulation. Whether it is citizen suits to enforce rights under the Civil Rights Act 1964, the Electronic Communications Privacy Act, the Consumer Product Safety Act or the American Disabilities Act, she finds private enforcement of such low frequency as not to have a major impact on the authority of these regulatory regimes in American society. Civil action using the Racketeer Influenced and Corrupt Organizations (RICO) statute is another font of citizen enforcement for which many once held high hopes; Bucy (2002a: 22) found, however, that civil RICO plaintiffs had the awful success rate of three victories in 145 civil RICO cases. Her conclusions are almost as dismal about the effectiveness of the citizen suit provisions that have been included in most environmental and many consumer protection statutes enacted in the US since 1970.

The problem is that citizen suit provisions attached to public environmental and consumer protection laws provide no effective way for citizens to learn about violations. '[T]hey also fail to coordinate public and private prosecutive efforts adequately, fail to offer adequate incentives for counsel to represent plaintiffs in citizen suits, and fail to offer an incentive for those willing to disclose inside information about environmental violations' (Bucy 2002a: 43). Bucy's conclusion is that the special power of private justice is that it can mobilize two things that public enforcement fails to elicit: inside information and entrepreneurial legal talent. Simply providing a right for citizens to initiate actions under a public regulatory law, or providing for class actions, has mostly failed in US legal history to mobilize the best of these two special capabilities of private justice for serving the public good. Insiders who provide information on lawbreaking to outsiders face high costs for their organizational careers. Hence private enforcement laws must be crafted to deliver great rewards for the provision of private enforcement. Similarly, unless private enforcement of environmental laws delivers high rewards to entrepreneurial legal talent, that talent will continue to serve interests in gaming the law rather than complying with it.

> No matter how talented or dedicated our public law enforcement personnel may be nor how many resources our society commits to regulatory efforts, a public regulatory system will always lack the one resource that is indispensable to effective detection and deterrence of complex economic wrongdoing: inside information . . . Private justice can supply the resource of inside information. Because of the necessary and nonsubstitutable nature of this resource, private justice is not just one option for addressing economic banditry in a global, computerized world; it is the best option. (Bucy 2002a: 5)

Bucy finds that private environmental suits averaged 37.4 a year in the US between 1987 and 2000, insufficient for a major impact on regulatory compliance. She finds much greater success of the qui tam provisions of the federal False Claims Act (FCA) in leveraging 237.5 actions per year. 'Comparing the amount of judgments obtained in citizen suits and qui tam FCA actions is even more dramatic. From 1988 through 2000, qui tam FCA judgments totalled $3.9 billion; judgments in environmental citizen suits totalled $16.6 million, or 0.43% of the qui tam FCA aggregate amount' (Bucy 2002a: 43).

Since then Bucy's contrast has become much more dramatic, as 2001–06 False Claims Act qui tam judgments for these six years were several times the 13-year total in her comparison for 1987–2000. Bucy argues we need to understand why qui tam has been so much more successful in drawing out whistle-blowers and drawing in entrepreneurial legal talent with high ethical standards. So what is qui tam and why does it show the way to a major possible transformation of regulatory capitalism?

THE HISTORY OF QUI TAM

Qui tam is shorthand for the Latin, *qui tam pro domino rege, quam pro se ipso in hoc parte sequitur*: 'He who sues as much for the King as for himself.' Qui tam first emerged in statutory form in thirteenth-century England. It rewarded private prosecutors with half the penalties imposed on wrongdoers by the courts. During the fourteenth and fifteenth centuries qui tam was heavily used and abused. While it compensated for the general non-existence of public investigative and prosecutorial capability, professional bounty hunters and informers often fabricated evidence and framed suspects to get their half of the penalty. English law responded to the abuse at first by reducing the plaintiff's share of the penalty, leaving its payment to the discretion of the judge, and finally by abolishing it in the Common Informers Act of 1951. Perhaps closer to the truth is that the Crown appropriated exclusive rights to prosecutorial abuse because it became lucrative in the late Middle Ages, especially with the advent of forfeiture laws (Bucy 2002b: 911). As Friedman (1996: 107) put it: 'the right to run courts and collect fines was a valuable property right . . . Both kings and barons regarded the power to enforce the law as a potential source of income.'

Qui tam survived with more of a presence in the American colony where state institutions were weaker than in England. It was invigorated by President Lincoln in 1863 with the False Claims Act. His war effort was suffering from the delivery of defective military supplies and failure to deliver contracted supplies at all. Lincoln was desperate for a solution to this problem of defence contractors cheating the Union Army at a time when the Attorney-General's office was in its infancy and quite incapable of prosecutorial effectiveness against a military-industrial complex that emerged for the first time. Hence the Act rewarded private suits for false claims against the government with a bounty. Abuse of this renewed qui tam also became rife and again it fell into disuse. That changed in 1986 when Senator Grassley introduced amendments to the False Claims Act to control abuse in effect by making private prosecutors more accountable to public ones. As a result, the False Claims Act quickly became the state's primary weapon to fight fraud against itself (Department of Justice 2003). My argument is that by the late twentieth century, the state had a capability to metagovern private prosecution that was quite beyond the fifteenth-century English state and the nineteenth-century American Union. Hence, a regulatory strategy that had previously repeatedly collapsed under its own abuses was finally ripe for sustainable effectiveness in the era of regulatory capitalism. This is not to say modern qui tam is without abuse (see Askanase 2003); it is only to say that the abuse was no longer so shocking and systematic as to make the law politically unpopular.

The number of qui tam cases filed under the False Claims Act was only 33 in 1987, passed 100 for the first time in 1992, passed 200 in 1994, passed 300 in 1996 and has never fallen below that number since. Qui tam settlements and judgments passed a million dollars for the first time in 1989, $100 million in 1992, $1 billion in 2000 and remained above that in every year since, apart from 2004 (Phillips and Cohen 2007). Fraud against the government's health-care system has been the fastest growing domain for qui tam suits and accounts for the largest share of recoveries, though the original motivator of both the 1863 and 1986 legislation, defence contracting fraud, remains the second largest contributor. While in 1987, only 7 per cent of new fraud matters in the Department of Defence were qui tam cases, since 2000 88 per cent have been qui tam (Phillips and Cohen 2007: Fraud Statistics – Department of Defense). Statutes similar to the False Claims Act to enable qui tam for fraud against the government have now also been enacted in at least nine states – California, Florida, Hawaii, Delaware, Nevada, Illinois, Tennessee, Louisiana and Texas – the District of Columbia (Foster and Havian 2000: 2; Bucy 2002a: 48), New York City and Chicago (www.ffhsj.com).

The initiative for False Claims Act cases normally comes from whistleblowers within a wealthy corporation alleged to have perpetrated fraud against the government. The whistle-blower goes to a law firm that specializes in qui tam suits. It is important to note that whistle-blowers, NGOs and others who launch qui tam suits are not required to have been harmed by the defendant's conduct in any way. This is not private law to recover personal losses as in tort; it is a private right to enforce public law encouraged with reward for doing so. Whistle-blowers and other plaintiffs file lawsuits 'under seal', so that they are concealed from the public and the defendant until the government has time to decide if it wants to join the lawsuit. If the state then runs the case successfully on the basis of information in the initial filing, the whistle-blower gets at least 15 per cent of what the state recovers in the suit, with the court having discretion to award up to 25 per cent. If the government decides not to join the lawsuit, the plaintiff who wins on their own gets a guaranteed 25 per cent and up to 30 per cent.

Qui tam is therefore a solution to the problem that whistle-blowers tend to be permanently tainted as employees. Once they have blown the whistle, they find their career stalls within the firm they have informed upon. If their competence is in defence contracting or supply of pharmaceuticals to hospitals, they find that other contractors in those sectors also will not hire a whistle-blower. It is emotionally agonizing to turn in friends. One survey of 90 whistle-blowers found 54 per cent said they were harassed at work, 82 per cent claimed harassment from superiors, 80 per cent physical deterioration and 86 per cent 'negative emotional consequences, including feelings of depression, powerlessness, isolation, anxiety and anger' (Bucy 2004c: 314). Qui tam provides a financial incentive for whistle-blowers to put up with all this in cases where the government has been defrauded of very large amounts of money. If, as a result of the qui tam suit, the government takes action and recovers $30 million from a pharmaceutical manufacturer or a defence contractor, the whistle-blower's share will range from $3 to $6 million – an amount that can generate an investment return sufficient for retirement, or sufficient to start up a small business. Quite a healthy incentive for senior managers in organizations that commit large frauds to become a whistle-blower. The larger the organization, the bigger the fraud and the deeper the pockets of the fraudster, the more economically remunerative qui tam is for whistle-blowers. This is why qui tam has come of age in the era of the mega-corporation.

Recent American qui tam has proved less rife with abuse than its English precursor because the whistle-blower against, say, a defence contractor who fraudulently extracts payments from the Pentagon must first give the Department of Justice a chance to take over the action. Justice decides to take on most of the meritorious False Claims Act actions because if the case is meritorious and Justice declines to take it over, the whistle-blower's legal team can still take a private action and win twice as large a percentage of the recovered false claims, leaving the revenue poorer and the Justice Department embarrassed by an error of judgement. On the other hand, legal counsel for a whistle-blower with an unmeritorious case will counsel caution once the Department of Justice declines to take over the prosecution. In that circumstance, they must bear all the enforcement costs and risks and must go before a judge who knows that this is a qui tam case the Department of Justice has found in want of merit. Moreover the Justice Department can submit to the court that in the public interest the case should be dismissed.

A virtuous circle of accountability is created by the networking of whistle-blowers with whistle-blower-protection NGOs who refer them to specialized law firms, who share an epistemic community with Justice Department lawyers who are qui tam specialists. Law firms want to be reputable in the eyes of whistle-blower support NGOs on the one hand, and in the eyes of the Justice Department on the other.[1] The market for qui tam legal work in the United States, unlike some other legal markets, meets the conditions for a market in professional virtue (in the terms of the previous chapter of this book). It follows that if the litigators specializing in qui tam suspect that the plaintiff is vexatious, say attempting to frame their employer, lawyers will be reluctant to lend their expertise to a venture that might lose them the case, the fees that come from winning, and their reputation as both a winning and an ethical qui tam litigator.

The networked governance quality of the qui tam enterprise creates a circle of accountability in which whistle-blower, NGO, law firm, Justice Department and judge are each checking abuse of process by one another. This was not the world of the fourteenth-century professional bounty hunter roaming from town to town, dragging alleged felons before a magistrate without any sifting of their allegations either by professional police, prosecutors, law firms or NGOs who are concerned about their reputation locally because they are repeat players. Hence the corporatized world of regulatory capitalism is a world of fatter targets for qui tam, but also one of more networked checks and balances against framing the fat target. Moreover, because the fat target of the twenty-first century is a sophisticated organization that can mobilize procedural safeguards in its defence more readily than the fourteenth-century trader dragged before the court from his market stall, the risk of the defendant being framed is radically reduced. Qui tam is a market that works as a market because rewards are rich and open to contest, and it is a market in professional virtue.

These are some of the respects in which qui tam is a remedy whose time has come with the era of regulatory capitalism. Advocates of qui tam who pre-dated the 1986 amendments to the False Claims Act that so transformed enforcement of fraud against the US state, had a much wider vision of the arenas where qui tam might apply (Crumplar 1975; Fisse and Braithwaite 1983: 251–4). They conceived of whistle-blowers from Enron, Arthur Andersen, Merrill Lynch or others that shook Wall Street in the current decade being able to file their sealed complaint with the Securities and Exchange Commission. Pamela Bucy (2002a: 11) showed that there were Enron insiders who might have been given a financial interest at an early stage in blowing the whistle to get a qui tam payout. While Bucy finds regulatory reform lessons from Enron, she thinks the biggest lessons are about private enforcement reform to enlist knowledgeable insiders to the public interest:

> Reforming existing laws on contributions to 401(k) retirement plans, tax shelters, accounting firms' conflicts of interests, and disclosure requirements for

> derivatives (the type of financial arrangement Enron was able, legally, to keep off its books) should all be considered. But there is a limit to what public regulation can do. Humans are too creative for regulators to anticipate all of the ways greed can overcome judgments and morals. Even if that were not the case, the cost, disruption and injury to a growing and changing economy make massive public regulation unfeasible. Enlisting the resource of inside information; knowledgeable insiders who are willing to alert regulators to malfeasance before or as it is occurring, is the only effective and efficient way to police wrongdoing motivated by economic gain. An effective private justice institutional design can provide this resource. (Bucy 2002a: 10–11)

The pre-1986 advocates of new qui tam laws also conceived of consumer groups working with whistle-blowers to lodge sealed complaints that would give the Federal Trade Commission, the Consumer Product Safety Commission or the Food and Drug Administration an opportunity to join in a major antitrust or consumer protection case. This literature also worked through some of the checks and balances that could be deployed for public legal officers to supervise or pre-empt private qui tam and to craft enabling laws to ensure that qui tam actions could be dismissed by the court if they compromised the integrity of a publicly articulated enforcement policy.

Bucy (2002a: 68) correctly conceives genius in the 'dual-plaintiff design' of the False Claims Act that sees both collaboration between private and public regulators and mutual checking and balancing of each other's mistakes and abuses. Defendants' reputations, for example, are protected while allegations are kept under seal and the competing readings of their justice by public and private regulators are put in contest. This makes for a more circumspect approach than, say, tort litigation, in which the private litigant has an untrammelled incentive to maximize the reputational assault in order to induce conditions for the most favourable settlement. More than that, the dual-plaintiff design of post-1986 qui tam 'provides a structured way for private justice litigants and regulators to maintain a dialog about regulatory policy, and for regulators to provide case-specific guidance and oversight of private litigants' (Bucy 2002a: 69). The first part of this Bucy quote is about what Parker (1999) and Braithwaite and Parker (1999) discuss as the responsive institutional design ideal of enabling the justice of the people to bubble up into the justice of the law, the second part to the ideal of the justice of the law filtering down into the justice of the people. Chapter 7 explores other paths to realizing these twin ideals.

One of the attractive features of qui tam in contemporary conditions is that there is a natural constraint on the most obvious kind of violence to the integrity of a public enforcement policy. This is the violence of using the tool for minor cases that clog the courts. It is hard to imagine whistle-blowers finding it worthwhile to risk litigation in cases where the recovery by the state was less than a six-figure sum. Should they win, the whistle-blower would gain little or nothing from their cut of the recovery after they had paid their lawyers' fees. Lawyers with the competence to win complex qui tam cases will not take them on when they are minor matters that cannot sustain the contingency fees that are generally the basis for their compensation. This is not to deny that qui tam does involve risks of over-enforcement and a consequential drag on economic efficiency, uncertainty and disruption to the lives of the innocent. Prudent judicial custodians of the institution need to be watchful for this. Also, the Department of Justice needs to be vigilant with the right the False Claims Act gives it to submit that the matter be dismissed in the public interest. Finally, the legislature must stand ready to fine-tune the level of qui tam payouts and regulate contingency fees; empirically, if over-enforcement becomes the major problem, the first response should be to reduce the statutory percentage of the payout received by plaintiffs, not to repeal the law.[2] Moreover, policy learning and adjustments can be made to how oversight of qui tam by the Department of Justice and by the courts works. Bucy makes a strong case that the current design of qui tam under the False Claims Act leaves the risk of over-enforcement small compared to its potential to remedy rampant under-enforcement.

On the under-enforcement side, Bucy (2004a: 617) cites the story of Michael R. Lissack, brilliant investment banker, a Smith Barney managing director at an unusually young age. He anonymously called a US Attorney's office to explain to them a massive 'yield burning' fraud phenomenon that was completely unfamiliar to the law enforcement community. After repeated efforts to alert and educate law enforcement anonymously for 18 months, Lissack filed a qui tam lawsuit against national and regional investment banks. It was ultimately settled with 30 banks for $200 million. Not only did Lissack's suit recover a huge sum for the Treasury that had been lost to an enforcement failure, kindred recoveries followed in its wake, to the state of California for example. More importantly, the embarrassment of the exposure of the under-enforcement catalysed policy reform at both the Securities and Exchange Commission and the Internal Revenue Service to deal with a systemic problem they had found too difficult to comprehend and tackle (Bucy 2004a: 618). Mr Lissack seemed to be smarter, better informed and more tenacious than the public enforcers.

Qui tam might also motivate whistle-blowers to take action in cases that are at the less serious end, yet serious enough to justify attention from the courts because of the inevitability of chronic under-enforcement. During my decade as a part-time Commissioner with Australia's national antitrust and consumer protection agency it seemed clear that price-fixing by petrol (gas) stations was rife in rural Australia. Because it was difficult to find whistle-blowers (who had no incentive to inform on their employer), investigation costs were high and prospects of success very low. So only major suspected petrol price-fixing was a priority for investigation.

Imagine an all-too-common kind of Australian rural town with 1000 residents and farmers who buy their petrol from just two outlets in the town that always charge exactly the same price. In the course of a decade, townsfolk, farmers and travellers through the town spend many millions of dollars at these two petrol stations. A whistle-blower files a complaint of price-fixing maintained throughout that decade. It shows prices artificially inflated by more than 10 per cent. The ill-gotten gains therefore amount to many hundreds of thousands of dollars, possibly millions. The appropriate antitrust penalty must, of course, considerably exceed the ill-gotten gains, otherwise it is rational to take one's chances of getting away with it and simply hand over the illegal profits if caught. That is why the False Claims Act provides for treble damages. So the penalty might be attractive enough for the petrol-price whistle-blower, indeed might be enough to justify a court order for the sale of the petrol stations to new owners to pay the fine, even an order to hand over of one of the stations to the whistle-blower to cover his share of the fine. So we can see how it is possible to craft qui tam to make it rational for private enforcement to occur in circumstances where public enforcement is quite impossible. In the world of rural petrol price-fixing enforcement imagined in this paragraph, antitrust offenders would feel vulnerable to a new kind of itinerant bounty hunter – the truck driver who notices that the two retailers in a town have the same price and always move their prices at the same time. The truck driver takes a retirement job at one of the stations to get the insider evidence of price-fixing and waits for his day to win a handsome qui tam boost to his retirement nest egg.

The circumstances I describe are an important public policy problem in Australia, where rural people have become the new poor of our society, yet miss out on all the protections of the regulatory state available in the city. In the move from the police economy discussed in Chapter 1 (in which the local constable was responsible for all forms of commercial cheating in a country town) to the galaxy of specialized regulatory agencies which only find it economic to base inspectors in offices in major cities, rural citizens are the big losers. Qui tam is a tool that might take the enforcement capability of a private constable back into our rural living spaces. Indeed, it could be politically and economically rational for a local council to pay for a regulatory constable who over time recovered much of the secure salary the council provides him or her through occasional qui tam victories before the local magistrate in collaboration with local whistle-blowers. One of the areas they might ply with private enforcement might be labour standards violations against rural workers, a domain where, as we see in the next section, trade unions are the more plausible private prosecutors. As we move on to consider that option, we must not lose sight of the fact that regulatory capitalism has let rural people down. Regulatory capitalism is designed by city dwellers for city dwellers. It needs redesign to reverse the sad effects for those who live in villages and farms of the abolition of the multidisciplinary constable. Peel's invention of paramilitary police preoccuptied with the discipline of crime control was a disaster for the village dwellers of all the world's nations, especially their poorer ones. The remedy may be qui tam combined with a reinvention of rural constables as multidisciplinary regulators of plural forms of domination.

NGOS AS PRIVATE PROSECUTORS

In certain areas there is a long history of NGOs as private prosecutors and private regulatory inspectors. Coal-mine safety is one in Australia (Braithwaite 1985), as is abuse of animals where the Royal Society for the Prevention of Cruelty to Animals has long had inspection and prosecution powers. Early in the twentieth century, citizens of New Jersey could bring civil actions against those who mistreat animals to recover a statutory $100 penalty, with half to be paid to the Society for the Prevention of Cruelty to Animals (Fischer 1973: 778). The New Jersey Society for the Prevention of Cruelty to Animals of a century ago could do fund-raising by being vigilant for opportunities to gather the handsome sum of $50 for the society through civil actions against the very evil that was its mission to eradicate.

Foster and Havian (2000) documented the considerable number of False Claims Act environmental suits that began to emerge in the 1990s. Many were for overcharging the government on clean-up work that was not done or done only partially. Some of these cases developed a theory of 'reverse false claims', meaning avoiding obligations to pay the state. Say a contract with the state includes a requirement to dispose of hazardous waste in compliance with specific regulations, 'then it could be sued for false claims if it certifies to the government that it has disposed of the waste properly but has not done so' (Foster and Havian 2000: 2). Some of the germinal environmental cases were filed by the Natural Resources Defense Council.

Such NGO-initiated cases also open the possibility of NGOs launching False Claims Act cases on behalf of workers whose labour rights are violated. Of course, the scope for this is extremely restricted by the requirement to show a false claim against the government. So the statutory reform needed is access of private citizens to qui tam actions for failure to honour statutory labour standards. Trade unions could be counted on to use such a tool to sue employers on behalf of workers. Let us return to our rural

Australian town and imagine that a local pastoralist has sent packing a team of ten itinerant shearers who have just sheared tens of thousands of sheep for him. He refuses to pay them. Or imagine that the local supermarket has illegally made redundant ten workers, without back pay. You might wonder how it could be economic for a union to launch a qui tam case that recovers only 15 per cent of the salaries of ten poorly paid workers. Yet even in our least likely case of enforcement effectiveness in outback Australia, the same formula as applies in False Claims Act cases for frauds against the US government could actually generate viable returns. First, the False Claims Act provides not just for recovery of the monies defrauded. It pays treble damages. Second, the Act provides for a penalty of between $5500 and $11 000 per false claim.[3] Bucy (2002a: 105–50) advocates applying the same penalty principles to major frauds against financial markets and environmental protection. Translating those principles to private qui tam suits to enforce Australian rural labour rights, the pastoralist and the township supermarket owner would be liable to recovery of three times the wages illegally withheld from the ten workers plus up to $110 000 (10 × $11 000) in per claim penalties. So even in this least likely case of rural labour rights enforcement on behalf of a handful of workers, it is not inconceivable that trade union officials could learn to run such cases in a way that gets the workers their just entitlements and covers the union's costs in doing so.

In the case of the factory in the city where hundreds of workers are underpaid, the viability of labour law qui tam is of course greater. Moreover trade unions do not need to cover all their costs to make qui tam a brilliant enforcement tool for them. Unions do not exist to make a profit; they exist to enforce labour standards; they expect to spend money in the pursuit of that objective. They also seek to secure that objective by increasing union membership. A vibrant membership base is the lifeblood of trade union effectiveness, economically and politically. If half the rural workers for whom it recovers wage entitlements through a qui tam suit join up in appreciation, the fact that the union fails to cover its costs in the suit might not worry it. Moreover, a trade union would use the qui tam threat most commonly to lever a negotiated settlement with the workers in return for keeping the allegations out of the courts and out of the local rural press. A responsive trade union regulator would value qui tam for the influence it would give them from the higher reaches of its private enforcement pyramid.

So the prescription would be to define a wider range of regulatory laws where citizen qui tam suits could be used beyond fraud against the government. This could certainly include environmental laws and labour rights where treble damages and significant per-worker-claim penalties could apply in a way similar to the False Claims Act. Private enforcement policy might be made more restrictive with labour law by barring it if the government agency responsible for labour standards takes any enforcement action consistent with its enforcement policy, even if that is not a prosecution. So, if an Occupational Health and Safety (OHS) agency takes a restorative justice route and successfully negotiates an enforceable undertaking that is credible to the court in terms of the agency's published enforcement policy, then the court would strike down any private qui tam suit by a trade union. The idea of this is to give the firm an incentive to call in the OHS agency and start negotiating an enforceable undertaking that is credible in order to fend off private prosecutions.

In the large-firm sector where OHS inspections are frequent, private prosecutions can be a check and balance on capture of the regulator. An important motivation for a trade union in taking the risks of large legal costs from a private action would be the desire to expose a captured regulator and thereby create the conditions for the appointment of more aggressive enforcers of the law. In the small-firm, outwork and underground sectors, the value of private prosecutions would be to create some deterrence in conditions where neither regular OHS inspections nor OHS compliance systems are likely to be operative. In the conditions of our contemporary deregulated labour market, it might make sense to make multi-pronged union legal attacks on lawless, unsafe work in these sectors viable by simultaneously allowing for private treble damages qui tam suits for underpayment of minimum wages, absence of workers' compensation insurance and other breaches of all labour laws.

A structural analysis of such robust private prosecution capability is that it might attract union litigation not so much to make money as to spearhead unionization pushes in workplaces, the costs of which might be fully or partially funded by the legal actions. The other side of the structural analysis is that it would create conditions where employers actually lobby for the resourcing of government inspectorates to displace 'rogue' union enforcers. A similar kind of analysis could be mounted for motivating employers to lobby for resources for environmental regulators to enforce their laws to prevent 'rogue' environmental NGO qui tam enforcers. In the next section, however, we stick with the OHS challenge to reflect on whether qui tam would be a threat to restorative and responsive justice.

TRIPARTITE RESTORATIVE AND RESPONSIVE JUSTICE

From a restorative justice perspective, there can be virtue in allowing private law enforcement. Restorative justice is partly about empowering victims of injustice and qualifying historically recent state monopolies of enforcement. It is restorative justice thinking in German criminal law, for example, that sees today rape trials often with two prosecutors present – one representing the state, the other the victim (often funded by state legal aid) (Frey 2004). Restorative justice philosophy is about equal consideration for the justice claims of defendants, victims and communities affected by the alleged crime.

With OHS, the idea of the state, workers and employers all being able to take credible enforcement action against each other is that each will display an enforcement pyramid to the others that will motivate all to sit together in the restorative justice circle to engage in a genuine way with conversational regulation (Black 1998). The state displays a hierarchy of state enforcement actions that might range from improvement notices to mandating the preparation of a safety case, to prosecution and deregistration and a good many things in between. There is virtue in workers having more rungs in their enforcement pyramids than go-slows, work-to-rules and stop-work meetings, with qui tam suits as a less draconian possibility before resorting to a fully fledged strike. Responsive regulatory theory therefore raises the question whether qui tam might enable reduction in the days lost from industrial disputes in modern economies. Employers have the most subtle range of enforcement tools, from reprimands, to reassignment to less attractive tasks, withholding bonuses or promotions, up to dismissal. Both NGOs (like unions) and employers also have a range of ways they can regulate the state, ranging from political pressure, to adverse publicity to lawsuits requiring them to exercise public powers properly.

The more clear it is that business, NGOs and government all have quite a range of escalatory options to deploy against the other two, the more sense it makes for the three to sit down together and see if they can discover a path to a win-win-win solution. Ayres and Braithwaite (1992: especially ch. 3) argued that the logic of tripartite responsive regulation is that it creates incentives for dialogic problem-solving, as opposed to punitive regulation. The paradox of the pyramid is that capability to escalate to really severe sanctions is necessary to motivate restorative justice at the base of the pyramid.

Restorative justice means a process where all the stakeholders in an alleged injustice have an opportunity to discuss its consequences and what might be done to right the wrong. It is about sitting in a circle discussing who has been hurt and then the victim being able to describe in their own words how they are coping with the hurt and what they are looking for to repair that harm and prevent it from happening again. It is about the virtue of active responsibility, as opposed to the passive responsibility of holding someone responsible for what they have done in the past. Active responsibility means taking responsibility for putting things right in the future. So a common strategy in preparing for a restorative justice conference is to encourage everyone before the conference to think of any ways they might be willing to own a bit of responsibility for the past by offering to do something to make things better for the future.

Often restorative justice conferences break down because no one wants to own responsibility. When that happens, the skilled facilitator of a business regulatory conference adjourns. She then widens the circle again and again until she finds someone who will own responsibility. If an executive who was directly responsible for an OHS violation digs her heels in, claiming neither she nor the company has any responsibility, then we can widen the circle to include her boss. Perhaps the boss proves to be an even tougher nut in refusing to accept any responsibility on the part of the employer. Then the circle can be widened to that person's boss or boss's boss as discussed in the previous chapter. The advantage the facilitator has as she widens the circle is that statistically she is likely eventually to hit a softer target who can be motivated by shame or moral suasion to offer to take some steps to fix the problem and prevent reoccurrence. The disadvantage the recalcitrant offender has is that she knows that the facilitator deploying this strategy is likely eventually to reach a level of the organization where good relations with the government over a conflict that is spinning out into something larger than it should is going to result in her being told to fix the problem at the end of the process. So why not avoid all that grief and be a constructive problem-solver up front?

So conceived, the circle is a more efficient strategy than iterated OHS prosecutions against workers, manufacturers, suppliers, designers, franchisers, contractors, subcontractors, managers, directors and other duty-holders to own whatever bit of the responsibility is rightly theirs for what went wrong. The circle is about avoiding holding actors to totalizing conceptions of responsibility: 'It was your fault, not mine.' It is about trying to create a contagion of someone starting the process by saying 'Well I think I should take responsibility for ensuring that next time this is done, because if I had done that on this occasion, the spillage of the chemical may never have happened.' Overdetermined multiple responsibility for acting in the future to prevent what has gone wrong in the past is also the best hope for taking safety 'beyond compliance' (Gunningham and Sinclair 2002; Gunningham et al. 2003), forging together creative problem-solving strategies that might never have been seen in a process that focuses on deciding who to single out for blame.

In criminal law, the evidence that restorative justice prevents future crime better than courtroom prosecutions is becoming stronger (Braithwaite 2002; Bonta et al. 2006; Sherman and Strang 2007). However, I have argued that this is only so, at least in many contexts, because the restorative justice circle occurs against a background of the perceived inexorability of escalation to seriously punitive justice if an offender tries to just walk away from their responsibility. So the argument in *Restorative Justice and Responsive Regulation* (Braithwaite 2002) is that restorative justice needs a regulatory pyramid, even if it is only the implicit one of a parent or teacher saying that bullying another child is not something that will be allowed to stand. The safety of the bullied child will be addressed and the harm repaired, one way or another. The parent or teacher projects an image of invincibility. He or she may not be sure what form escalation will take, but whatever it takes, he or she is not going to walk away and leave this child unprotected from bullying with the injustice of the bullying unconfronted. The attitude we should want workplace OHS inspectors to adopt (whether they are from government, unions or the business itself) to OHS abuses should be no less than that inexorable will to confront and solve the problem, and learn from it. This is the context within which to see the greatest potential of a qui tam reform to labour law – in lending credibility to trade unions threatening enforcement escalation in those niches where employers feel invulnerable to enforcement by state inspectors.

Learning leads to the final virtue of the restorative justice circle. The evidence is that communication problems, which often mean failure to learn from the same mistake being made many times before, underlie many serious OHS violations (Braithwaite 1985). Having all the stakeholders in the circle sharing their experience of the problem in their own voice is a better way of promoting learning than having the problem reduced to legal concepts in the words of lawyers who act as mouthpieces for the stakeholders in a courtroom. Inspectors who identify problems, but who resist telling participants how to fix them, also do better at promoting learning and stakeholder ownership of responsibility. In these learning circles, the state is just one stakeholder. Most of the work of repair and future prevention is done by the other stakeholders who are closer to the action. For all that, the media conference announcing the mega-penalty accomplished through a qui tam suit is suggested as a crucial enabler for the warm and fuzzy work of restorative OHS. That is why it is crucial for the law to prevent litigious qui tam from pre-empting or killing off restorative justice when restorative justice is working well in securing health and safety.

The simple way to do that is for a regulatory agency to have an enforcement policy that privileges restorative justice at the base of an enforcement pyramid. When the regulator moves effectively through restorative justice to deal with the problem in compliance with that enforcement policy, the qui tam litigation does not proceed (though the whistle-blower still has a claim to 15 per cent of the penalties voluntarily paid through the restorative justice agreement). Enforcement policies should give whistle-blowers a right to participate in such restorative justice circles.

OPENING ACCOUNTS TO PRIVATE ENFORCEMENT ENTREPRENEURS

Pamela Bucy's (2002a: 79) most fundamental insight is that the 'more complex and interconnected our world, the more essential inside information becomes to effective regulatory efforts'. This is conceived here as an insight about the nature of regulatory capitalism. False Claims Act powers of qui tam explicitly do not apply to tax fraud in the US. They should, if we take economic justice seriously. The fundamental problem of tax enforcement is that a great many among the very rich use corporate shelters, financial engineering around tax laws, international arbitrage and tax havens to avoid most of the liabilities the law expects them to pay. Or they use them to pay no tax at all. It is hard to overestimate what a large driver of the widening gap between the very rich and mainstream society this is, particularly in the United States (Johnston 2003; Braithwaite 2005). Tax enforcement failure is an information failure problem. The smart money is always a generation ahead of the financial engineering comprehension of tax authorities, as we saw in Chapter 2. Therefore, as with other kinds of complex fraud against the government, the solution is to draw out whistle-blowers. In tax that would be easy because the revenue loss from the biggest scams is so large. That is why the United States excludes qui tam from application to false tax claims. It would be too effective. It would cause too much business activity to shift out of the United States to avoid it and too many campaign contributions to dry up.

Ironically, in the same year of the False Claims Act reforms in the US, Christopher Hood (1986), building on Becker and Stigler's (1974) work on the privatization of law enforcement, argued that while privatizing British tax enforcement would have its problems, these were less than in other domains of law enforcement. There have been other proposals to foster private regulation of tax that merit consideration with or without financial qui tam. In 2002, ranking US Republican on the Senate Finance Committee, the same Charles E. Grassley who had introduced the transformative False Claims Act amendments of 1986, indeed the same senator who was a key player in much of the nursing home-regulatory reform of recent decades discussed elsewhere in this book, called for public disclosure of corporate tax returns (Stratton 2002: 220). The call was motivated by the vast difference between the numbers in Enron and WorldCom's tax returns and their financial statements to the stock exchange. The argument was that if investors had access to the tax return data, analysts might have detected the fraudulent books before the company went down. Canellos and Kleinbard (2002: 2) have argued that this would not work: what would be more useful for both tax auditors and investors would be to have access to a public book-tax reconciliation schedule that would 'provide a useful platform for highlighting transactions which are likely to involve manipulation for tax and accounting concepts'. Theodore Sims (2002) suggested that making corporate returns available in a useful form on a website would enable a system of rewards for private auditors (bounty hunters) who brought new tax shelters to light. To motivate private auditors to pick over corporate tax returns in search of shelters, Sims suggests a bounty of, say, 20 cents in every dollar recovered by the tax authority payable by the taxpayer to the private auditor on top of any other tax penalty. 'The most effective way of channelling sufficient resources into prevention is to make it as profitable to police corporate shelters as it has obviously become to purvey them' (Sims 2002: 736). Requiring public companies to make public a book-tax reconciliation schedule as part of the social contract that also grants them limited liability does not seem an unreasonable intrusion into their privacy. If this reform were combined with the False Claims Act applying to false claims in tax returns, private auditors of tax shelters might use the book-tax reconciliation schedule to target likely multimillion dollar tax cheats, and then draw out the right whistle-blower to share in a qui tam recovery for the Treasury.

PRIVATE JUSTICE AND DEVELOPING ECONOMIES

If qui tam is an idea whose time has come with the maturing of regulatory capitalism, are developing economies ready for it? First, do developing countries have the concentrations of corporate wealth that would provide qui tam targets with deep enough pockets? My first thought was that it would work with only some developing countries with which I am familiar – Indonesia, the Philippines, Thailand – that have a crony capitalism that concentrates wealth incredibly. In these three countries the ten families with the greatest share ownership control half the corporate sector; in Hong Kong and Korea the top ten families control one-third (Partnoy 2000: 770). Yet when I thought of the extremely poor countries that I knew best – Papua New Guinea and the Solomon Islands – none of the indigenous cronies who run things seemed to have deep enough pockets to make qui tam legal practice a particularly viable business. Then I realized I was wrong. What about the companies who are doing most to destroy the future of the Solomon Islands – the Asian logging companies who rip out the forests, often without permits or in breach of the conditions of permits they do have, who pay little tax and get away with this because they have corrupted the political system. They are destroying not only the extraordinary environment of the Solomon Islands, something they are also doing in Papua New Guinea's tropical forests; they are also destroying the agricultural base of future generations of villagers who comprise most of the population. Then in Papua New Guinea I began to think of the, mostly Anglo-Australian, mining companies that have also caused massive, reckless environmental destruction. Companies like BHP-Billiton and Rio Tinto have among the deepest pockets in the world, as do the banks and accounting firms that work for them.

Where would the entrepreneurial legal talent come from in a poor, tiny country like the Solomon Islands to take on a major Asian logging conglomerate in a qui tam suit? Initially of course it would come from international NGOs, who if they were good capacity-builders would train local lawyers working beside them to take over from them. International NGOs like Avocats sans Frontiers, working with development agencies like the World Bank who support legal capacity-building, could also help with learning the lessons of English and American history from qui tam. Public prosecutorial and civil justice oversight capability in the Solomon Islands is not as weak as it was in the office of Abraham Lincoln's Attorney-General, but it is closer to that than to the US Justice Department today. Lincoln did not have legal governance capacity-building support from private and public foreign aid that could be mobilized to monitor abuse of qui tam in the Solomon Islands. So I would actually suspect that environmental and financial qui tam laws of the sort drafted by Pamela Bucy (2002a: 105–50) would actually be one of the better things the Solomon Islands could do to tackle the biggest problems it faces.

We must also remember that some developing societies such as India have strong democratic states with substantial, sophisticated bureaucracies and courts. Many 'failed states' such as Afghanistan are strong societies with formidable regulatory capacities in civil society through institutions such as *jirga* (Wardak 2004). One policy option for rural areas of developing countries is to revert to something closer to the pre-industrial ideal of policing, where a local constable (like a District Officer in British colonial administration) was not a specialist in policing crime, but regulated business as well. In the Internet age, generalist police/regulatory constables could be paid and trained as part-time information points on what approaches a village court might take to dealing with environmental harm caused by a local business. Equally, however, as in the discussion above of petrol price-fixing in the Australian rural town, when larger national or international organizations with deep enough pockets are commercially plundering a village, the local constable would be trained in how to network with legal NGOs or private qui tam lawyers in the capital. In the Solomon Islands and Papua New Guinea it is tragic to observe local police ignore logging that clearly fails to comply with regulatory laws because they see that as the responsibility of Forestry Department bureaucrats far away in the capital.

Qui tam in effect networks whistle-blowers with law firms, state regulators and prosecutors, extending the intelligence, evidence-gathering and litigation capabilities of the state in big, difficult cases. The reason qui tam was invented in thirteenth-century England at around the same time that village-level generalist police was invented was to compensate for weakness in state regulatory capacity. Across the globe today it still might be true that where state capacity is weakest the case for reliance on qui tam is strongest. Obversely, where state regulatory capacity is strong, private prosecution to fill gaps left gaping by failed public enforcement is less critical. In this sense, qui tam in the US should be a least likely case (Eckstein 1975) of qui tam adding value. The fact that it clearly has added value there might give hope that qui tam might prove valuable in weak states where opportunities to substitute for failed state enforcement are more plentiful.

On the other hand, if the court system and justice bureaucracy themselves in a developing country are so inefficient or corrupt that they cannot cope with surges of qui tam actions, then these greater opportunities may simply not be practically available to be seized. Even in such circumstances, a strategy that can rely on private resources to do much of the justice bureaucracy's work for it has more prospects than reliance on a wholly public process. The Grassley proposals on making corporate tax returns more effectively public on the Internet so that a private tax auditing industry might emerge need not depend on courts. It could work by practitioners in this new private market in tax virtue taking the finding of their private analysis to the public tax authority. If the tax authority administratively assesses an extra $10 million in tax that the corporation voluntarily pays or settles (that is what normally happens), then the private tax auditor might win her $2 million qui tam payout without approaching a court.

Note also how the private auditor can help make responsive regulation work by being a check on corrupt tax officers, prosecutors and other officials (Ayres and Braithwaite 1992: ch. 3). When the corrupt official reaches a cosy settlement with the corporation that fails to collect the tax owed, the private auditor has an interest in exposing this to his administrative and political masters who have an interest in higher tax collections, and to the courts if necessary, in order to collect the full bounty owed to the private auditor. Cooter and Garoupa (2000) show that one of the attractive features of bounties (combined with immunities for any minor roles a whistle-blower played in the crime) is that they can create conditions where criminals cannot trust each other. Corruption unravels when each partner in a crime is also a potential bounty hunter. An important feature of qui tam here is that only the first to lodge the qui tam suit can collect the bounty. Hence, there are disincentives among those with incriminating knowledge to sit back and hope the problem goes away; there are incentives to be the first into the Justice Department with that knowledge. Both the corrupt regulator who takes bribes and the executive who pays them are vulnerable to this incentive to be the 'first in time' to the Justice Department.

Enforcement of labour standards is another area where qui tam would mostly work by threatening the private prosecution in order to trigger settlement negotiations, while rarely in practice having to rely on an overburdened court system. If the international trade union movement managed to get this kind of private enforcement capability implemented in developing countries through Free Trade Agreements, the International Labour Organization (ILO) and World Trade Organization (WTO) negotiations, they could also be used by multi-stakeholder initiatives for global labour rights. The idea would be that an organization like the Fair Labor Association would threaten qui tam actions against both developing country manufacturers who breach the labour laws of that country and the multinationals behind the brand who benefit from those breaches. Because globally strategic qui tam test case litigation might be self-funding, it would be a credible new lever for the weak to negotiate settlements of underpaid wages and other labour rights.

Networking with lawyers who specialize in qui tam actions against multinational companies would be networking with lawyers who in some cases could mount actions in foreign courts against multinationals – thereby obviating the need to rely on courts in the poor country. While it is unimaginable that False Claims statutes to compensate developing states could be enforced in Western courts, in tort cases like the Bhopal chemical pollution disaster in India and the litigation against BHP (now BHP-Billiton) by Papua New Guinea villagers over the destruction of their livelihoods by the pollution of the Fly River, globally networked law firms have had major impacts on multinationals.

Whatever the level of the governance deficits in developing societies, in an era of networked governance, weaker actors can enrol stronger ones to their projects if they are clever. Anne-Marie Slaughter's (2004) work suggests that the globe is strewn with disaggregated bits of strong states that might be enrolled by weak states (and by weak NGOs). The developing country civil aviation regulator can enrol the US Federal Aviation Administration to stand up to an airline that flouts safety standards in the developing country; and the developing country health regulator can enrol the Food and Drug Administration to audit the unsafe clinical trials on a new drug being conducted on its people. Developing nation NGOs may be weak, but are becoming stronger both in their own right and in their capacity to enrol Northern NGOs and international regulatory organizations into projects to compensate for the weak regulatory capacities of developing states. Responsive escalation up a regulatory pyramid can hence be accomplished not only by escalating state intervention, but also, as Peter Drahos (2004a; 2004b; 2004c) has suggested, by escalating the networking of new tentacles of domestic and transnational governance.

The core idea of responsive regulation as a strategy actually has special salience for resource-poor states. This is the idea that no regulator has the resources consistently to enforce the law across the board and therefore limited enforcement resources need to be focused at the peak of an enforcement pyramid. Networking escalation is an interesting elaboration of how to make the most of limited regulatory capacity. Qui tam is a statutory private justice reform that instead of substituting public with private justice, institutionalizes collaborative networking that enables more credible regulatory escalation. Mobilizing public virtue to regulate private vice is not the only path around capacity deficits. Private markets in virtue can also be mobilized to regulate vice, indeed to flip markets in vice to markets in virtue. Where state capacity is weakest, both qui tam and responsive escalation via networking with progressively more private and public enforcers should pay the highest dividends. Moreover, networking regulatory partnerships also structurally reduces the benefits of capture and corruption in those developing economies that are endemically prone to corruption. Responsive regulation is a worrying strategy in corrupt societies because it puts more discretion in the hands of regulatory bureaucrats who can use that discretion to increase the returns to corruption. Both the strategies of networking around state incapacity and mobilizing private markets for enforcing virtue have the attractive feature of exposing and preventing regulatory corruption.

CONCLUSION

In the era of transnationally networked governance and globalizing regulatory capitalism, the kind of hybrid private–public law enforcement of qui tam can contribute more to regulatory pyramids than either the private prosecutions of centuries past or purely public enforcement. In the United States the market for qui tam legal work is much more a market in virtue than the market for tort law. Qui tam lawyers also do more to keep public prosecutors honest than tort lawyers. Silencing and emotional emasculation of whistle-blowers is a form of domination with devastating consequences in modern societies. Qui tam gives whistle-blowers a voice by giving them an improved instead of a diminished financial future. This can help democracies become more vital republics in which legal institutions enable the injustices of the people that are most suppressed by forces of economic domination to bubble up into the justice of the law. At the same time it has an innovative strategy for giving public reason a path to constrain excesses of private litigation, albeit one where the private citizen ultimately can reject the counsel of the Justice Department and contest it in the courts.

Some might see it as a threat to the doctrine of the separation of powers to allow a court to back a private prosecutor against a contrary view from the public prosecutor, implicitly sending a message from the judicial to the executive branch that 'you were wrong not to prosecute this'. No, a republican who values freedom as non-domination (Braithwaite 1997; Pettit 1997) cannot want a separation of powers where each branch of governance is left alone to misuse power without too much interference within its own sphere from the other branches of government. Rather, for the complex world of regulatory capitalism, republican freedom requires many separations of private and public powers, not just three branches of state governance. This republican ideal is for each separated power to be sufficiently autonomous from the many other centres of power not to be dominated by them. Yet part of this resilience against domination comes from their very interdependence with all of those other branches of power. No single branch of governance is allowed to dominate because, as it seeks to dominate another branch, that branch's interdependence with third and fourth branches will protect its semi-autonomy.

A concrete instantiation of this republican ideal is a world where public prosecutors, private markets for legal work, and courts can together help whistle-blowers escape the domination of business criminals. Equally, courts and private qui tam litigants can join to defeat the joint domination of business criminals and an executive branch captured by them. Yet the same institutional design also allows for the joining of the separated powers of the court and the public prosecutor to protect an innocent business from a vexatious whistle-blower. It is a messy ideal of cross-cutting deliberation of public reason. The best ideals are a bit messy and redundant. They have to be because domination can come from so many unexpected directions.

NOTES

1. Moreover, as Bucy (2002a: 58) explains: '[T]he goals of realtors [private qui tam plaintiffs] is to convince the DOJ [Department of Justice] of a case's merit so that the DOJ will

intervene to take "primary responsibility" for the case. Realtors' counsel does this by presenting to the DOJ, at the time of the complaint it filed (under seal), a thorough, well-thought-out, carefully researched report describing exactly how fraud was committed and how it can be proven in the highly complex, regulatory area of government contracting. The demanding nature of this task requires skilled counsel and deters unskilled or inexperienced counsel. Such an undertaking is simply too difficult and time-consuming for inexperienced counsel, especially if – as is almost certain – counsel is working on a contingency fee basis.'

In a subsequent study, Bucy (2004b: 1039) reported an American Bar Association survey of the False Claims Act private bar that showed 51 per cent to have attended a 'top 25' undergraduate institution, 71 per cent a 'top 25' law school, 48 per cent to have served in the Justice Department, 23 per cent to have served as a law clerk to a federal judge, 43 per cent to hold a leadership role in their law firm and 32 per cent to have authored three or more publications in the False Claims Act field.

2. The implicit normative position here is that there is nothing inherently wrong with legislating for contingency fees to be shared between whistle-blowers and their lawyers. The previous chapter argued that contingent remuneration of tax practitioners on the basis of the reduction in tax liability they secure for their client should be banned. That was because those tax contingency fees engender a market in vice. The argument in this chapter is that qui tam contingencies create a market in virtue. Law should therefore be designed specifically to allow those contingencies, including for tax enforcement.

3. See 28 C.F.R.§ 85.3(a)(9)(2002).

4. The nodal governance critique of responsive regulation[1]

There are many critiques of responsive regulation (for example, Black 1997; Haines 1997; 2005b; Pearce and Tombs 1997; Gunningham and Grabosky 1998; Glasbeek 2002; Tombs 2002; Vincent-Jones 2002; Scott 2004; Yeung 2004; Barton 2006; Maxwell and Decker 2006; Nielsen 2006; Parker 2006; Feld and Frey 2007; Gunningham 2007; Rawlings 2007; Waller 2007; Wood and Shearing 2007). It is not the purpose of this chapter to address all the insightful lines of attack that have been made on the theory, just some that are centrally relevant to the regulatory capitalism theme of this book. The most common criticism is the least accurate: that responsive regulation is a statist theory, merely about what state regulators should do. Were it true, this really would be an important critique in terms of its relevance to an era of networked governance. The reason some have made this critique relates to the way they have focused upon the first two chapters of the most influential presentation of the theory in the book by Ian Ayres and John Braithwaite (1992) titled *Responsive Regulation*. Even with that book, it is a strange critique in that chapter 3 is about tripartism. Chapter 3 is about the way state regulators are prone to capture, corruption and weak accountability unless there are third players of the game who are neither business nor state players. Moreover, earlier writings on enforced self-regulation (Braithwaite 1982) and on the regulatory pyramid (Braithwaite 1985) were embued with learnings from mine-safety research that found unionized mines to be safer, that the regulation of individual mines by the head office safety department, by management–worker safety committees and by elected trade union inspectors were together more important than state inspection, yet were empowered by state inspection.

Nevertheless, one can understand why younger scholars who were born into the era of regulatory capitalism see *Responsive Regulation* as a book that is overly statist in its obsessions. The core chapters were written right at the end of the Reagan presidency and near the end of Thatcherism in Britain. It was a reflection back on the debates of that era. First, it was about the empirical claim that it was wrong to view it as an era of privatization and deregulation, a theme revisited in Chapter 1 of this book. Second, Ayres and Braithwaite's book (1992) was about how unproductive the regulatory policy debate had been during that time. For the entire period from Watergate to the demise of Margaret Thatcher we saw a glorious battle between those defending deregulation, led by the Chicago school of economists, versus defenders of the New Deal and of the post-Watergate crackdown on corporate crime. First, I must explain the basics of the theory. Then I mount some critiques of responsive regulation I do wish to accept because they involve a more rounded, adaptive, nodal understanding than mine of how to get things done in the era of regulatory capitalism. The next section is a rehash of Ayres and Braithwaite (1992) and Braithwaite (2002). Those familiar with these works can skip it.

CORE IDEAS OF RESTORATIVE AND RESPONSIVE REGULATION

The basic idea of responsive regulation is that regulators should be responsive to the conduct of those they seek to regulate in deciding whether a more or less interventionist response is needed. Rule enforcers should be responsive to how effectively citizens or corporations are regulating themselves before deciding whether to escalate intervention. The dissatisfaction with the business regulation debate that motivated Ian Ayres and I to write *Responsive Regulation* was with the unproductive see-sawing in policy ascendancy between those who argued that business people are rational actors who only understand the bottom line (and who therefore must be consistently punished for their lawbreaking) versus those who believe business people are responsible citizens who can be persuaded to come into compliance. The latter tend to gain the ascendancy during long booms that are free of crisis, while the punitivists get the upper hand when capitalism is punctuated by crises (Chapter 2, this book). In different contexts there is a lot of truth in both positions. This means that both consistent punishment and consistent persuasion are foolish strategies. The hard question is how do we decide when to punish and when to persuade. What makes the question so difficult is that attempts to regulate conduct do not simply succeed or fail. Often they backfire, making compliance worse. So the tragedy of consistent punishment of wrongdoers of a certain type is that our consistency will regularly cause us to make things worse for future victims of the wrongdoing.

The most distinctive part of responsive regulation is the regulatory pyramid. It is an attempt to solve the puzzle of when to punish and when to persuade. At the base of the pyramid is the most restorative dialogue-based approach we can craft for securing compliance with a just law. Of

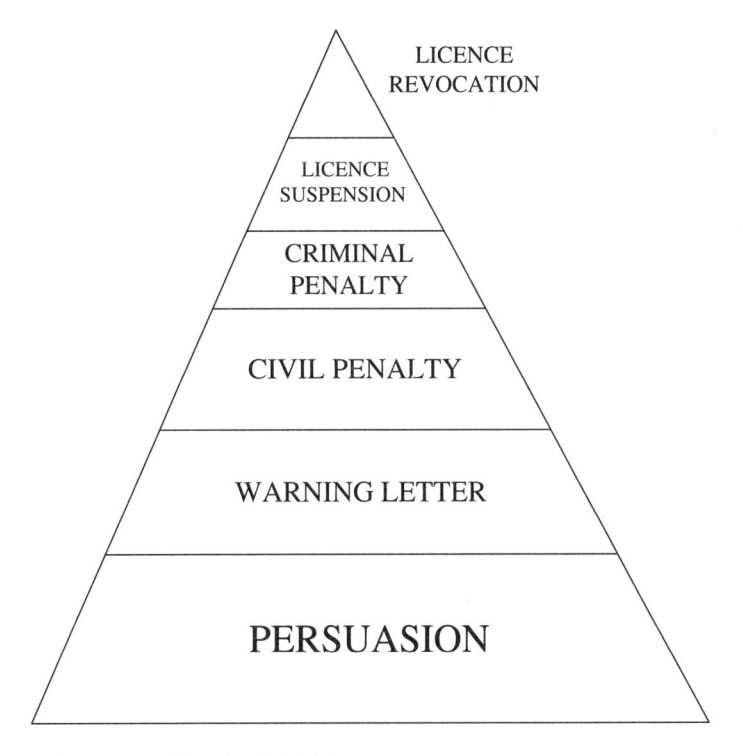

```
                    LICENCE
                   REVOCATION
                  ───────────
                    LICENCE
                   SUSPENSION
                 ──────────────
                   CRIMINAL
                    PENALTY
               ──────────────────
                  CIVIL PENALTY
             ────────────────────────
                 WARNING LETTER
         ──────────────────────────────

                    PERSUASION
```

Source: Ayres and Braithwaite (1992: 35).

Figure 4.1 An example of a regulatory pyramid

course if it is a law of doubtful justice, we can expect the dialogue to be mainly about the justice of the law (and this is a good thing from the civic republican perspective that provided the normative motivation for the theory – Braithwaite and Pettit 1990; Pettit 1997). As we move up the pyramid, more and more demanding and punitive interventions in peoples' lives are involved. The idea of the pyramid is that our presumption should always be to start at the base of the pyramid first. Then escalate to somewhat punitive approaches only reluctantly and only when dialogue fails. Then escalate to even more punitive approaches only when the more modest forms of punishment fail. Figure 4.1 is an example of a responsive business regulatory pyramid from Ayres and Braithwaite (1992: 35). The regulator here escalates with the recalcitrant company from persuasion to a warning to civil penalties to criminal penalties and ultimately to corporate capital punishment – permanently revoking the company's licence to operate.

The crucial point is that it is a dynamic model. It is not about specifying in advance which are the types of matters that should be dealt with at the base of the pyramid, which are the more serious ones that should be in the middle and which are the most egregious for the peak of the pyramid. Even with the most serious matters – flouting legal obligations to operate a nuclear power plant safely that risks thousands of lives – we stick with the presumption that it is better to start with dialogue at the base of the pyramid. A presumption means that however serious the crime, our normal response is to try dialogue first for dealing with it, and to only override the presumption if there are compelling reasons for doing so. Of course, there will be such reasons at times – the man who has killed one hostage and threatens to kill another may have to be shot without a trial, the assault offender who during the criminal process vows to go after the victim again and kill her should be locked up.

As we move up the pyramid in response to a failure to elicit reform and repair, we often reach the point where, finally, reform and repair is forthcoming. At that point responsive regulation means that we must put escalation up the pyramid into reverse and de-escalate down the pyramid. The pyramid is firm yet forgiving in its demands for compliance. Reform must be rewarded just as recalcitrant refusal to reform will ultimately be punished.

Responsive regulation has been an influential policy idea because it formulated a way of reconciling the clear empirical evidence that sometimes punishment works and sometimes it backfires, and likewise with persuasion (Braithwaite 1985; Ayres and Braithwaite 1992). The pyramidal presumption of persuasion gives the cheaper and more respectful option a chance to work first. The more costly punitive attempts at control are thus held in reserve for the minority of cases where persuasion fails. Yet it is also common for persuasion to fail. When it does, the most common reason is that a business actor is being a rational calculator about the likely costs of law enforcement compared with the gains from breaking the law. Escalation through progressively more deterrent penalties will often take the rational calculator up to the point where it will become rational to comply. Quite often, however, the business regulator finds that they try restorative justice and it fails; they try escalating up through more and more punitive options and they all fail to deter. This happens for a number of reasons. One is the so-called deterrence trap (Coffee 1981), where no level of financial deterrent can make compliance economically rational. Perhaps the most common reason in business regulation for successive failure of restorative justice and deterrence is that non-compliance is neither about a lack of goodwill to comply nor about rational calculation to cheat. It is about management not having the competence to comply. The manager of the nuclear power plant simply does not have the engineering know-how to take on a

The nodal governance critique of responsive regulation 91

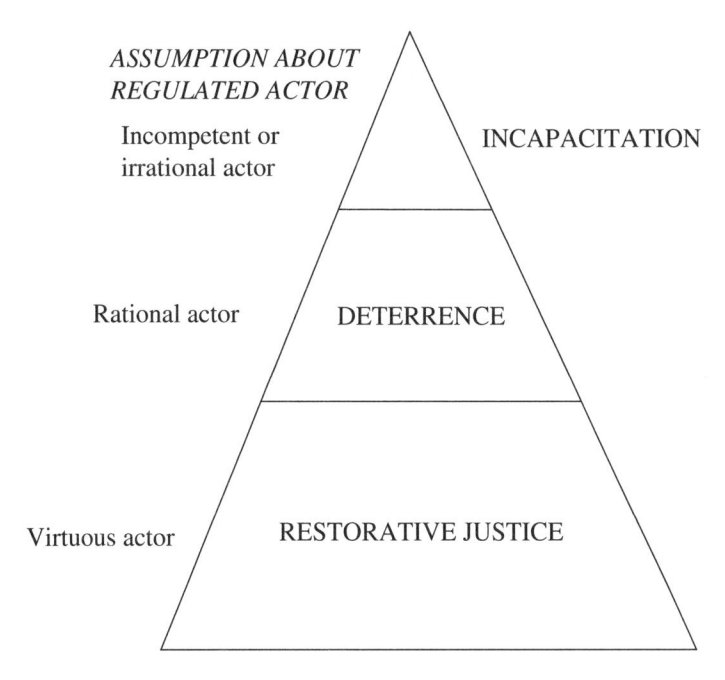

Figure 4.2 Towards an integration of restorative, deterrent and incapacitative justice

level of responsibility this demanding. He or she must be moved from the job. Indeed, if the entire management system of a company is not up to the task, the company must lose its licence to operate a nuclear power plant. So when deterrence fails, the idea of the pyramid is that incapacitation is the next port of call (see Figure 4.2).

Restorative justice is an approach where at the base of a regulatory pyramid, all the stakeholders affected by an injustice have an opportunity to discuss how they have been hurt by it, to discuss their needs and what might be done to repair the harm and prevent recurrence. It is also an approach informed by a set of values that defines not only a just legal order, but a caring civil society. These values are, for me, derived from the foundational republican value of freedom as non-domination (Braithwaite 2002: 12–16), though others who share the same restorative justice values motivate them from different foundations (for example, Zehr 1995; 2002). The design of Figure 4.2 responds to the fact that restorative justice, deterrence and incapacitation are all limited and flawed theories of compliance. What the pyramid does is to cover the weaknesses of one theory with the strengths of another.

The ordering of strategies in the pyramid is not just about putting the less costly, less coercive, more respectful options lower down in order to save money and preserve the republican value of freedom as non-domination. It is also that by only resorting to more dominating, less respectful forms of social control when more dialogic forms have been tried first, coercive control comes to be seen as more legitimate. When regulation is seen as more legitimate, more procedurally fair, compliance with the law is more likely (Tyler 1990; Tyler and Blader 2000; Tyler and Huo 2001). Astute business regulators often explicitly set up this legitimacy. During a restorative justice dialogue over an offence, the inspector will say there will be no penalty this time, but that she hopes the manager understands that if she returns and finds the company has slipped back out of compliance again, under the rules she will have no choice but to refer it to the prosecutions unit. When the manager agrees, yes this is understood, a future prosecution will likely be viewed as fair. Under this theory, therefore, privileging restorative justice at the base of the pyramid builds legitimacy and therefore compliance.

There is also a rational choice account of why the pyramid works. System capacity overload (Pontell 1978) results in a pretence of consistent law enforcement where in practice enforcement is spread around thinly and weakly. Unfortunately, this problem will be at its worst where crime is worst. Hardened offenders learn that the odds of serious punishment are low for any particular infraction. Tools like tax audits that are supposed to be about deterrence are frequently exercises that backfire by teaching hardened tax cheats just how much they are capable of getting away with (Kinsey 1986: 416). The reluctance to escalate under the responsive pyramid model means that enforcement has the virtue of being highly selective in a principled way. Moreover, the display of the pyramid itself channels the rational actor down to the base of the pyramid. Non-compliance comes to be seen (accurately) as a slippery slope that will inexorably lead to a sticky end. In effect what the pyramid does is solve the system capacity problem with punishment by making punishment cheap. The pyramid says unless you punish yourself for lawbreaking through an agreed action plan near the base of the pyramid, we will punish you much more severely higher up the pyramid (and we stand ready to go as high as we have to). So it is cheaper for the rational firm to punish itself (as by agreeing to payouts to victims, community service, paying for new corporate compliance systems). Once the pyramid accomplishes a world where most punishment is self-punishment, there is no longer a crisis of capacity to deliver punishment where it is needed. One of the messages the pyramid gives is that 'if you keep breaking the law it is going to be cheap for us to hurt you because you are going to help us hurt you' (Ayres and Braithwaite 1992: ch. 2).

Paternoster and Simpson's (1996) research on intentions to commit four types of corporate crime by Master of Business Administration (MBA) students reveals the inefficiency of going straight to a deterrence strategy. Paternoster and Simpson found that where the MBAs held personal moral codes, these were more important than rational calculations of sanction threats in predicting compliance (though the latter were important too). It follows that for the majority of these future business leaders, appeals to business ethics (as by confronting them with the consequences for the victims of a corporate crime) will work better than sanction threats. So it is best to try such ethical appeals first and then escalate to deterrence for that minority for whom deterrence works better than ethical appeals.

According to responsive regulatory theory, what we want is a legal system where citizens learn that responsiveness is the way our legal institutions work. Once they see the legal system as a responsive regulatory system, they know that there will be a chance to argue about unjust laws (as opposed to being forced into a lower court production line or a plea bargain). But they will also see that game-playing to avoid legal obligations, failure to listen to persuasive arguments about the harm their actions are doing and what must be done to repair it, will inexorably lead to regulatory escalation. The forces of law are listening, fair and therefore legitimate, but also seen as somewhat invincible. The deterrence superiority of the active deterrence of the pyramid, as opposed to the passive deterrence of a fixed scale of penalties that is consistently imposed for different offences is developed in Braithwaite (2002: ch. 4).

In the punishment versus persuasion debates among regulatory scholars, while advocates of consistent punishment argued that cynical businesses abuse offers of cooperation (which they do if cooperation is not backed up by enforcement capability), advocates of consistent persuasion argued that punishment and persuasion involve incompatible imperatives. Theorists of this second sort believe that threat and coercion undermine goodwill and therefore the trust that makes cooperative compliance work. This indeed can also be pointedly true. How can we but corrupt restorative justice values if we seek to coerce them? The first point to make is factual. Very few criminal offenders who participate in restorative justice processes would be sitting in the room without a certain amount of coercion. Without their detection and/or arrest, without the spectre of the alternative of a criminal trial, they simply would not cooperate with a process that puts their behaviour under public scrutiny. No coercion, no restorative justice (in most cases).

The question seems not one of how to avoid coercion, but how to avoid the escalation of coercion and how to avoid threats. A paradox of the pyramid is that to the extent that we can absolutely guarantee a commitment to escalate if steps are not taken to prevent the recurrence of lawbreaking, then escalation beyond the lower levels of the pyramid will rarely occur. This is the image of invincibility making self-regulation inevitable. Without locked-in commitment to escalation where reform does not occur to fix the problem, the system capacity crisis will rebound. The fundamental resource of responsive regulation is the belief of citizens in inexorability.

Restorative justice works best with a spectre of punishment in the background, threatening in the background but never threatened in the foreground. Where punishment is thrust into the foreground even by implied threats, other-regarding deliberation is made difficult because the offender is invited to deliberate in a self-regarding way – out of concern to protect the self from punishment. This is not the way to engender empathy with the victim, internalization of the values of the law and the values of restorative justice, the sequence of remorse, apology and forgiveness that can transform lives in permanent ways. In contrast, contingent threats at best could only change lives in immediately contingent ways. The job of responsive regulators is to treat offenders as worthy of trust because the evidence is that, when they do this, regulation more often achieves its objectives (Braithwaite 1998).

NETWORKED ESCALATION WHEN ACTORS ARE WEAK

Haines (1997) formulates one critique of responsive regulation in terms of the existence of a dual economy. A handful of sophisticated large corporations that dominate high-risk sectors like the chemicals industry are complemented by hundreds of smaller, often marginally viable, chemicals firms, especially downstream. Regulated self-regulation that requires firms to put demanding compliance systems in place is something chemicals multinationals can cope with, but not marginal firms. Nor can state regulators cope with getting around on a regular basis to the multitude of small businesses that need most monitoring and help. This when responsive escalation requires iterated encounters that prompt movement up and down the pyramid.

Here is a serious challenge to the general applicability of responsive regulation for which there is no fully satisfactory answer. Nevertheless, three types of moves can help respond. One is the move made by the leading chemical industry self-regulation scheme, Responsible Care (Gunningham and Grabosky 1998). Empirically, small chemicals firms are dependent on the multinationals. They either supply the multinationals, buy from them, or both. This means while it is fiscally impossible for state regulators to be in regular contact with all these little firms, it is impossible for the chemicals majors *not* to be in regular contact with them. Their business depends on it. The Responsible Care strategy is to make their reputation depend on it as well. An upstream–downstream community of shared fate (Rees 1994) is constituted by making major chemicals companies responsible for the way their products are used by those they trade with upstream and downstream. This is a kind of reverse reputational engineering compared with what chemicals companies used to do to avoid scandal. They used to spin off the most hazardous parts of their operation to independent suppliers or reprocessors (Fisse and Braithwaite 1983: ch. 6). Then when fish died in a polluted river, the chemicals multinational would point the finger at the small company that was doing this dirty work at the behest of the multinational.

A similar strategy was used by multinational footwear and clothing manufacturers to avoid labour standards in developed economies. They became marketing, design, fashion and brand-image organizations that spun off actual production to sweatshops in poor nations. State labour standards regulators in these nations were too poorly resourced to inspect the suppliers regularly, while the factories were jurisdictionally beyond the reach of regulators from the home country of the multinational. Regulators that Cashore et al. (2004) call non-state market driven have sought to break this impasse by creating a community of fate between the Nikes, Reeboks and the developing country manufacturers of running shoes. Some non-state market-driven certification schemes such as the Forest Stewardship Council are joint ventures, in the latter case between environmental NGOs and retailers who refuse to buy wood products that are not certified as meeting the Forest Stewardship Council standards.

Adverse publicity and the market power of consumers and retailers to withdraw their decision to purchase are the levers these regimes use against stronger actors to make them regulate weaker actors. When this works, making the multinational become the regulator solves the problem of regulator weakness and want of jurisdiction. But it does not solve the problem of the regulated developing-country manufacturer having weak capabilities to regulate itself. This is where we make the second move to salvage some effectiveness for responsive regulation from the weak actor critique.

These regimes might not only require multinationals to regulate weak organizations within their upstream–downstream community of fate, but also to *help* them. Regulatory policy can create capacity-building obligations upstream and downstream for large corporates. This is part of the most recent general theoretical move in responsive regulation: to complement an emphasis on obligations to 'pick problems and fix them' (Sparrow 2000) with obligations to 'pick strengths and expand them' (see Chapter 6, this volume). The idea is that strengths expand to absorb weaknesses. For example, if something is not getting done in an organization, we can tackle that in two ways: by fixing the problem of lazy employees who are not doing it (perhaps fire or retrain them); or by increasing the number of energetic, highly motivated employees who take on new challenges when they see something undone that ought to be done. Hence, Braithwaite et al. (2007) modified responsive regulation by complementing a regulatory pyramid with a strength-building pyramid. This idea is illustrated in Chapter 5 with the regulatory challenge of cultivating the intellectual commons.

There is a burgeoning literature on where the great many non-state market-driven regulators such as the Marine Stewardship Council (Cashore et al. 2004) and self-regulatory organizations such as Responsible Care do and do not work in terms of either upstream–downstream regulatory obligations or capacity-building obligations. This book does not tackle the detailed task of reviewing that evidence. Most of the regulatory failure is contextual to the poor system design of particular non-state market-driven or self-regulatory organizations. Yet a general problem is that the industries they regulate are usually much better resourced and more politically powerful than they are.

This leads to the third general response to the problem of actors being too politically weak or resource-poor to be able to make responsive regulation work. Peter Drahos (2004b) first developed this idea of the pyramid of networked escalation. When a regulator (say a developing country regulator) does not have the resources to credibly escalate monitoring and enforcement, it instead enrols network partners who at a particular time on a particular issue in a particular place have more resources than they do. Figure 4.3 represents the core idea of the pyramid of networked escalation. Instead of escalating to increasingly interventionist sanctions that the regulator mobilizes itself, the regulator enrols increasing numbers of more potent network partners to escalate pressure on the regulated firm. For example, a securities regulator in a developing country might enrol a multinational accounting firm to produce a report on the compliance of one of its client firms and then monitor implementation of responsive reform to fix the problems revealed by the monitoring, including monitoring of whether managers are disciplined or dismissed when they fail to act. A weak developing-country regulator can enrol (and be enrolled by) both transnational and village networks, private and other public sector organizations, NGOs, professions, disparate types of network partners. Empirically, Braithwaite et al. (2007) found British nursing-home inspectorates to be weak regulatory agencies, in both legal powers and resources. Yet they accomplished a great deal of improvement in quality of care by creative networking even of organizations as powerful as banks. Banks become reluctant to lend money to homes when inspectors put up on the Internet excoriating inspection reports.

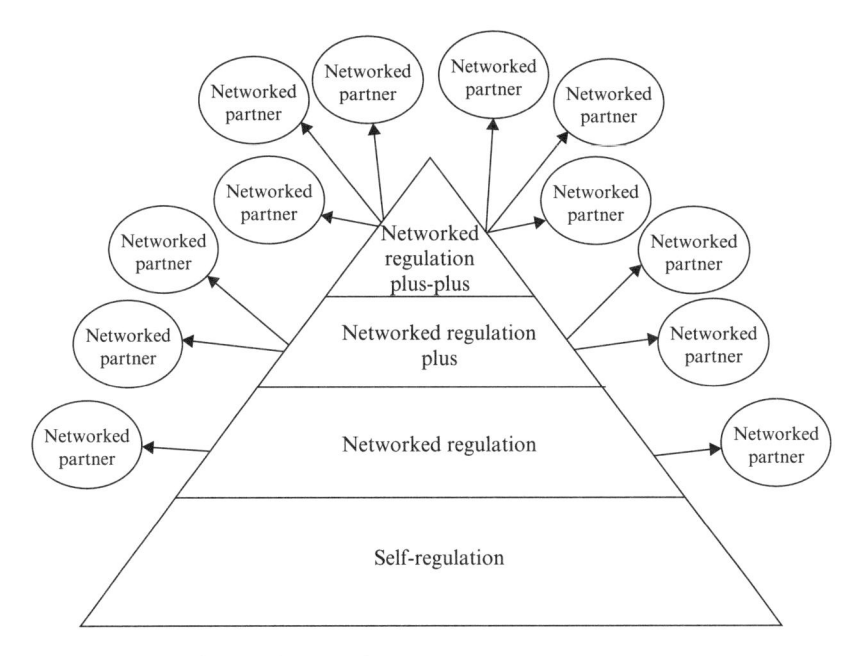

The nodal governance critique of responsive regulation 97

Source: Adapted from Drahos (2004b).

Figure 4.3 A pyramid of networked escalation

There can be a linkage between the three general strategies we have discussed to respond to the problem of actors being too resource-poor to make responsive regulation work – (1) creating an upstream–downstream community of shared fate that links the reputational fate of powerful actors to those of weak ones; (2) requiring strong companies to build out from the strengths of weak ones; and (3) networked pyramidal escalation. A non-state market-driven regulator can create an upstream–downstream community of fate that requires strong firms to assist weak firms to build out from their strengths; and then it might regulate how well this is done with a networked pyramid.

WHY THE NETWORKED PYRAMID IS IMPOVERISHED FROM A NODAL GOVERNANCE PERSPECTIVE

Wood and Shearing (2007: 106–7) explain that police forces have long had de facto enforcement pyramids under the doctrine of a 'continuum of force':

> This idea encourages police to speak softly, to carry a big stick (in the form of a firearm that can be used to kill others) and to escalate up from soft talk, through physical constraint, through to deadly force in ways that respond to the levels of compliance to their directions. (Wood and Shearing 2007: 106)

Wood and Shearing then explain how recent shifts in police thinking in countries such as Canada emphasize more horizontal and partnering moves. This policy shift is about expanding the governance imagination of police officers 'who are encouraged to operate with greater fluidity and agility across a wide range of resources' (Wood and Shearing 2007: 107). Compared with the 'continuum of force' doctrine, these more recent doctrines put greater emphasis on horizontal scanning for creative ways to be responsive to the particularities of the situation.

> In our work with very poor communities we have found that once people get together within deliberative forums in which they are encouraged to stretch their imagination, they discover that not only do they have many resources available to them that can be used to govern effectively, but they have resources that can be used to enrol more powerful actors . . . (Wood and Shearing 2007: 107)

Escalating hierarchically up an enforcement pyramid is still an option. While in some contexts softer options should be used first, in others it will be better to use harder resources first, then drop back to softer resources after credibility has been established. The attuned police officer will do a diagnosis of the particular situation as a professional trained to scan the environment for local resources that can produce a local result, before scanning upwards to more institutionally remote solutions that might be offered by a court, a restraining order, an eviction from public housing, for example. Responsiveness was, of course, always about what works depending on the situation. And a presumption for starting at the base of the pyramid was always only a presumption.

When the terrorist pulled the gun to shoot the hostage, responsive regulation always said the best option might be to short-circuit any thought of dialogue and have the sniper take him out. But it also said, do not automatically think that because this person is a terrorist with a gun and a hostage that a fatal bullet is mandated. If you talk to him you might even discover that your intelligence is wrong and he is an innocent Brazilian. Never dismiss the possibility that having the right kinds of conversations might persuade you to reframe the normative objectives that should be salient in the situation: No, these conversations persuade me that it would not be right to invade Iraq to prevent the spread of weapons of mass destruction and the spread of terrorism.

While realizing that failing to escalate immediately to maximum force may cost a life, always test in your mind the range of less lethal options first.

Perhaps as you scan up the pyramid of options, you dismiss dialogue as too risky in this situation, and a lethal shot would be excessive force. A shot in the ground from behind cover or in the tyres of the car may be a hard response that seizes control of the situation and allows moving down to softer approaches.

Using this judgement, the responsive regulatory presumption in favour of the lowest level of force likely to work still rules. However, the officer's mind is opened to the possibility that escalating immediately to quite a hard option will so create an image of invincibility that, at the end of the day, less force will be used to calm the situation than if he or she opts to escalate up through a range of lesser interventions that fail. In addition, however, the officer's mind might be opened to either a graduated reduction in tension or radical de-escalation, for example by allowing the wife of a violent man to talk to him with love about surrender.

A set of principles of nodal governance for responsive regulation might be formulated on this foundation provided by Wood and Shearing (2007). They apply as much to civil society regulators as to state regulators:

1. Never escalate to hard options without considering all the available softer regulatory interventions. If the situation gives you time, engage in a brainstorming dialogue to discover them. Be open to reframing the norm to be secured on the basis of that dialogue.
2. Use restorative justice dialogue to bubble up norm improvement, including law reform and radical deregulation.
3. Have a preference for 'governing by providing' over 'governing by regulating'. Try to solve problems by providing resources to the potential target of regulation when those gifts might motivate them to govern themselves.
4. Jump immediately to a coercive option when quick diagnosis suggests this will achieve the result with less force overall than a sequence of failed escalations.
5. When you do not yourself have the power to control the situation, consider networking with partners horizontally, or better still with partners who can *de-escalate* coercion, before considering vertical escalation.
6. If you need to escalate vertically, but lack the power or resources to do that, scan creatively and optimistically for potential network partners with resources you lack. Search also for other weak actors whose combined power tied in a node governs the situation with greater power than the sum of its parts.
7. If you want to regulate to achieve a result with minimum force, belong to an organization with symbols that signify a capability and resolve to escalate right up to the peak of a regulatory pyramid that is threatening

in the background (but rarely threatened in the foreground). Belong to an organization that both *walks softly* and carries a big stick. If you do not belong to such an organization, network with someone who does.[2]

To put some flesh on the bare bones of these principles, the next section uses some data collected in 2006 (with Leah Dunn) on police peace-keeping in war-torn Timor Leste. It is used to illustrate how one actor, which happens to be a rather colourful kind of international actor, has a regulatory strategy that more or less follows these principles.

GUNS 'N' ROSES

When the wounds of the terrible war in Timor were reopened in May 2006 with firefights between the police and the military, and rock and knife fights among youth gangs, the Australian and New Zealand military quickly quelled the worst fighting and handed over to police who initially were predominantly Australian Federal Police (AFP). These police mostly had a kindly, minimum use of force, community-policing philosophy. After the military had confiscated a considerable proportion of the guns, the main policing problem was large gangs of young men attacking either each other or the police by raining rocks and metal darts (that can kill) upon them. When the Australian police found themselves at risk and unable to handle these situations, they would call in a formed police unit – specialist riot police. Initially this was a unit of the GNR, the Guarda Nacional Republicana from Portugal.

There was significant tension between the AFP and GNR in Timor and between the diplomatic objectives of their two governments. While the kinder and gentler community police of the AFP were often critical of the alleged brutality of the GNR in kicking young men while they were on the ground, beating them after arrest, and the like, they were at the same time in awe of them and genuinely grateful for saving their lives on many occasions. The AFP in Timor were not particularly elite police units; the GNR were. They were a formed police unit trained for managing riots. The GNR had served four four-month tours in Iraq without losing an officer before doing the same in Timor. They were young men with magnificent physiques, rippling torsos from weight training that they were wont to display while exercising on the beach. Young Timor combatants respected the GNR, much less so the AFP. In Timor, a country where food is scarce for a number of months each year, everyone is thin. Some of Timor's young toughs referred to the AFP as Awfully Fat Policemen, the GNR as Guns 'n' Roses. We found that they could be sweet as a rose in the way they collaborated with Timorese gangs; but they also certainly deployed much more formidable automatic weapons and riot control technology than the AFP and were better trained in using it well.

The GNR had experienced a lot of psychological training in understanding crowds. They had been taught that different cultures respond to different riot control techniques. Horses work well in some cultures. In some societies a fear of large dogs is common, especially if rabies is a problem. Dogs do not fare well in a shower of rocks at 20 paces however. One GNR officer, who had extensive experience in France, said French demonstrators are used to tear gas and allow themselves to be steered with tear gas to a locale where the police are happy for them to demonstrate. They had found that tear gas was almost never a good option in close encounters within Timorese villages where old people and babies tended not to be able to avoid collateral damage from the gas. Water canons were good in narrow Portuguese streets: when directed from vehicles that were almost as wide as the street, water canons could easily push rioters away up a street. Water is also more effective in chilling a mob in cold climates. Neither condition applied in Timor's tropical villages.

The GNR had been trained to be responsive to both the people they were controlling and to the space. If you make the mistake of pushing the crowd towards a wall they will instinctively push back like animals. You must visualize an exit, steer them to it and get a herd effect through it. Sometimes this means telling them that this is where you want them to flee, for example when you fire the tear gas. 'There are always two or three solutions.' We could illustrate in various ways from our fieldwork notes how the GNR are trained to be responsive to the particularities of the situation, by which they mean mainly the people, their leaders and the space.

The commander of the 146 GNR in Timor Leste in 2006 gave us a PowerPoint presentation on their philosophy of 'gradual [graduated] use of force' that made it clear that they had a pyramid of sorts. At its simplest level this is a pyramid that escalates from community policing delivered mainly by the Australian Federal Police and New Zealand Police initially (with some support from GNR), to GNR enforcement, to military enforcement.

The GNR commander also explained the more elaborated pyramid in Figure 4.4. The preferred response at the base of this pyramid was again to solve the problem before it got out of hand through community policing. They played football with local young men, provided Portuguese football jerseys to teams who were assumed to be based on martial arts groups around which gangs formed. The GNR networks through the Catholic church; the church is one of the most powerful nodes of governance in Timor Leste. The GNR does charity work like sort out the water supply in a village. In a remarkable parallel with one of Clifford Shearing's findings

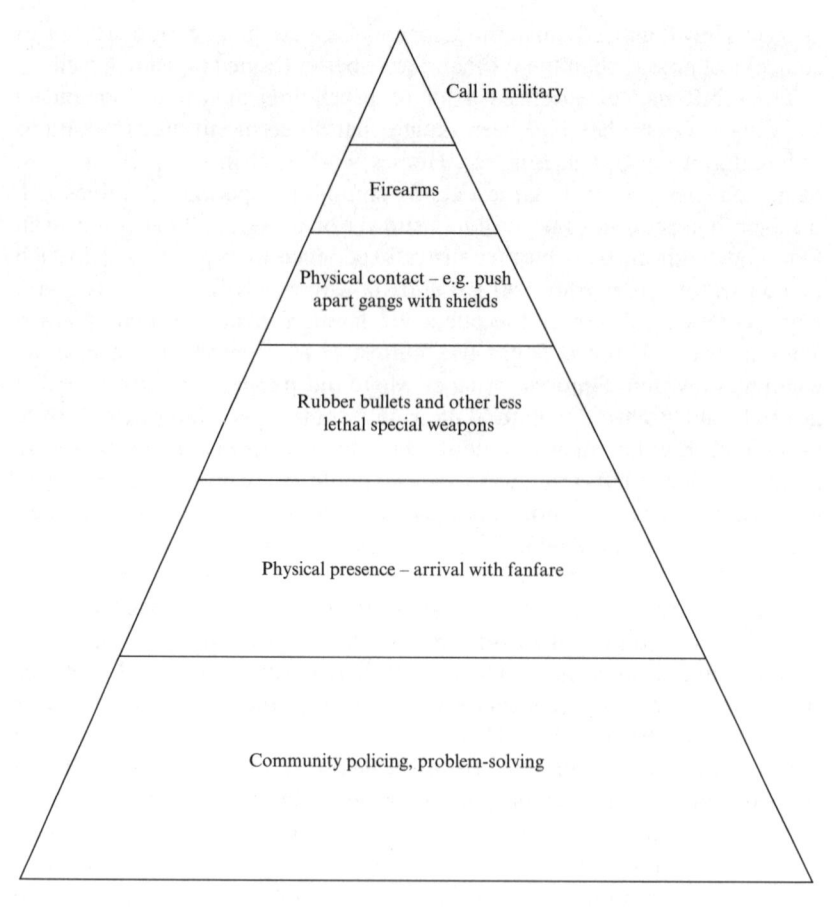

Figure 4.4 GNR gang-fighting control pyramid in Timor Leste

about turn-taking at the water tap being a root cause of conflict in South African squatter settlements, not only had the GNR found this here, we also observed the New Zealand police run a community policing consultation in Timor at which water pump conflict was raised by the chiefs and the police agreed to get one of the humanitarian NGOs to prioritize their village for a new pump. The GNR gave out food and sweets to children on all and sundry occasions, shared their water bottles with them when things were hot and tense (opened so they could not sell them!). Consistent with the principle of governing through gifts (see also Ayling et al. 2006) rather than regulation, they would also call in their medical teams to help injured combatants:

> Senior GNR Officer: We had a bad rock and knife fight. Three AFP officers and I confronted the situation. After assessing the situation, we called for reinforcements. Noticed there were parties injured on both sides. So there is an opportunity for a helping and calming strategy while waiting for backup. I went to the first group, calling them away from the other group, saying 'You have an injury; we will help you.' Called in our medical team. Then I went to the other group and did the same for their injured. You use the motive to unify them on their own problem rather than on fighting the other. Then you can start talking to them to move to a truce.

The GNR philosophy is to be genuinely interested in solving their problem in the moment. While it is not the police role to solve their deeper social problems, the police must be seen to be genuinely interested in their grievances. If what they want is to speak to the media about that grievance, the GNR had no problem with calling in journalists for them to talk to. On other occasions they brought in politicians to discuss their grievances – democratic policing. If what they wanted was to make a visible protest statement, steering of the crowd would be negotiated so the traffic could flow around them while allowing the crowd a highly visible space.

The next rung up the pyramid was 'Physical presence – arrival with fanfare effect.' The commander said 'sometimes visuality is enough. The dark uniforms [he had explained earlier how the dark GNR uniforms had come to symbolize no-nonsense shutting down of gang fights, the blue uniforms of AFP gentle and timid community policing] the sirens are enough to move the crowd on and end hostilities.' Police from several countries told us it was common to be under attack from a shower of rocks; then as soon as the GNR arrived, young men would drop their rocks and disperse. This was indeed a cultivated image of invincibility as in responsive regulatory theory. The GNR philosophy was actually minimum use of force with the proviso of never making the mistake of being seen as ineffective because you use too little force.

> GNR Commander: Sometimes its better not to act immediately. You sit back and assess the situation, identify the leaders, etc, rather than take an ineffective action. Must keep the initiative once you act. If you act and fail to solve the problem, you will create a reaction from your adversary . . . If you don't have sufficient capacity, don't act – wait and identify the ones causing trouble . . .

In Europe tear gas tended to be the next escalation. Not in Timor Leste, for the reasons outlined above, where mostly rubber bullets were next, lobbed into the right space to disperse a mob in a planned direction. Occasionally, at this level of the pyramid, a 'bean bag' round was fired at the torso from a shotgun where the objective was to knock down, hurt and cause the leader to run ahead of a herd who might follow his or her flight.

Next on the hierarchy on the GNR commander's PowerPoint was 'physical contact', meaning, for example, physically grappling with two gangs by separating the formed police unit into two groups with shields that push the gangs apart. Firearms was said to be always the last option, used only when police were in danger. But actually an escalation beyond that was to call in the Australian or New Zealand military. While the GNR had machine guns that could be mounted on their armoured vehicle, their training was in crowd control rather than winning firefights, if that was what it came to. The military also had advantages of night-vision equipment, flares, snipers and could call in tanks and air support.

Once two fighting gangs were separated into two groups, the GNR wanted to collect intelligence and lay the foundations for community policing follow-up in meetings with chiefs and youth leaders the next day and over subsequent days in an attempt to settle grievances, solve root causes and work right through to reconciliation rituals to consolidate a peace if possible. One reason the GNR were mostly opposed to tear gas in the Timor context was that it would cause everyone to run before a post-riot conversation could be held on the spot to set up further dialogue.

> GNR Commander: Once you have a group separated from their adversary, you ask a leader for their version of what happened. Then people gather around to listen. This draws out competing versions of what happened and complaints from locals and passers-by. Helps draw in the stragglers who might re-start the fight with the other group.

We were told it can be good to say to the person you think is leader: 'You are the leader?' That gives the crowd an opportunity to tacitly lend him that authority. If the GNR has correctly identified the one to three leaders that they believe always exist in a mob, and they think they are good at observation that identifies them, the crowd will mutter agreement with a person's proffered leadership. Then 'they will follow what comes out of negotiation with him'. Another way is to ask 'who in the group will represent the group?' Leaders of the two formed police groups then converse with the two targeted gang leaders or sets of leaders: 'OK what's the problem. We'll sort it out together.' The riot can be governed by the two nodes (Table 4.1). This approach both creates a space between leaders and the mob that is following them and can separate the leaders of two gangs.

CONCLUSION

The original contribution of this chapter has been to draw on the way Wood and Shearing (2007) have built on the work of Peter Drahos to define

Table 4.1 How GNR uses principles of responsive nodal governance

New principles of responsive nodal governance	Examples of how the GNR uses them
1. Never escalate to hard options without considering all the available softer regulatory interventions. If the situation gives you time, engage in a brainstorming dialogue to discover them. Be open to reframing the norm to be secured on the basis of that dialogue	When both sides have serious injuries, try to draw them in to the project of helping their own instead of hurting the adversary
2. Use restorative justice dialogue to bubble up norm improvement, including law reform and radical deregulation	In the days and weeks after the riot, meet with elders and gang leaders to identify problems that can be fixed that are making people angry, and to enable reconciliation through working together on them
3. Have a preference for 'governing by providing' over 'governing by regulating'. Try to solve problems by providing resources to the potential target of regulation when those gifts might motivate them to govern themselves	If turn-taking at the tap causes fights to break out, get an extra tap into the camp for Internally Displaced Persons
4. Jump immediately to a coercive option when quick diagnosis suggests this will achieve the result with less force overall than a sequence of failed escalations	Do not try to physically separate two gangs if you are at risk of having insufficient officers so that they might force you to retreat, getting the upper hand, drawing more into the riot. Call in reinforcements, the army and/or special weapons
5. When you do not yourself have the power to control the situation, consider networking with partners horizontally, or better still with partners who can *de-escalate* coercion, before considering vertical escalation	Support a respected nun or priest who can open a front of dialogue. Bring in politicians or the media to listen to a grievance
6. If you need to escalate vertically, but lack the power resources to do that, scan creatively and	Network with village chiefs as well as the nuns in point 5

Table 4.1 (continued)

New principles of responsive nodal governance	Examples of how the GNR uses them
optimistically for potential network partners with resources you lack. Search also for other weak actors whose combined power tied in a node governs the situation with greater power than the sum of its parts	
7. If you want to regulate to achieve a result with minimum force, belong to an organization with symbols that signify a capability and resolve to escalate right up to the peak of a regulatory pyramid that is threatening in the background (but rarely threatened in the foreground). Belong to an organization that both *walks softly* and carries a big stick. If you do not belong to such an organization, network with someone who does	If you are the AFP, call in the GNR!

seven principles for a nodal governance of responsive regulation. One risk of responsive regulation is that by having regulatory officials focus on what strategies they should order at different rungs of different regulatory pyramids is that, as Sparrow (2000: 201) would put it, work becomes organized around tools instead of tools organized around work. Our principles are a partial remedy to that risk. They require us to scan horizontally and below for completely innovative strategies that are attuned to the particularities of a problem, and for horizontal network partners, before looking to escalated sanctions or networked escalation. When the rocks are flying and the GNR brings in a nun beloved by both fighting gangs, under the shelter of their shields, to reason with leaders of both sides, what are created are de-escalatory nodes of governance.[3]

Thus, a pathology of responsive regulation without our seven nodal principles is that it not only suffers Sparrow's worry about the need always to keep the problem in front of us and our tools behind us, it also has the Wood and Shearing (2007) worry of looking excessively vertically in the search for tools and network partners, to the neglect of scanning sideways and below. Shearing and Ericson (1991) speak of what we might call horizontal sensibilities, like police who learn to 'act like you are on vacation' instead of acting as if they are comtemplating tougher stuff. Wood and Shearing (2007) agree this does not eliminate the need to plan for escalation up a regulatory pyramid. Regulators need to accrue clout by signalling the extent of their coercive capability to escalate to something that will bring the most egregious and powerful rule-violators to heel. They need to plan it in advance, first, because they need to signal their pyramid. Second, regulatory officials need to know that their boss will back them if they escalate in circumstances of a certain kind.

An ideal of restorative and responsive justice is not only to filter the justice of the law (for example, a human rights culture) down into the justice of the people, it is also to bubble up the justice of the people into the justice of the law and how it is enforced. When the GNR organize a meeting with chiefs and youth leaders to learn the lessons from a shoot-out, when they invite politicians and/or the media to sit down with rioting young people so they can understand and tell the story of the kind of legislative or policy change these young people seek, nodes of governance are created that can bubble up local stories and local solutions into the national policy story book. Chapter 7 attempts to elaborate how to begin to grapple with this most difficult challenge of restorative and responsive justice of bubbling up local stories, lessons and solutions into the national policy story book and the national law. We have barely begun to learn how to do that.

Reframing in light of local sensibilities is one thing horizontal scanning for local justice options can do better than formal national justice. One of Clifford Shearing's (2001) most famous reframing stories is of the nodal governance of theft of tools in a factory. Instead of defining the theft as crime and punishing it, all tools were constituted as a tool library. Workers could now take what they wanted without having to smuggle it out. But tools had to come back within a short space of time, and did. Yet another the United Nations (UN) police in Timor Leste rediscovered was reframing a violence problem as a problem of ordering access to that precious commodity – water. One point of such reframing is to reorient justice to the future-oriented solution to problems at the root of people's miseries, away from ritualism (a topic we return to in Chapter 6). Clifford Shearing believes that the kind of justice people in poor, violence-ridden communities in places like South Africa most want is justice as a better future, justice as realistic hope. One way to prevent them from escalating up their pyramid of street violence to exact revenge is to secure a pause where a reframing conversation can occur – with a nun, a politician or even a police officer – that displaces momentum towards justice as revenge with ideas for justice as a better future. Yes, instead of throwing rocks at them for pushing us away from the tap, let us work together with World Vision for that plan for an additional tap.

Another point of local contestation and reframing of what is normatively at stake in a regulatory regime is to render the regime more meaningfully accountable in a democracy. Accountability, too, is at its richest when it simultaneously has vertical dimensions (say accountability to a human rights commissioner enforcing national legal rights) and horizontal dimensions (a mother calling the police to account in a restorative justice conference for excessive force during the arrest of her child). This theme we return to in the final chapter.

NOTES

1. Thanks to Jen Wood, Christine Parker and Clifford Shearing for helpful comments on this chapter.
2. In Dupont's (2006) network analysis of private and public security in Montreal, he found that 52 per cent of the bridges that linked two organizations were a single individual.
3. We interviewed a nun who had done this. She had converted her convent into a camp for internally displaced persons. On various occasions when rock fights broke out between different factions near the convent, she had bravely walked between the two groups to broker peace when she knew she was loved and trusted by gang leaders on both sides. During the famous rock attack outside the Solomon Islands Parliament in 2006 in which more than 30 Australian police were injured by rocks, some very seriously, a group of respected women leaders offered to face the rocks to plead for peace from the rioters. In some Melanesian societies, it is difficult for men to keep fighting when bodies of women stand in the way; this gives women a special kind of peace-making role that requires a special kind of courage. In the case of the riot at the Solomon Islands Parliament, the Australian police, perhaps wrongly, perhaps rightly, judged that they should not accept the women leaders' offer as it would put them too much at risk.

5. Regulatory capitalism, business models and the knowledge economy
Janet Hope, Dianne Nicol and John Braithwaite

We saw in Chapter 1 that the emergence of regulatory capitalism is predicated upon a knowledge economy governed by networks. Knowledge economies are fuelled by innovation. In the global knowledge economy of the twenty-first century, the dominant institutional mechanism for fostering innovation is intellectual property; but intellectual property rights are not the only possible means of encouraging innovation. Instead of being granted a series of patents, Thomas Edison might have been given a tax holiday on profits derived from the fruits of his inventions, or a share of the taxes other companies paid as a result of exploiting a licence to use the inventions. He might have been awarded something akin to a national creative arts fellowship, or rewarded for his contributions through a statutory automatic licensing scheme like the copyright collection schemes administered in Australia by the Australian Performers Rights Association for musical works and the Copyright Agency Limited for literary works.

In fact, the heavy reliance on standardized monopoly privileges that characterizes innovation policy in today's global economy is a relatively recent phenomenon. Historically, a more institutionally nuanced approach prevailed.[1] The sovereigns of the Middle Ages used their power over the creation of privileges to develop non-exclusive forms of reward such as tax exemptions or bonus payments. Venice, for example, used special funds or special positions to reward those who were skilled in the making of canons (Mandich 1960). Even when these privileges took the form of exclusive rights of manufacture, the term of the right was a matter of negotiation between the inventor and the sovereign. Unlike today, patent terms were not uniform.

The twentieth century saw states shift towards much greater dependence on the blunt instrument of patent law to promote national competitiveness in the knowledge economy. As a result, we live in a world where power derives less from the control of capital and labour, and more from the control of abstract objects such as patents, copyright and trademarks (Drahos 2002). In the era of industrial capitalism, owning the best factories was the way to become a tycoon. Nowadays, if a pharmaceutical company were given a choice between acquiring all the factories of its most powerful competitor and its most valuable patents, it would choose the patents.

To explain this trend, we need perhaps look no further than Adam Smith's warning that business leaders always prefer to use their power to secure monopolies that exclude the threat that competition poses to their profits. But whatever the reason, the decision to configure incentives to innovate primarily as rights to exclude others from exploiting the fruits of invention gives rise to contests between markets in virtue and markets in vice (see Chapter 2). Here, the market in virtue is a market in innovation that is rewarded and energized by intellectual property rights. The market in vice is a market in locking up knowledge that would benefit humankind were it freely shared.

MONOPOLIZATION OF INNOVATION THROUGH INTELLECTUAL PROPERTY

Why do we consider monopolistic practices with respect to intellectual resources a market in vice? The conventional assumption is that intellectual property monopolies are essential to innovation, either as an incentive to private investment or as a means of coordinating the exchange of information needed to enable cooperative and cumulative development. But as Benkler (2006: 49) emphasizes, such monopolies have both static and dynamic costs: they allow producers to charge a non-zero price for goods (information) that have a zero marginal cost, and they raise the price of information inputs into future rounds of innovation. Both types of costs contribute to a range of pernicious effects in fields where intellectual property rights are numerous, poorly defined and/or overly broad.

In both medical and agricultural biotechnology, for example, scholars have issued warnings of a potential 'tragedy of the anticommons' (Heller and Eisenberg 1998). A tragedy of the *commons* occurs when common resources, such as grazing land or fisheries, are destroyed through overuse because no individual user has an incentive to conserve them based on private property rights (Hardin 1968). A tragedy of the *anticommons* occurs when numerous overlapping property rights and reach-through licence agreements seal off an arena of knowledge to the wider community of potential users. A distinct but related problem occurs where broad intellectual property rights are granted over foundational technology in new areas of research (Merges and Nelson 1990; Scotchmer 1991). Holders of these broad rights have the capacity to block off whole areas of innovation if they follow the traditional monopolistic exclusionary model in exercising their patent rights.

The tragedy of the anticommons and monopolistic exploitation of broad blocking rights both deprive follow-on innovators of access to and freedom to operate with information inputs and thereby impact on society more broadly. Even where these blockages can be overcome through workarounds such as conducting research and development (R&D) offshore or engaging in mergers with owners of complementary intellectual assets, they may have adverse structural effects, raising barriers to entry and reducing competition.[2] Besides raising the prices for innovative products, such practices concentrate the capacity to innovate in the hands of actors who have little incentive to innovate, except in ways that promise to generate supra-normal profits while sustaining the structural status quo.

The impact of these combined effects can be seen most clearly in agricultural biotechnology. Empirical evidence suggests that public sector researchers in rich countries are affected by a patent-induced tragedy of the anticommons, exacerbating neglect of agricultural research and development conducted for the benefit of people living in poor countries that have little indigenous capacity for biotechnology innovation (Kryder et al. 2000; Delmer et al. 2003). Meanwhile, the private sector has avoided anticommons tragedy only at the cost of a radical restructuring that has dramatically reduced competition, leading to the exclusion of players who might be interested in serving markets that are insufficiently lucrative to be attractive to agronomic systems giants such as Monsanto. Higher prices for agricultural inputs and research tools are passed down the line to farmers and end-consumers. Effective biosafety regulation is undermined when the capacity to conduct biotechnology R&D is restricted to those who stand to gain by minimizing regulatory interference. Traditional agricultural practices such as the saving of seeds, necessary to preserve the diversity of genetic resources under threat from the widespread adoption of monocultural farming, are rendered difficult or impossible by the use of intellectual property fences and technological locks such as the 'terminator' gene complex.

Underpinning this and other markets in intellectual property vice is a global regulatory regime that greatly expands monopoly rights: the TRIPS (Trade-Related Intellectual Property Rights) Agreement under the World Trade Organization. The TRIPS Agreement ratcheted up the length and international enforceability of patents and a variety of other intellectual property monopolies (Drahos 2002). Since TRIPS came into force in 1995, the US and the European Union (EU) have further ratcheted up intellectual property regulation across the world system through a series of bilateral 'free trade' agreements (Drahos 2001; 2004c). This remarkably successful push to propertize intellectual resources globally has reinforced opportunities for locking up knowledge at the expense of rewarding innovation. It has redistributed wealth from over 90 per cent of the world's nations that are net importers of intellectual property rights to a handful of wealthy nations that are net exporters. It has created a world where we see the risk of patented drugs to treat AIDS being kept beyond the reach of AIDS victims in poor nations by monopoly prices. Yet we argue in this chapter that there exist weapons of the weak that can be deployed to counter these effects.

REVERSING INFORMATION LOCK-DOWN

This chapter explores the considerable scope for responsive regulatory strategies to flip markets in vice to markets in virtue. The little we know about the empirics of these markets suggests that information lock-down need not triumph over continuously reinvigorated innovation. Open-source software is a case in point. As dominant software corporations widen their control of the architecture of the information economy, free and open-source software arises as a counter-control movement. In the up-cycle, owners of software monopolies restrict access to computer code, thereby achieving private architectural regulation of information spaces; then competition is restored by counter-regulation that guarantees code will be both readily accessible and unencumbered. Thus, open source manifests the cyclical nature of regulation and counter-regulation under regulatory capitalism, as discussed in Chapter 2.

In the software context, open source relates to copyright licensing. Copyright, no less than patents, constitutes contests between markets in virtue and markets in vice. Within the business life of the most successful copyright owner in history – Bill Gates of Microsoft – we see in play markets in both vice and virtue. On the one hand, we see the virtuous life of a man who accumulates wealth by supplying innovative software that solves the information problems of people at prices they can afford, and then gives much of that wealth away to solve other problems of the world's poor. On the other hand, we see Microsoft as the target of successful European suits for anti-competitive practices that deployed its domination of the architecture of computing and the Internet to exclude competition. Gates has been the consummate tactician of architectural regulation of cyberspace to secure monopoly. We contend that it is possible to ensure that the virtuous contributions of a Bill Gates exceed the harm his architectural regulation inflicts in excluding competition. This might be accomplished by responsive regulation of his own architectural regulation.

Public regulation by European Commission antitrust enforcement (or national antitrust) has not been the most important counter to Bill Gates's architectural regulation. Rather, it is private regulation that has most effectively clipped his anti-competitive conduct. This private regulation has come from software creators employing open-source licensing and business models. Open-source developers distribute their software together with the relevant source code so that the code can be adapted and improved by anyone who acquires a machine-readable (binary or executable) form of the program. All open-source code is covered by a licence that guarantees every software recipient the right to compete with the licensor-developer as a distributor – whether for profit or not – of both the original software and any improvements he or she might make. Some open-source licences can also be used to prevent licensees using copyright to exclude others from copying and improving on those improvements.[3] Open-source business models not only enable price competition with Microsoft, they attract innovative users who want the freedom to adapt and improve the software they buy or share. All the big players, from IBM to Sun Microsystems to Microsoft, have been forced to accommodate the open-source phenomenon in one way or another.

Why do innovators find it attractive to exploit their innovations using open-source strategies? Individual hobbyists and researchers engage in open-source development for the sake of personal rewards such as fun, learning and a sense of belonging to a community. For innovators with a public interest mission, these strategies offer a way to achieve the benefits of technology transfer without creating new barriers to access and use. An open-source approach can preserve freedom to operate for the innovator and others in contexts where there is a threat that important new technologies may be appropriated for exclusive use. Open-source strategies can enhance an organization's reputation and learning capacity. For self-interested innovators operating in a commercial environment, broad dissemination of a new technology on open-source terms has the additional advantage of expanding markets for complementary goods and services. If the innovator is also a user of the technology, sharing technology development with other prospective users can generate substantial cost savings and/or productivity gains, substantially reducing capital barriers to entry. Such strategies can also be used to alter the competitive landscape, for example to undermine a competitor's proprietary offerings or to ensure competition among one's own suppliers.

Although open source is primarily a software phenomenon, the glimmerings of an open-source movement can also be seen in biotechnology. This is a field in which monopolistic obstacles to ongoing innovation are particularly troubling because of the pressing global demand for technologies that contribute to better health care, food security and environmental sustainability. Open source-style biotechnology patent licences and material transfer agreements represent just one of a range of devices that might be used to flip markets in vice to markets in virtue in the context of biotechnology research and development.

Other licence-based models that can be used to promote the exchange of information needed for ongoing innovation include clearing houses, patent pooling, cross licensing and other mechanisms for clustering of licences. A variety of types of clearing houses are already in existence. They range from mere databases of information, to network coordination to facilitate exchange of actual technologies, through to royalty collecting agencies (Krattiger 2004; Nicol and Hope 2006; Van Overwalle et al. 2006; Van Zimmeren et al. 2006). Peter Drahos (2000) has suggested that clearing houses can be global rather than national in scope and targeted on redistributively strategic problems for developing countries such as indigenous knowledge. Clearing houses of this nature are likely to be particularly useful in niches that are technologically obscure, as well as those obscured by secrecy[4] or geographical remoteness for a potential partner.

Patent pooling is another aspect of the market in intellectual property virtue – though depending on the strategist's intentions, it can also be part of a market in vice, as when patent pools have been used to conceal cartels from competition authorities (Drahos 2002). Arrangements of this type enable the consolidation of patent rights so that negotiating licences is streamlined and transaction costs are consequently reduced.

These strategies rely on pre-existing intellectual property rights. Another possibility is to bypass intellectual property rights completely, focusing instead on the advantages to be gained by straightforward dissemination in the absence of intellectual property rights. This strategy, which harks back to the traditional norms of publication of scientific results and exchange of research materials, is sometimes referred to as 'open access' to distinguish it from open source, in which the innovator does obtain intellectual property protection but exploits it in a way that does not exclude others from accessing or using the protected technology.

In this chapter we focus on the applicability of open source-style licensing and other anti-monopoly devices, mainly using patenting of biotechnological inventions as an illustration. None of these devices offers a 'one size fits all' solution to the problem of information lock-down. Each has its own advantages and disadvantages that make it more or less suitable for any given application. What all have in common is that they represent private forms of regulation that can be deployed at a grass-roots level by actors with little institutional power and relatively few resources. At the same time, each device has the capacity to make effective use of extra power and resources as and when they become available. They are therefore well suited to illustrate pyramidal approaches to regulation that move incrementally from less costly interventions with broader potential application through to higher cost strategies targeted towards a narrower range of targets.

CONSTRUCTING A COLLABORATION-STRENGTHENING PYRAMID

In the remainder of this chapter, we argue that open-source and other anti-monopoly devices can play a vital role in reinforcing the market in intellectual property virtue while helping to contain the market in intellectual property vice. To make this argument we refer to two kinds of pyramids: the strengths-based pyramid and the regulatory pyramid. A strengths-based pyramid promotes virtue; a regulatory pyramid restrains vice. We distinguish the design principles of a regulatory enforcement pyramid and a strengths-based pyramid in Table 5.1.

To see how the two approaches can be integrated, consider the interaction of strengths-based and regulatory pyramids in the context of nursing home regulation as proposed by Braithwaite et al. (2007) (Figure 5.1).

In the intellectual property context, a strengths-based pyramid seeks to promote uses of intellectual property rights that maximize the exchange of information and materials needed for ongoing innovation without negating the benefits of intellectual property as an incentive and/or coordination mechanism. A regulatory pyramid focuses on restraining the incursion of intellectual property rights into spheres where innovation would be better served by other institutional mechanisms (such as traditional data access practices). It also seeks to mitigate those uses of existing intellectual property (IP) rights that are most damaging to ongoing innovation. Both forms of pyramidal governance are responsive in that intervention is minimal by default, escalating only in response to emerging risks or opportunities.

In this section we explore the possibility of a 'collaboration-strengthening' pyramid (Figure 5.2) that nurtures open source and other initiatives that seek

Table 5.1 Design principles for strengths-based versus regulatory enforcement pyramids

Regulatory pyramid	Strengths-based pyramid
Risk assessment	Opportunities assessment
Fear	Hope
Prompt response before problem escalates	Wait patiently to support strengths that bubble up from below
Pushing standards above a floor	Pulling standards through a ceiling

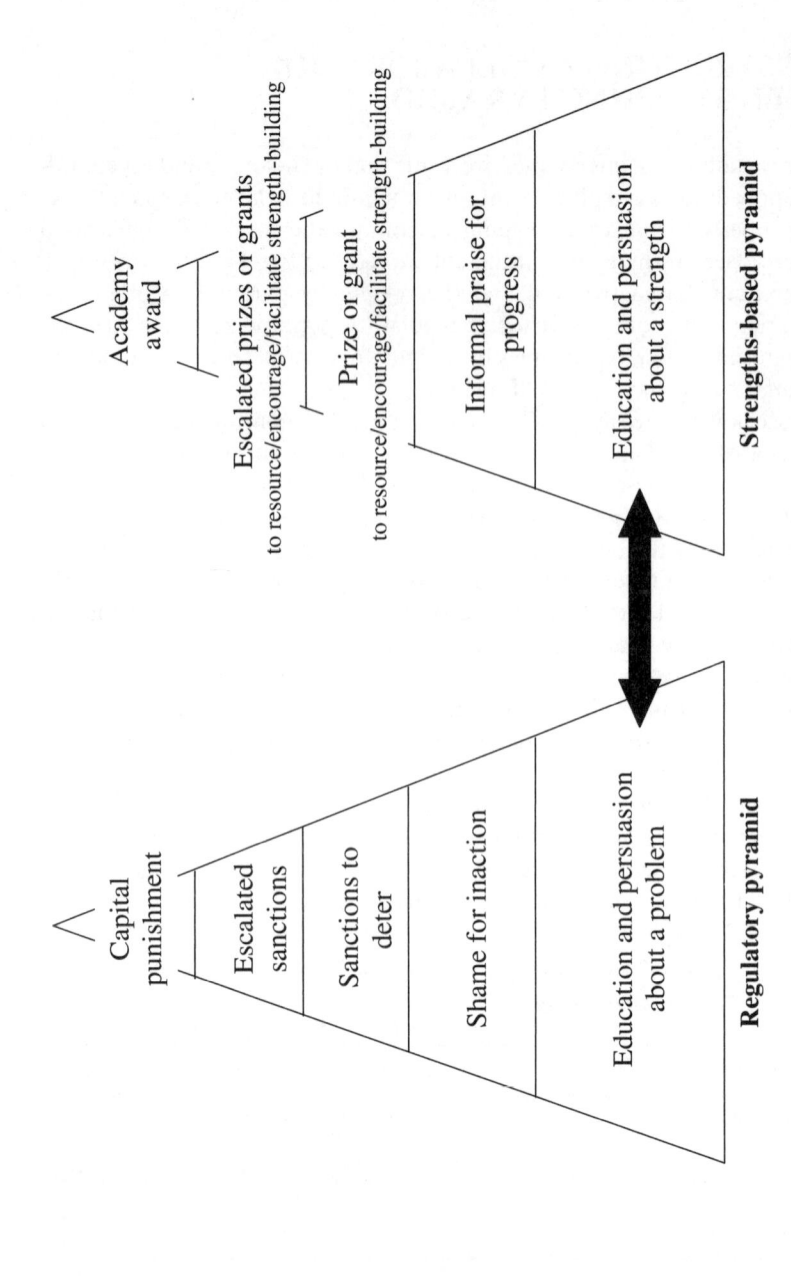

Figure 5.1 One possible approach to integrating a strengths-based pyramid with a regulatory pyramid based on the work on nursing-home regulation by Braithwaite et al. (2007)

Figure 5.2   One possible collaboration-strengthening pyramid for a knowledge economy

Pyramid (bottom to top):

- Research that documents and disseminates understanding of the plurality of collaborative IP mechanisms and associated business models and the niches where they might fit
- Foster widespread, well-informed deliberation about the benefits and challenges of implementing particular mechanisms in relevant fields
- Enable experimental implementation of promising models
- Safeguard and mainstream successful implementations; establish incentives for wider adoption
- Recognize those who use intellectual property rights to foster collaboration

to expand the freedom to share knowledge that is subject to private ownership. Figure 5.2 describes generic escalations of collaboration-strengthening, while the accompanying text suggests various more specific ways of implementing the different rungs of the pyramid. The idea is that different kinds of actors (NGOs, states, scientists) in different countries will find very different kinds of pyramids useful (in terms of specific entries on different rungs) from the standpoint of their vision of how to promote a more collaborative knowledge economy. Our approach builds on actors' existing efforts to exploit intellectual property rights in ways that promote innovation. The corresponding regulatory pyramid – the 'monopoly-regulating' pyramid – is elaborated in the next section. Both these pyramids might be considered by the myriad types of actors involved in the networked governance of regulatory capitalism. In Chapter 4 we made the point that actors need not have the capacity themselves to mobilize the action required at every level of a pyramid they seek to contribute towards building. They can seek to make their humble contribution at a certain level of a pyramid, while lobbying others (like states) to mobilize other levels they cannot themselves manage. And they can enrol the greater power of others at nodes in a network of governance.

The first task in constructing a collaboration-strengthening pyramid is to identify existing strengths in the management of intellectual property in biotechnology. In a series of surveys and interviews with participants in the Australian medical biotechnology industry, Nicol and Nielsen (2003) found that innovators often sold patents and licences too cheaply, or not at all, without the creativity that might have been applied to crafting win-win licensing deals. This led Nicol and Nielsen to conclude that there was a need for research that opened the minds of non-US, non-European biotechnology start-ups in comparatively partner-poor business environments (like Australia) to the wide variety of licence-based business models that are possible. At around the same time, researchers in other jurisdictions were reaching similar conclusions (for example, Benkler 2004; Ebersole et al. 2005; Van Overwalle et al. 2006).

In response to this perceived need, Dianne Nicol and Janet Hope are developing a typology of the great variety of intellectual property-based models that have the potential to open up data access practices in biotechnology, from open source to patent pooling. The idea is to develop a number of disparate licensing and patent-pooling models, in part by translating successful strategies in other industry sectors, and also by using existing knowledge of current licensing practices in biotechnology. The models will go through a refinement process following interviews with biotechnology innovators and will then be tested using case studies in niche areas. Then the idea is to reflect on the ecology of those business models – which models fit which niches in the global business environment. Let us assume this ecological model is indeed the nature of the game – matching technically complex ideas to commercial niches that may be geographically remote and obscure to the naked eye even of a brilliant biotechnologist. The basic problem is one of not being able to find the niche or, if it is found, forcing a square business model into a round niche. One Hope and Nicol hypothesis is that the standard biotechnology business model of monopolizing patents that an innovator develops and then on-sells to a bigger monopolist may not always be the most appropriate model, either from the perspective of the innovator or from the broader social perspective.

Research that documents and disseminates understanding of the plurality of business models available and the range of niches where they might fit itself forms a possible base for our collaboration-strengthening pyramid (see Figure 5.2). The reason this strategy belongs at the bottom of the pyramid is that, being the least interventionist, lowest-cost strategy imaginable, it would be prudent for anyone who wishes to promote a market in virtue to invest in it first. Even if mainstream biotechnology industry participants are conservative when it comes to intellectual property strategy, there exist in biotechnology (as in other industries) entrepreneurs who search out new knowledge, understanding that they need to explore new ideas to improve the partnering critical to expanding the influence and market returns from their invention. It follows that just publishing good research of this kind in academic or trade journals, on the Internet or in the mainstream media might help reinforce more open patterns of exchange. Nicol and Hope are conducting their present business model research in the context of the Australian biotechnology sector. Our hypothesis is that, at the base of collaboration-strengthening pyramids, research is needed across the gamut of technological and geographical sectors.

A minor escalation of this kind of market-information-enhancing investment would be to take action that fosters deliberation about specific mechanisms for encouraging collaborative uses of intellectual property rights. The aim would be to engage a diverse range of actors, each with her unique perspective and expertise, in discussions about the potential costs, benefits and challenges associated with implementing a particular approach. One possible intervention at this rung of the pyramid would be to present a proposal that is sufficiently concrete to generate detailed feedback and, ideally, provide a platform for subsequent interventions. An example is Maurer, Rai and Sali's (2004) paper describing a 'Tropical diseases initiative' that seeks to implement open source-style development in relation to pharmaceuticals. The paper was published in an open-access medical journal in order to reach the widest possible audience with the relevant technical knowledge and interests in drug development. Another example is the work of Greg Graff and his colleagues at the University of California, Berkeley, in detailing an intellectual property clearing house for agricultural biotechnology (Graff and Zilberman 2001). Similarly, the first steps in the creation of a patent pool-type arrangement for humanitarian use of the technology for Golden Rice production were a satellite meeting at the World Food Prize Symposium in 2000 and the creation of a Golden Rice Humanitarian Board by Ingo Potrykus and other key players involved in the development of the technology (Potrykus 2001).

A further low-level intervention aimed at encouraging open and informed deliberation would be to establish a website that incorporates both information about a particular mechanism or implementation and an online discussion forum or email list where interested parties can interact, ideally in a way that permits others to witness and learn from the interaction (as when an email list is publicly archived on the Internet). A proposal might also be raised at professional meetings and workshops where the interaction can take place in real time and space instead of in cyberspace. The forum might be a concurrent session at a larger meeting; alternatively, a player with sufficient funds might choose to sponsor a dedicated meeting.

At the same rung of the pyramid, one could establish training workshops on how master practitioners of non-monopolistic business models collaborate across business networks to match the right business model to the right niche at the right point on the globe. The 'open space' workshop methodology (Heft 2002) has developed simple methods for allowing participants to find the set of dialogue partners that are best for them within the open floorspace of a diverse set of clustered meetings of minds. Each little cluster produces their own one to two page workshop report on future collaboration options, with 'to do' lists, contact lists and agendas for future conversations.

The next rung of the collaboration-strengthening pyramid involves enabling the experimental implementation of promising mechanisms. Consider as an example open-source licensing of biotechnology patents and related know-how and materials. As Hope (2007) notes in her book, *Biobazaar: The Open Source Revolution and Biotechnology*, a variety of biotechnology initiatives have consciously adopted one or a combination of the key principles of open-source licensing and development in an attempt to overcome some of the challenges posed by an increasingly complex intellectual property landscape. These include a Canadian proposal for a General Public Licence for plant germplasm (Michaels 1999), a draft licence (never adopted) for Human Genome Project sequence data (Sulston and Ferry 2002), the data access policy of the International Haplotype Mapping ('HapMap') Project (Gitter 2007), the Tropical Diseases Initiative (Maurer et al. 2004), Science Commons (sciencecommons.org/), Biological Innovation for Open Society (BIOS) (Dennis 2004) and proposals for Equitable Access and Neglected Disease Licences (Kapczynski et al. 2005). Still in the planning stage is Brazil's Network for Open Scientific Innovation.

All these efforts represent interventions at the third rung of our strengths-based pyramid, in that all are aimed at implementing the open-source approach in the new sphere of biotechnology. The range of interventions represented in these examples gives an indication of the variety of ways different actors can engage with a strengths-based pyramid. Both CAMBIA's BioForge and The Synaptic Leap have developed software tools and a web environment to allow researchers to collaborate via the Internet in ways that resemble the methods of software developers. Tom Michaels, Amy Kapczynski and others have drafted possible open source-style licence provisions; Science Commons, an offshoot of the Creative Commons initiative, is working to develop a full suite of model licences. CAMBIA has licensed specific technologies on open source-like terms, while philanthropies and government agencies have provided funding to employ staff to develop the initiative further.

Open source fits very well within a collaboration-strengthening pyramid because one of the attractions of open-source methods for opening up information exchange is that they involve minimal upfront investment on the part of technology developers. Would-be leaders of open-source technology development initiatives 'seed' new projects with contributions that need not be refined beyond demonstrating sufficient promise to attract further contributions. If the project proves interesting, other developers will invest their own resources according to their own interests and capacities. If not, nobody has incurred significant losses and the project's technology content remains available for others to incorporate into future development initiatives. Yet despite low start-up and subsequent barriers to open source-style collaboration, would-be regulators could usefully make a range of interventions to promote the success of either a particular project or the movement as a whole.

Like particular implementations of open-source biotechnology, efforts to put a clearing-house model into practice belong on the third rung of our strengths-based pyramid. It might be supposed that the base level of intervention required to kick-start clearing-house initiatives is somewhat higher than for open source because the clearing-house approach is likely to require collective action on the part of multiple intellectual property owners. But experience in relation to the Public Intellectual Property Resource for Agriculture (PIPRA) – an organization at the more elaborate end of the institutional spectrum – suggests that low-level interventions can be invaluable in paving the way for later developments. We have seen that the first steps towards the establishment of PIPRA were taken by academic researchers in the field of agricultural and resource economics, who drew attention to the market in intellectual property vice described earlier and suggested an agricultural biotechnology clearing house as a solution. According to Graff and Zilberman (2001: 1), such a clearing house would aim to 'reduce transaction costs and other market failures that hinder the exchange of IP, creating pathways through the patent thicket and giving freedom-to-operate with proprietary biotechnologies'.

This base-level intervention was followed by interventions at the second rung of the pyramid, including a round-table workshop to explore the desirability and feasibility of implementing the clearing-house model. In sponsoring this workshop, the Giannini Foundation, the Farm Foundation, the Rockefeller Foundation, and the University of California brought the academic proposal closer to realization. Later, supporters of the clearing-house initiative arranged for professional facilitators to take over much of the work of negotiating a MOU (memorandum of understanding) among participating institutions. This was a third-level intervention, targeted at practical implementation of a specific clearing-house proposal. Other interventions at this level included the establishment of PIPRA as a legal entity, the hiring of paid staff and the creation of a network of *pro bono* advisers.

Patent pools can also follow the same pattern. The patent pool-type arrangement that has been established for humanitarian use of the technology for production of Golden Rice is another clear example of how intellectual property vice might be translated into virtue. Golden Rice has been genetically engineered to synthesize beta-carotene as a means of combating vitamin A deficiency, which impairs the development of immune systems, particularly in children, increasing their susceptibility to a whole range of infectious diseases. The Rockefeller Foundation and the EU, the Swiss Federal Office for Education and Science and the Swiss Federal Institute of Technology funded the project to develop the technology, led by Ingo Potrykus in Switzerland and Peter Beyer in Germany. The ultimate aim was to supply the product for free to subsistence farmers in developing countries (Potrykus 2001). Major inroads were made into the development of the technology in the 1990s in collaboration with Zeneca (which later merged with Novartis to become Syngenta), but by 2000 it was estimated that in order to secure freedom to use the technology it would be necessary to negotiate licences for all of the 70 or so overlapping patents and other property rights over the technology, which were owned by 32 different companies and universities (Kryder et al. 2000). The magnitude of this task would appear at first sight to be overwhelming, but it turned out that the patent landscape was much less complex in Europe and developing countries than in the US. Agreement on the necessary contractual arrangements to establish freedom to operate was achieved with less than six months of negotiations. Zeneca was able to negotiate with other commercial rights holders to license their intellectual property free of charge for the sole purpose of the Golden Rice Project. Zeneca then licensed back the combined package of necessary intellectual property to the Golden Rice Humanitarian Board. Syngenta continues to donate new technological developments to the board (goldenrice.org), illustrating the willingness of the private sector to act virtuously in response to dire humanitarian need.

The success of the Golden Rice initiative has led others at lower rungs on the collaboration-strengthening pyramid to advocate patent pool-type arrangements in other areas of biotechnology, including the development of a vaccine for the SARS virus (Simon et al. 2005) and in human diagnostic testing (Ebersole et al. 2005; Verbeure et al. 2006). In order to keep pools of this nature virtuous, it is wise to include public involvement in pool governance (Caulfield et al. 2006). For example, the pool might have an independent governance body whose decisions would be open to public scrutiny and which would be required to balance the necessity of industry involvement, the interests of researchers, ethical issues, and the desire to keep licensing terms reasonable to ensure that the public has access to valuable technologies. Putting these governance measures in place in relation to a particular patent pool would require intervention at the third level of our collaboration-strengthening pyramid. Review by competition authorities of the proposed pool structure may also be necessary. This is a nice illustration of the need for the dual institutional design of a capacity-building pyramid such as Figure 5.2 and a monopoly-regulating pyramid with antitrust enforcement capabilities soon to be considered in Figure 5.3. The regulatory pyramid can check the capture by monopolists of capacity-building initiatives within the strengths-based pyramid.

One important aspect of third-level interventions designed to enable experimental implementation of particular mechanisms is to generate and incorporate information about the success or failure of the experiment. Is there an ongoing need for this type of mechanism in this particular field? What are the strengths and weaknesses of the particular model being implemented in the light of practical experience? How can implementation efforts be tweaked to build on strengths and eliminate weaknesses? These questions must be asked and answered to ensure that the process is one of iterative learning and improvement.

The next level of the collaboration-strengthening pyramid relates to experiments that have proved successful. At this stage, implementations may begin to pose a competitive threat to industry incumbents operating within markets in intellectual property vice and require protection from backlash. A successful effort may also attract imitators that detract from its credibility as a means of promoting knowledge exchange when they fail to meet appropriate standards of openness. Possible interventions aimed at safeguarding successful implementations include the formation of standards bodies and the establishment of certification programmes along the lines of that administered in the software world by the Open Source Initiative. Licensing standards, best practice guidelines and certification programmes would also serve the purpose of promulgating the principles of successful implementation, facilitating broader adoption of the relevant model.

Other interventions that belong at this level of the pyramid are those that seek to mainstream a particular mechanism as an element of an overall innovation strategy, whether at a corporate, state or international level. In the US, the National Institutes of Health offer 'glue grants' specifically to promote large-scale collaborative projects. Taking open-source biotechnology as an example, philanthropic organizations such as the Gates Foundation or government funding bodies such as the (Australian) National Health and Medical Research Council might choose to prioritize the funding of projects that employ open-source methods or offer grants to enable open-source collaborators to obtain professional technical, legal or marketing advice. Firms such as Health Management Organizations or government agencies that act as bulk purchasers of biotechnology products such as drugs or seeds could offer procurement contracts preferentially to open-source developers or distributors; government laboratories could choose to use open-source research tools wherever available. Companies and research institutions could permit or encourage employees to spend a proportion of their work hours contributing to open-source projects, or they might allow employees to use spare equipment or other resources such as laboratory consumables for the purposes of making such a contribution. In relation to patent pooling, a similar mainstreaming intervention would be for governments to mandate participation in a particular patent pool as a condition of obtaining the necessary licences to operate in a given industry.

Another example from this level of the pyramid is the establishment of state-funded industry–university research clusters such as the Cooperative Research Centres programme, funded after competitive bids to the Australian Research Council (www.arc.gov). Under such programmes millions in taxpayer funds are contributed to collaborative teams of industry and university innovation workers. The university and industry partners are also required to show their commitment by putting large sums of their own cash into the research effort as well as infrastructure and personnel. The big research money flows are from taxpayers to university researchers to reward those types of researchers whom industry partners believe have potential to generate commercial opportunities. The implicit strategy of such programmes is that it is cheaper to pay off academics to turn their talents to national R&D priorities that will build innovation clusters of shared knowledge than it is to bribe businesses to do so. Business should be doing it in any case in response to the market if there really are good opportunities out there. The second implicit idea of such programmes is that it is better that a nation's best university researchers have their research priorities steered by public rather than private money. Private money poses a greater risk that a nation's best minds will be turned to closing off rather than opening up the intellectual commons. Our best minds should not be excessively distracted from pursuing what they see as the most foundational, as opposed to the most lucrative, insights. And fine minds are more easily recruited to public projects that expand their scholarly influence across an open commons than to secret private projects where publication can be more fraught.

In their current format, these research clusters tend to rely on the traditional monopolist model for intellectual property management and distribution. Universities tend to sell or license patented pharmaceutical technologies to pharmaceutical multinationals because they see no other way of achieving global market distribution. But industry could be co-opted into these clusters by public funding that promotes scientific exchange because they still have an interest in having the best scientific minds in the country working with them rather than their national competitors. They also have an interest in supporting public programmes that prevent the finest scientists from fleeing the country to work with international competitors. Philosophically, some of these programmes need to be more attentive to awarding the biggest grants to the most pro-collaboration proposals and to ensuring that it is not the public money that is co-opted by the private sector into monopoly-oriented projects. Otherwise this institutional device for fostering innovation could backfire into strengthening the market in intellectual property vice.

We live in a world where the Queen of England is more likely to award a knighthood to Bill Gates than to Richard Stallman (the inspiration and instigator of the free software movement). Knighthoods, Academy awards and Nobel Prizes are important not only for their potential to reward selfless dedication to the commonweal (Brennan and Pettit 2004), but also for what they signal about the values and the good works that matter. Hence, while it is a good idea to disperse rewards to many by making Drahos's (2000) idea of an indigenous knowledge clearing house work well, it would add extra value for the United Nations Educational, Scientific, and Cultural Organization (UNESCO) each year to lionize a person or organization who has made a special lifetime contribution to facilitating a flow of benefits from indigenous knowledge to indigenous peoples, while making indigenous knowledges part of the common heritage of humanity that reinforces biodiversity with cultural diversity. Prizes may be given out at national or international levels by any credible awards body; Stallman might be unlikely to receive a knighthood, but his Free Software Foundation issues an annual Award for the Advancement of Free Software. Australian programmer Andrew Tridgell won this prize in 2005, two years after receiving The Bulletin Magazine's nomination as Australia's smartest information and communications technology person. Other potential forms of recognition, corresponding to the apex of our proposed pyramid, include *Time Magazine*'s Person of the Year award, tributes in major journals (in the biotechnology field, for example, *Nature* or *Science* – in 2006

Ingo Potrykus and Peter Beyer were named in *Nature Biotechnology* as the two people who had made the most significant contribution to agricultural biotechnology in the last ten years (Jayaraman et al. 2006)), a change in the rules of the Nobel Prize to make virtuous uses of any relevant intellectual property rights a condition of the award, or the attendance of heads of state at media conferences announcing scientific and technological breakthroughs (as when both UK and US heads of state appeared at the press conference announcing publication of the draft human genome sequence). We do not wish to advocate which are the best kinds of prizes or awards to give out. We simply float the idea of cultural recognition for shunning intellectual property vice in favour of extraordinary feats of service to the common knowledge heritage of humanity.

Nor would we want to suggest that we think the particular pyramid in Figure 5.2 has all the best possible entries in the right order. All we wish to accomplish in this chapter is three things: first, to introduce some of the virtues of the idea of a collaboration-strengthening pyramid; second, to make the pyramid less abstract than it would be if we failed to illustrate with concrete policy possibilities for populating different levels of the pyramid; and, third, to illustrate the idea that at the base of the pyramid we should choose strategies that are minimally interventionist and minimally costly, yet that have relevance to the widest possible community of innovators.

The idea of a strengths-enhancing pyramid (Braithwaite et al. 2007; ch. 10) is that as we move up it, we move to targeting progressively more costly rewards on progressively smaller target groups. There is an 'economy of esteem' (Brennan and Pettit 2004) in the conceptualization of the pyramid as we move from the most modest honour of being cited in a paper by the likes of Nicol and Hope as a biotechnology open-source innovator, to being lauded on the homepage of the leading biotechnology licensing clearing house, to the considerable honour of winning a competition as a chief investigator or principal partner in an Australian Research Council Cooperative Research Centre competition, to being toasted by the Director-General of UNESCO in Paris. There is more than just an economy of esteem in play here; there is also an economy of capital formation. The Cooperative Research Centre and the UNESCO Prize are about cash as well as caché. Hope and Nicol hope their work will be read not just to see who is cited, but also to learn about new ways of thinking about how to make money! Nevertheless, in Braithwaite et al.'s (2007) theorizing of dual regulatory and strengths-based pyramids, the emotional economy of pride is important in the latter and the emotional economy of shame, as we now illustrate, is important in the responsive regulatory pyramid.

OPTIONS FOR A PYRAMID TO RESPONSIVELY REGULATE MONOPOLIZATION OF INTELLECTUAL RESOURCES

In this section we consider the range of tools that might be deployed to populate a regulatory pyramid to counter monopolization of intellectual resources. While the pyramid in Figure 5.2 is substantially about rewarding and expanding virtuous uses of intellectual property rights, the regulatory pyramid, which is represented diagrammatically in Figure 5.3, is about sanctioning and containing the vicious effects of intellectual property rights.

The availability of patents for foundational biotechnological inventions creates the necessary precursor to monopolization of intellectual resources. Yet existing studies in the US, Europe and Australia have not found that owners of such patents routinely use their patent rights in a monopolistic way, so as to block off whole areas of research. Nor have they found a full-blown anticommons problem, at least in the area of biomedicine. There are isolated examples of blocking behaviour in biomedicine where foundational technologies are at stake, but these tend to be the exception rather than the norm (but cf. Murray and Stern 2005). Nor have they found that owners of foundational patents routinely use their patent rights in a monopolistic way, so as to block off whole areas of research (OECD 2002; Nicol and Nielsen 2003; Walsh et al. 2003a). In agriculture, as we saw at the start of this chapter, the evidence of monopolistic vices is more compelling.

In an Ernst & Young (1999), survey 21 per cent of biotechnology companies said that they had abandoned a project because it was blocked by another company's intellectual property rights. In Nicol and Nielsen (2003: 140), 18 per cent of biomedical organizations reported suffering frustrations in the progress of their research as a result of patent blockages and there was scant evidence of the existence of an anticommons as such (2003: 194–5). It is acknowledged that *any* blocking off of research areas could have negative repercussions on downstream innovation,[5] yet one must expect some jostling between competitors in any new area of technology. The stated purpose of the patent system, after all, is to create state-sanctioned monopolies to encourage innovation, so it is inevitable that some territory will be fenced off. The critical issue is to find the right balance. Because we know that 90 per cent of patents in the 1990s were never used (Ernst & Young 1999),[6] and because all the empirical studies find growing risks that intellectual property could be used in ways that could have a detrimental effect in innovation (Nicol and Nielsen 2003; Walsh et al. 2003a), a larger sleeper problem than the extant research reveals may be looming. That is, as history accumulates more patents acquired for

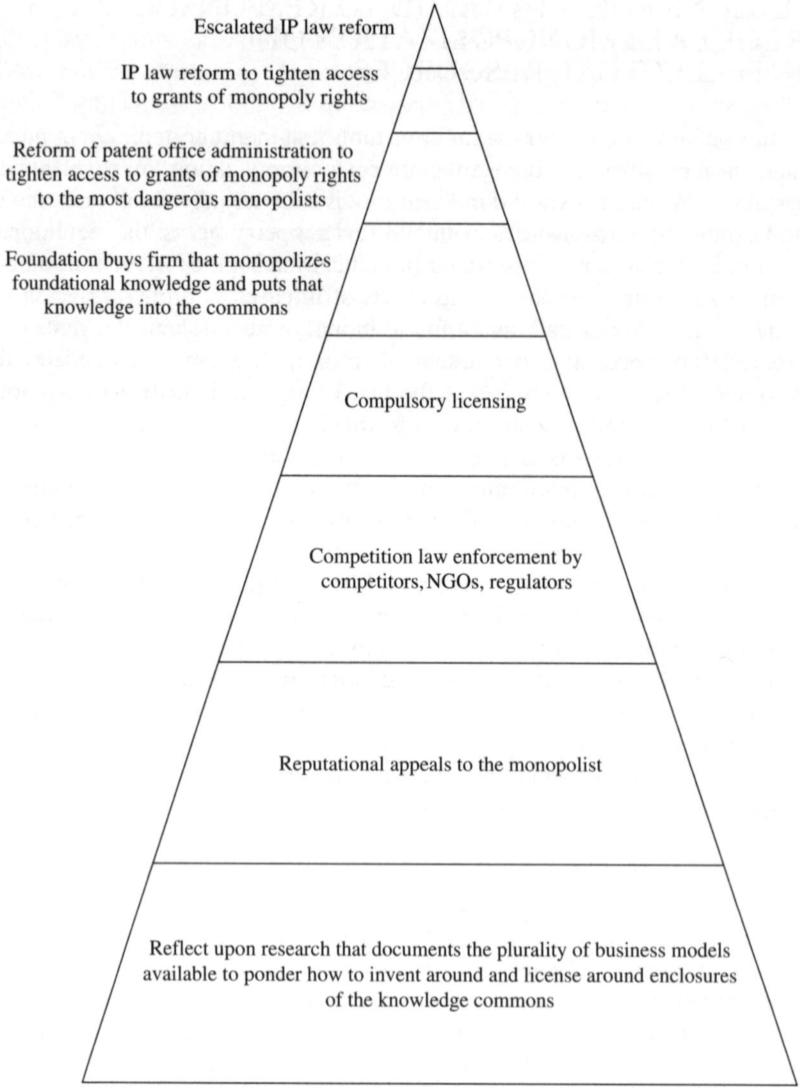
Escalated IP law reform
IP law reform to tighten access to grants of monopoly rights
Reform of patent office administration to tighten access to grants of monopoly rights to the most dangerous monopolists
Foundation buys firm that monopolizes foundational knowledge and puts that knowledge into the commons
Compulsory licensing
Competition law enforcement by competitors, NGOs, regulators
Reputational appeals to the monopolist
Reflect upon research that documents the plurality of business models available to ponder how to invent around and license around enclosures of the knowledge commons

Figure 5.3 One possible pyramid for regulating abuse of monopoly power through intellectual property rights

blocking reasons and as the patent landscape gets more and more complex, monopoly vices might progressively fester around these blockages.

The worst manifestation of this is where large patent portfolios are acquired specifically in order to discourage innovation by others through various blocking strategies that involve seeing the direction a competitor is headed and deliberately creating patentable roadblocks along that path. Specific blocking techniques include 'clustering' (patenting around one's own core patents), 'bracketing' (patenting around a competitor's core patents), 'blitzkrieg' (patenting a large number of similar or related devices or molecular entities), 'blanketing' (mining every step in a manufacturing process with patents claiming minor modifications), 'flooding' (acquiring many patents on minor or incremental variations on technology developed by another company), 'fencing' (blocking certain lines or directions of research and development using a series of patents) and 'surrounding' (enclosing a key patent with minor patents that collectively block its effective commercial use) (Macdonald 2004). None of these strategies requires the patent owner to actually use or permit others to use the patented technology. A whole host of other strategies are employed to firm up such monopolistic positions, including mergers and acquisitions of small players for defensive purposes, cherry-picking technology to transfer from the public sector to cut off virtuous new innovations, and utilizing the threat of litigation and all its associated costs to temper the behaviour of the risk averse.

One of the virtues of responsive regulation is that it is a dynamic regulatory model that responds to changes in the environment to be regulated with the minimum level of intervention required to solve the problem. If the problem does fester, escalatory capability is planned for, indeed signalled to those who intentionally promote the problem.

The regulatory pyramid in Figure 5.3 has an education and persuasion approach at its base as the presumptively preferred approach, as do the pyramids in Figures 5.1 and 5.2. Figures 5.2 and 5.3 have more or less the same base: reflect upon research that documents the plurality of business models available to ponder how to invent around and license around and discourage enclosures of the intellectual commons. To solve the problem of monopolization of intellectual resources, the first solution for an organization affected by say a blocking patent is to see if it can invent around it, or obtain a licence at reasonable cost, or enter into a cross-licensing arrangement with the blocking firm. Or it can move across to the collaboration-strengthening pyramid of Figure 5.2 – successfully advocate for patent pooling or join an open source-style collaboration that over time might collectively invent around the blockage. The empirical research implies consideration of inventing around as the main game at the base of the pyramid: Nicol and Nielsen (2003: 212) found two-thirds of the biotechnology researchers they interviewed to have 'frequently' invented around patents.

Where monopolies of intellectual resources cannot be circumvented by any practical strategy, reputational appeal to the monopolist is one simple strategy that can work. Many readers are doubtless thinking this an implausible suggestion: monopolists do not give away their monopolies because they are bad for their reputation. Actually they do. When we academics borrow a book from a colleague who wrote it and then photocopy some pages from it, perhaps multiple copies to discuss in our research group, we do not worry that the colleague might act against us for breach of copyright. The reason we go ahead and break the law without worrying that our victim will act against us is that this would be terrible for his or her professional reputation. Imagine if he or she were silly enough to write to his or her publisher, reporting that we had reproduced a dozen copies of a section of his or her book. Apart from writing back to their author that this *de minimis* breach would not justify the costs of copyright enforcement, the publisher would explain to the author that it is reluctant to jeopardize its reputation in scholarly communities by prosecuting academics for photocopying for research purposes.

It is not just at the *de minimis* end of the property rights continuum that reputational appeals can produce offers to waive monopoly rights. We have seen this on the part of the major owners of patents in drugs to treat AIDS in developing countries. While this gesture was made to rehabilitate corporate reputations that had been savaged in the aftermath of the catastrophic effect of TRIPS on access to affordable medicines in developing countries, and while it was an utterly inadequate response to the magnitude of the problem, there can be little doubt that it has saved a very large number of lives in Africa.

Perhaps the most consequential reputational reluctance to enforce monopoly rights was found in Nicol and Nielsen's (2003: 257) empirical research among Australian biotechnology organizations. They found companies were loath to enforce patents against researchers in research institutions both because of the damage it would do to the image of the company and because research institutions tend not to have such deep pockets that they will be generous and quick to settle. That research also suggests that a similar situation may exist in the diagnostics sector (Nicol and Nielsen 2005: 317). The damage that can be done to a company's reputation through aggressive exercise of their monopoly rights is illustrated by the negative publicity that Myriad Diagnostics received in Europe and Canada as a result of its attempts to enforce its BRCA patents against public hospitals testing for increased susceptibility to breast cancer. While such bad publicity does not necessarily cause rogue players to modify their behaviour, it may discourage more widespread adoption of such practices. In this age where corporate social responsibility is the catch-cry, patent holders may become increasingly reluctant to enforce their rights against organizations seen to be acting for the public benefit.

The next rung up our regulatory pyramid is competition law enforcement. This might be undertaken by a company adversely affected by their competitor using an intellectual property right to block entry into their market. It might be launched by NGOs concerned about anti-competitive conduct rendering medicines unaffordable to the poor. Or it might be launched by a national antitrust agency or an international organization such as the European Commission. While all of these auspices have been used to launch strategic competition cases, and while such competition law actions have become available since the 1990s as an option in most of the world's jurisdictions, empirically all these options are infrequently used in most societies. Yet one can point to important cases such as the consent decree Ciba-Geigy and Sandoz entered into with US antitrust authorities when they merged to form Novartis. The decree required them to broadly license their human gene therapy patents to foster competition in that area (Ciba-Geigy Limited, 123 F.T.C. 842 (1997)). Over the past decade, the European Commission has become much more active in intellectual property competition law cases, and has become willing to tackle big targets like Microsoft. Experts increasingly see widened scope for competition law enforcement against monopolistic overreach of intellectual property rights (Drexl 2005; Fink 2005; Fox 2005; Janis 2005; Ullrich 2005).

Competition law enforcement does not have to be frequent to matter as just one step among a range of escalatory options. Competition authorities can have a policy of requiring complainants in intellectual property cases to explore the options lower in the pyramid before it will consider an investigation. It would be naive to expect competition authorities to become proactively competent at penetrating the secrecy and scientific complexity surrounding thickets of biotechnology patents. However, they could reach out to the biotechnology sector in a variety of ways, for example, through their agents in law firms specializing in competition law (Parker 2002) to educate potential whistle-blowers in biotechnology firms, research organizations and patent offices to step forward and educate the antitrust regulators as to why a particular thicket of patents is being used to undermine competition in an unusually damaging way. When such education campaigns by competition regulators are well done, they promote the responsive regulatory objective of enforcement being threatened in the background even if it is rarely actually threatened in the foreground. The targeted education campaign can help create a climate within a strategic industry sector that a business model of simply monopolizing intellectual resources will be unsustainable because it can be attacked not only by a variety of competing business models, but it might be attacked legally by a variety of types of actors who might be moved to defend the commons through law enforcement. Competition authorities can encourage firms to engage with conversational forms of regulation that reach agreement on how to head off such attacks before the event, for example by submitting proposed arrangements to them for review as in Business Review Letters submitted to the US Department of Justice, or authorization applications to the competition authority in other jurisdictions such as Australia.

The next rung up the enforcement ladder is statutory compulsory licensing, as opposed to licences issued as part of a competition law settlement (Scherer 2000: 327–42; Reichman and Hasenzahl 2003: 26–33). Compulsory licensing provides a licence to work the invention without the authorization of the owner of an intellectual property right, either broadly or narrowly, in order to achieve specified public benefits such as the promotion of competition or protecting public health. It is a remedy explicitly allowed by TRIPS (despite US pharmaceutical industry lobbying to ban compulsory licensing), explicitly provided for in the laws of most countries, even the US. Compulsory licensing can have a number of uses, ranging from the supply of medicines for the treatment of HIV-AIDS to remedying the effects of anti-competitive practices in a range of markets. The mere threat of a compulsory licence in some circumstances may be enough to bring a patent holder to the bargaining table. The provisions can be cumbersome and expensive to use, though this is hardly true of government use provisions that normally only require an official to authorize use.

Compulsory licensing simply cannot solve some problems. A compulsory licence granted to a competitor by nation X may not be a lot of use to the competitor if the main markets they need to compete in are those of nations Y and Z and there are blocking patents in Y and Z. Second, national governments feel that if they enforce compulsory licences US trade officials will punish them (at the behest of US industry lobbyists who fear the spread of compulsory licensing in domains such as pharmaceuticals). Because US trade negotiators have made the circumscription of compulsory licensing a major issue in bilateral trade negotiations, most nations fear its use will cost them other trade and security concessions from the US (Drahos 2007) and possibly the EU. Third, nations are particularly unlikely to be attracted to ordering a research-intensive company operating within their borders to license when most of the beneficiaries of the licence will be outside their borders.

Nation states, however, are not the only actors in the world system who can act to defend the intellectual commons. If a sufficiently fundamental form of knowledge were being locked up by a firm, a foundation[7] might be persuaded to purchase that firm, put the fundamental knowledge in the public domain, then sell it to a competitor with a more open business model.[8] While it may well be difficult for most charitable foundations to take on the purchase of a Glaxo or a Monsanto, even at the big end, it may be affordable for a big foundation. Bill Gates and his foundation might well be able to persuade one of the New York investment banks to buy Glaxo or Monsanto as long as Mr Gates wrote them a letter of guarantee that they would get their fee and the difference between the buying and selling price once it was sold on as a more (informationally) open concern. The foundation only needs enough money to cover this loss. And, of course, if the rationalizing non-monopolistic model for Monsanto is a brilliant one, then the Gates Foundation will actually make money out of the anti-monopolistic restructure. Like compulsory licensing, it is only an option. Even if Bill Gates and his friend Warren Buffet did not want to take on the restructure of hard cases like these ones, they (or some more pro-commons foundation) might be more willing to fund research that attempts to invent around the locked up technology, which is the strategy that PIPRA and CAMBIA have adopted. The argument to a foundation that funds a lot of research in this area might be that it can make a bigger contribution by putting this foundational knowledge into the public domain for all researchers to build on than by directly funding more research.

The same global political constraint that deters nations from compulsory licensing applies to the final three rungs of the pyramid – escalated reform of intellectual property law and its regulation to liberalize (as opposed to lock up) knowledge. The US really does not like nations that do this. Nor does the EU. Even though 90 per cent of the world's nations have an interest in shorter patent terms, for example – because they are net importers of patent rights, because they could reduce their public and private health bills greatly by having more cheaper off-patent drugs – their greater fear is of the market power of the US and the EU in trade negotiations and their power in security matters (Drahos 2007). Drahos and Braithwaite have argued that what is needed is Chinese and Indian leadership on compulsory licensing, because these are the countries with both the most profound interest in such a policy shift and countries that are increasingly too powerful themselves for the US and EU to bully (Drahos 2002; Braithwaite, J. 2004). Then Drahos and Braithwaite have argued that the G-20 group of developing economies at the World Trade Organization, led by Brazil, South Africa, India and China, should make ratcheting back to less monopolistic global intellectual property regulation a priority.

Hence, to bring the peak of the enforcement pyramid in Figure 5.3 to life, a long-run global political strategy is needed that reformers like Peter Drahos have assiduously promoted through working with NGOs like Oxfam, through endless lunches with Brazilian and other diplomats, and through public campaigning to oppose the signature of Australia's free trade agreement with the US. Yet so long as there are Peter Drahoses and Brazilian leaders who are interested in such a campaign, and so long as there are US intellectual property interests who fear and loathe them and that campaign (and there are), intellectual property monopolists actually do have inchoate fears about ending up at the peak of this regulatory pyramid. A debate about intellectual property law reforms that national governments are currently paralysed about taking seriously is of course a poor substitute for actual law reform. Yet the nice thing about a responsive regulatory pyramid is that it can work moderately well with a bad law (see, for example, the case of British nursing-home regulation in the 1980s and 1990s (Braithwaite et al. 2007)). One reason it can work with a bad law is that the spectre of the bad law being reformed into a good law can play on the minds of legal game-players. This, we conjecture, is why the US pharmaceutical industry offered to waiver its monopoly rights over patented AIDS drugs for some of those most in need of them in some of the world's poorest countries.

The British nursing-home inspector case (see also Chapter 6) also instructed us in how imaginative street-level bureaucrats can effect problem-solving regulatory administration with a bad law. In that case inspectors accomplished this by networking in threats from others (such as banks that might refuse lending when they see a damning inspection report on the Internet) when the law was effectively unavailable to back enforcement. Patent examiners are street-level bureaucrats not unlike the bureaucrats who issue licences to nursing homes. In sectors like biotechnology, competitors often complain of patent examiners granting overly broad claims (Nicol and Nielsen 2003: 252). Patent examination creates perfect conditions for regulatory capture because the applicant and the regulator are the only players at the point when the patent is granted (Ayres and Braithwaite 1992: ch. 3). One method of regulatory escalation would therefore be to bring a third player into the regulatory game. This third player could be an outside academic consultant or a person active in open-source and related NGO networks like the Open Source Initiative or the Electronic Frontier Foundation. Objective criteria might be used to select the target list of companies who would be moved from bipartite to tripartite patent examination.

Surveys of organizations in innovative sectors could be used to target companies that get the highest numbers of nominations for ownership of patents that cause respondents to abandon R&D programmes. Companies that own unusually large numbers of patents are obviously more able to deter innovation with a wall of patents than organizations who own none or only a few. Those owning more than a certain number of patents could be asked to provide evidence on how many have been commercially exploited, with the dozen firms which appear to have the lowest levels of patent exploitation being targeted for tripartite patent examination on all future applications.

Our point is that however monopoly-enhancing a nation's intellectual property laws are, its intellectual property administration can be risk-managed to escalate scrutiny of firms with a history of abuse of monopoly power. Since the most aggressive players of the patent game in certain sectors like pharmaceuticals do get away with ridiculously broad bipartite grants of monopoly power at times, a shift to targeted tripartite scrutiny is something they would not enjoy. While US trade negotiators are quite capable of punishing governments for regulatory administration that aggravates US firms, in general risk management strategies in patent administration will be a sufficiently micro issue to go under the radar of US trade negotiators and really would be a technically difficult kind of micro-management for them to handle. Moreover, one of the interesting places to start with reform of patent administration to tackle overly broad grants of monopoly rights would be within the US Patents and Trademarks Office (PTO), with the objective of defending the dynamism of US technology start-ups. Indeed, there is already momentum in this direction: the US PTO has been stepping back from the breadth of its early 1990s patenting (partly under pressure from the courts) (Nicol and Nielsen 2003: 87) and the Federal Trade Commission (2003) has been pressuring the PTO to open up its administrative processes to post-grant review and opposition.

The US PTO has already commenced in 2007 the first social software project to be wired to a legal decision-making process – a 'marriage of Wikipedia to the authority of Administrative Law' on a sample of patent examinations that will be subject to 'open review' (Noveck 2006: 123). While some fear this experiment, companies like IBM who believe they will benefit from a race to the top in patent examination quality, support it. Under the experiment, the examination decision remains with public patent examiners, but they use the information gleaned from open review. Targeted tripartite examination could be combined with open review, or used without it. The European Patent Office is also being urged by the European Parliament and others to consider a variety of shifts from insider governance to more participatory governance of patent administration (Drahos 2006b; European Technology Assessment Group 2007).

A targeted tripartite process could be used for public interest purposes: NGOs could bring test cases for particularly controversial patents. The benefit of such challenges is not just with regard to the particular patent that is challenged. Examination practice would have to change to reflect such precedents, applicants would be reluctant to lodge offensive claims, and patent holders would be reluctant to enforce their rights when the validity of their patent claims were in doubt. There is an emerging global epistemic community of patent examination; engagement with this epistemic community (as Peter Drahos is doing in a current Australian

Research Council grant with IP Australia) might enable reform of a global profession in a way that does not confront American power head on, indeed in a way that helps sustain the dynamism of American innovation.

While trimming some years off the duration of patent monopolies might also serve well the dynamism of American innovation and competitiveness, this really would be confronting starkly the power of leading American corporations who lobbied for longer patents globally. Hence, if abuse of patent monopolies worsens in the years ahead, it is difficult to imagine that a politically feasible response at the peak of our pyramid would be progressively to cut patent terms until behaviour improved. However, in Australia it has been politically possible in the current decade to significantly tighten up the novelty and inventive step criteria in its patent law (Patents Amendment Act 2001 (Cth)), even if it is tightening that has not gone far enough. So we know that at least some kinds of law reform to tighten access to grants of monopoly rights at the peak of our pyramid are possible. Another option at the peak of this pyramid is to look at law reform to improve access to technology protected by monopoly rights, rather than focusing solely on the grant of those rights. One option would be to provide carte blanche exemptions from infringement in certain limited circumstances as the US did in 1996 by giving doctors exemptions for patented surgical procedures used in hospitals.[9] If reputational threats began to fail to deter patent owners from enforcing their rights against scientists doing foundational work in research institutions, law reform to create an express research exemption would become quite feasible. Patent owners understand this; it may be one of the reasons for them being persuadable by reputational threats.

The form of intellectual property law has always been much more starkly a product of global interest group politics, in particular the money power of American business, than in most legal domains (Drahos 2002). There is little prospect for meeting of minds so that at some future point in history we arrive at a law that all sides view as imbued with integrity. No, for as long as we can foresee, the purchasers of pirated DVDs in a developing country will view themselves as striking a blow across the digital divide, or at least as not doing anything very wrong, while Hollywood will continue to view them as the criminals described in the warning at the beginning of the screening. One of the virtues of responsive regulation is that, in conditions where law of deep integrity and legitimacy across different interest groups is impossible, it can still offer a way forward to solve problems like enabling innovation (this chapter), protecting elderly Britons from abuse and neglect (Braithwaite et al. 2007), and building peace after armed conflict (Braithwaite 2002: ch. 6). That is not to deny that the world would be better off with an international law for regulating armed conflict and intellectual property rights that had deep integrity and legitimacy. It is just to say that we can get on with the job of regulating abuse of power without recourse to law, while lobbying for more decent laws as part of that very regulatory project. Moreover, non-state players like foundations, professions, the G-20, NGOs, universities and companies with open-source business models can get on with the job of regulating the anticommons and other monopolistic vices, and strengthening the commons following the very principles that render responsive regulation more effective when state law enforcement does it – a preference for restorative justice over punitive justice, favouring a culture of learning and root-cause analysis over a blame culture, procedural justice, respectful listening, avoidance of stigmatization, rituals of truth and reconciliation, escalation when justice is not restored (Ayres and Braithwaite 1992; Braithwaite 2002; Braithwaite et al. 2007).

This helps us to understand an important difference between regulatory and strengths-based pyramids. At the base of a regulatory pyramid, webs of regulation need to be soft and weak. If the regulatory constraint is unjust or unreasonable, regulated actors must be able to crash through the web and contest the regulatory order at higher levels of the pyramid – for example, in litigation that strikes down the regulation. It is at the peak of the pyramid that the net must be resilient enough to prevent the most nefarious sharks from crashing through it.

With a strengths-based pyramid, it is at the base that we have the strong net, a safety net, so no one falls through. No one misses the opportunity for an education to build their strengths, for example. But not everyone is singled out for special praise when they use that education to build a special strength. Not everyone will have further strength rewarded with postgraduate education and research grants. Few will win a million dollar grant or an Academy Award. Building welfare in the knowledge economy may seem a different matter from educating children, in this safety net sense. Actually, we do not see it as fundamentally different. At the base of Figure 5.2, the idea is for research that catches all worthy business models and their matching niches for analysis and consideration. Higher in the pyramid, only selected models will be worthy of scarce private and public investment dollars.

CONCLUSION

There is no structural inevitability of a tragedy of the commons or of a tragedy of the anticommons. Judicious blending of property rights and informal communal regulation of overgrazing and overfishing has defeated tragedies of the commons in many of the world's surviving agricultural societies for millennia (Ostrom et al. 1999; Chanock 2005: 349–50) and in some contemporary fisheries. Likewise, we have argued, sage balancing of property rights and regulation might defeat the market in intellectual property vice.

The era of regulatory capitalism is one of the knowledge economy and of pluralistic networked governance. In this chapter we have acquired some flavour of both the limitations of state regulation using sovereign national laws, and of the plurality of regulatory tools deployed by non-state actors, in such a world. While it is a world where wealth flows to those best at monopolizing the commercialization of new knowledge, new entertainment and new technologies, and these are almost exclusively the corporations of wealthy nations, we have argued it is an economy where monopoly is always vulnerable to networking around it. Within the social movement for freer circulation of knowledge we do see creative moves like humanitarian licence clauses that mandate preferential transfer of technology to developing economies. Western political power was used to crush transfer of technology to developing countries as a central UN priority for a New World Economic Order in the 1970s – particularly through UNCTAD (Braithwaite and Drahos 2000). Yet in the current decade we see some promise for less centralized rivulets of egalitarian technology transfer through the Internet, networking of small technology businesses, universities, foundations and social movements with an ideology of liberating the intellectual commons. Comparatively weak nations like Australia, visionary foundations, NGOs like Oxfam who are interested in a more open and egalitarian global knowledge economy, universities and libraries can be advocates for initiatives at the base of our two pyramids and for a variety of creative ways of moving up plural collaboration-strengthening pyramids and pyramids to regulate monopolistic practices.

These actors would all struggle for different kinds of pyramids if they became attracted to the idea of pyramidal regulation. That is OK. In a world of networked governance, all must plan their strategic action being mindful of how others in a network are doing their strategic planning (Metcalfe 1994). Indeed, the degree of cooperative action – itself a scarce resource – that is required to implement a given strategy is one factor that must be taken into account in this planning; actions that can be taken unilaterally, such as the donation of technology to the public under an 'academic' or 'permissive'-style open-source licence, are intrinsically less costly than those that require extensive coordination among network partners. This means reflection on the escalatory designs of both those who are your networked adversaries and those who are your network partners. Part of the theory of responsive regulation is that open display of the content of the pyramids we favour helps all players of all hues see possibilities for politics with superior win-win prospects at the base of the pyramids we proffer to them.

NOTES

1. We owe this point to Peter Drahos in comments on a draft of this chapter.
2. For a discussion of the many strategies industry participants may adopt to keep the wheels of innovation turning despite the friction created by intellectual property rights, see Walsh et al. (2003b).
3. Open-source licences that do this are referred to as copyleft licences. 'Academic' or 'permissive' open-source licenses allow downstream innovators greater freedom to appropriate improvements.
4. Not just habits of commercial secrecy, but indigenous traditions of secrecy to prevent co-optation or crushing of indigenous knowledge by outside influences.
5. Peter Drahos made the following comment on this interpretation: 'Only1 in 5! – given the importance of start-ups in biotech I think that this is significant. Then what about the companies that don't enter an area in the first place because of the patent position.'
6. This figure suggests that acquisition for blocking purposes may be common. However, we are not suggesting that all such patents were deliberately acquired for blocking purposes. While it is sometimes assumed that all published patent documents represent rights that can and will be enforced, some are actually defensive filings that are published but never prosecuted to grant. Although the practice of defensive filing has its drawbacks, including contributing to the perception on the part of potential users of a technology that their freedom to operate is blocked even when it is not, it is not necessarily incompatible with non-monopolistic business models (for data on the large numbers of gene patents that have been applied for and not pursued or granted and allowed to lapse, see Hopkins et al. (2006)).
7. The Rockefeller Foundation has supported the BIOS intitiative of the leading open source innovator CAMBIA and PIPRA, the latter also being supported by the McKnight Foundation.
8. It would probably be important to fire the old management team. This is because there is moral hazard in this escalation. Being bought out by a generous foundation is hardly escalated deterrence of monopoly, even if it is escalated incapacitation of a monopoly.
9. See 35 USC 287 (c).

6. Can regulatory ritualism be transcended?

WHY DOES REGULATORY CAPITALISM CONDUCE TO RITUALISM?

Public providers of services in the era of provider capitalism (until the 1970s) suffered much criticism for their inefficiencies. Yet they enjoyed a kind of legitimacy, based often on rather settled patterns of cross-subsidization and on a history of expanding access to services. So public telecommunications providers basked in the continuous improvement to service access that decades of technological progress in telecommunications allowed. And they drew legitimacy from settled cross-subsidization of rural by urban consumers, of residential by business users. A similar story might be told of public railways and many other services. Privatization unsettled these arrangements: competition made it difficult for business subsidization of residential users, and other cross-subsidizations, to survive, for example. This unsettling challenged the legitimacy of privatization. It fuelled demands for the privatized providers to be held more accountable to public values.

The political elites that drove privatization had to defend its legitimacy by building community service obligations and other accountabilities into privatization packages. Because their commitments were neoliberal, they believed in markets, but not in the importance of these accountabilities. The latter were palliatives to placate spooked publics who needed to be helped to learn how to trust the efficiency of markets. True believers in achieving any kind of outcome are rarely enthusiasts for accountabilities that might question their belief. Chief executive officers of private corporations who want to believe that their company is recording good profits do not enthuse about accountants who query whether their numbers tell as positive a story as claimed. Indeed, they tend to replace them with more docile auditors. This is why in both private corporate accountability and public accountability, audit tends to become over time a 'ritual of comfort' (Power 1997).

By rituals of comfort, Power means that audit is an institution of pacification rather than proof. The production of comfort reflects the institutional need for audit not to be too successful in fingering problems and creating discomfort by reporting them. It is also a form of verification that mostly avoids public dialogue through an opaque and dry paper ritual.

Braithwaite et al. (2007) have developed inductively the notion of regulatory ritualism from empirical work on nursing-home regulation in a way rather like Power's conception of rituals of comfort. Their interpretation of ritualism was inspired by Robert Merton (1968). Merton identified five types of adaptation to a normative order – conformity, innovation, ritualism, retreatism and rebellion – where the response can be either 'acceptance' (+), 'rejection' (−), or 'rejection of prevailing values and substitution of new values' (±) (see Table 6.1). We can apply Merton's model, with only a little distortion, to acceptance and rejection of regulatory goals and means to achieving those goals institutionalized in regulatory standards. Braithwaite et al.'s (2007) data found conformity, innovation, ritualism, retreatism and rebellion all evident in responses of nursing homes to their regulation. Conformity was found when nursing homes endorsed regulatory goals and adopted the recommended path for achieving them. Innovation breaks with conventional means, finding new ways of pursuing agreed regulatory objectives. Rejection of both regulatory goals and means was evident in the worst nursing homes, a condition called retreatism. When rejection of goals and means was accompanied by a switch to alternative goals and means, nursing homes fitted Merton's rebellion mode of adaptation. Rebellion becomes most evident when regulatory agencies change their standards and procedures. This leaves the fifth mode of adaptation – ritualism.

Ritualism is the adaptation that has progressively become the most daunting challenge of regulatory capitalism in domains beyond nursing home regulation. Michael Power (1997) has demonstrated the ritual of comfort phenomenon in quite a variety of domains. Ritualism means acceptance of institutionalised means for securing regulatory goals while losing focus on achieving the goals or outcomes themselves.

Table 6.1 Merton's typology of modes of individual adaptation

Modes of adaptation	Cultural goals	Institutionalized means
I. Conformity	+	+
II. Innovation	+	−
III. Ritualism	−	+
IV. Retreatism	−	−
V. Rebellion	±	±

Source: Merton (1968: 194).

We have seen that neoliberalism confronts legitimacy problems when electorates wish to see more accountability for corporate power in privatized markets. The result is a politics of grudging regulatory growth that conduces to regulatory ritualism. Those political leaders who would prefer to deregulate, but are forced by the electorate to actually increase regulation are often attracted to ritualistic regulation that gives the appearance of being tough without compelling major substantive change. Then when politicians come to power who really want regulation that forces improvement, they are paradoxically at risk of attack from conservative ritualists when they dismantle rituals that give the appearance of toughness in favour of reforms that deliver more substance.

Even if street-level bureaucrats (Lipsky 1980) with wide discretion are actually getting a lot done, it is hard for politicians to prove to the people in a simple way that this is so. And when the street-level bureaucrat abuses discretion in a way that leads to a public scandal, the politicians want to be able to invoke an accountability mechanism, a ritual of comfort that will create the appearance that checks are now in place to ensure this cannot happen again. Since years rather than months tend to separate major public scandals that engulf any given regulatory agency, chances are the politician will be lucky and all the big problems will remain submerged from public view during the rest of his or her incumbency. The minister's career will end in this portfolio with the successful appearance that his or her ritualistic accountability mechanism has worked.

VARIETIES OF RITUALISM

There is an infinite variety of ways regulators and regulatees can both be obsessed with means of achieving goals (such as inputs and processes) rather than the goals themselves. Various forms of ritualism will be used to illustrate: rule ritualism, protocol ritualism, documentation ritualism, scientific ritualism, random sampling ritualism and technological ritualism. The first to be considered is rule ritualism.

Historically what has happened in many regulatory domains in the US is a process where key political players became critical of broad, vaguely defined standards. At the macro-level, one would think the industry were losers from an accumulation of rules. Surely they resist this? But rules do not accumulate at the macro-level; they expand in a rather micro way. In these micro-dynamics, it is sometimes the industry that drives the accumulation of rules. When nursing home X is found non-compliant on a broad standard on which home Y in similar circumstances is found compliant, home X screams about inconsistency. It complains to its industry association about the vagueness of the standard leading to 'subjective' and 'unfair' judgements by inspectors. The industry association representing these members' grievances pleads for the standard to be 'tightened up'.

Paradoxically, when the regulator then consults with consumer groups on this grievance, for different reasons, they agree that the standards should be made more specific. They are concerned that vague standards are unenforceable. Legislators can then see opportunities to please both interest groups by rule-making that portrays the same rule change in slightly different ways to the two constituencies. They tell the industry association they are responding to their grievance about the rules being vague and unfair; they tell the consumer group that they too are frustrated with the failure of inspectors to clean up the industry by enforcing these rules. Legislators themselves think of the standards as so vague that they give inspectors too much discretion to subvert their legislative mandate.

On this, lawmakers and consumer groups often genuinely agree. Lawyers – in roles that include judging, legal drafting, and representing the conflicting interest groups – are professionally socialized to distrust vagueness in legal standards. So they reinforce the above streams of sentiment and help them converge into a river that runs in the direction of more rules that have greater specificity. Lawyers agree with advocacy groups that vague standards are hard to enforce; they agree with industry that vague standards result in abuse of discretion. In Braithwaite et al.'s (2007) data, social and medical scientists had a similar view on vagueness to the lawyers. Scientists believed in tight protocols to ensure that inspectors assess the same things in exactly the same way using precisely defined criteria. In the US, the gerontological establishment was a major contributor to the culture of distrust towards street-level bureaucrats. The scientists' solution to the discretion problem was to hem state inspectors in with detailed protocols that they were audited to follow by federal US inspectors who checked that state inspectors did their job.

Often the upshot is convergence among all the key players of the regulatory game in the United States that broad standards that are not tightly specified must be narrowed. In nursing-home regulation, the consequence was a long-run historical process of all these constituencies succeeding in having one broad standard broken down into two narrower standards; later each of those two standards may be subdivided again into two or more. By 1986 this process had reached the point in the US where there were over 500 federal standards, complemented in most states by at least that number of state standards, sometimes by many times that number (the Illinois code for nursing homes included over 5000 quality of care regulations in the 1980s – Tellis-Nyack et al. 1988: 10).

How do inspectors cope with checking compliance with more than a thousand standards? The answer is that they do not. Some of the standards are completely forgotten, not suppressed by any malevolent or captured political motive, just plain forgotten. Such forgotten standards are never cited. Then there are those that become familiar by some accident of enforcement history that gave prominence to a particular standard in a particular state. Referring to state regulations, one Midwestern nursing-home inspector said: 'We use 10 per cent of them repeatedly. You get into the habit of citing the same ones. Even though you could use others [for the same breach]. Most are never used.'

Braithwaite and Braithwaite (1995) have analysed a variety of ways in which the accumulated existence of a large number of standards in the US drives huge inter-state inconsistency and intra-state inconsistency in how the standards are enforced. When inspectors have an impossible number of standards to check, arbitrary factors will cause particular standards to be checked in some homes, neglected in others, causing endemic unreliability. Braithwaite and Braithwaite (1995) explored in this way the paradox of extremely low inter-inspector reliabilities of compliance for comparatively specific US standards compared with extremely high reliabilities (inter-rater kappa coefficients for total compliance scores ranging from 0.93 to 0.96) for the 31 broad and vague Australian standards in force at that time.

Hand in hand with a paradox of reliability is a paradox of discretion. More and more specific standards are written by lawmakers in the misplaced belief that this narrows the discretion of inspectors. The opposite is the truth: the larger the smorgasbord of standards, the greater the discretion of regulators to pick and choose an enforcement cocktail tailored to meet their own objective. A proliferation of more specific laws is a resource to expand discretion, not a limitation upon it (Baldwin and Hawkins 1984).

The beauty of a small number of broad standards is that one can design a regulatory process to ensure that the ticking of a met rating means that a proper process of information-gathering and inspection team deliberation has occurred on that standard. Inspectors also have a superior capacity to stand back to document the wider patterns in the problems they have identified, to see the wood for the trees. The ritual of pretending to solve a problem by writing a new rule aggregates at the micro-level in a way that at the macro-level makes the system of rules unreliable and unserviceable for regulatory purposes.

The same argument against the proliferation of standards can be extended to the proliferation of protocols for rating standards. Protocols can work well in the context of a social science evaluation, but fail in practice because in the evaluation study the protocol does not have to compete for limited time with 30 other protocols. There are other reasons why a protocol that succeeds in the evaluation study fails in inspection practice. An evaluation might show that a protocol of putting a tick in a box for the name of every resident that participates in each activity can be done reliably. Moreover, scores from following the protocol are validated against more sophisticated detailed assessments of the effectiveness of activities programmes. Unfortunately, however, what was valid at the evaluation stage quickly becomes invalid at the implementation stage.

Regulated firms are quick learners in the business of getting good inspection results. If ticks in activities boxes are what count, droves of sleeping nursing-home residents are wheeled into activities programmes to get the numbers up. Never mind that the quality of the activities programme will be compromised by the clutter of sleeping bodies; it is beating the protocol that counts.

This pathology of protocols is just a specific illustration of the more general problem of formalized regulation forgetting that 'policy problems can be solved only by taking account of numerous interdependent and highly variable factors which oblige decision-makers to manage a kind of cybernetic process involving tentative probe, feedback, adjustment, and reconciliation' (Schuck 1979: 29). The pursuit of precision, either by protocols or by the proliferation of ever-narrower rules, causes an unreliability that is a symptom of a deeper and many-sided malaise of regulatory failure. This is especially depressing since the pursuit of precision usually fails in its own terms – it fails to deliver precision. There might have been 30 or 40 US regulations for every one in Australia at the time of Braithwaite and Braithwaite's (1995) reliability research, but the American standards still seemed vague. In the language game of regulation, the problem of one vague concept is solved by splitting into three vague concepts or by defining protocols with other vague concepts. An alternative to the perpetual struggle to get the words right is to concentrate more on getting the processes of dialogue right. Certainly there is merit in keeping the words simple. This is a necessary precondition to accomplish processes of dialogue that will deliver reliable judgements on those simple words.

DOCUMENTATION RITUALISM

Braithwaite et al. (2007) accumulated a great deal of evidence that when nursing homes are required to document compliance even with very simple protocols, such as a two-hourly turning schedule, evidence of protocol-compliance was often fabricated. A study by Schnelle et al. (2003) of 779 residents in 30 US nursing homes found that recorded incontinence was associated with documentation of two care processes: evaluation of the resident's incontinence history and toileting assistance rendered by staff. The disturbing thing was that, among residents capable of accurately reporting their care, no difference was found in the reported frequency of toileting assistance between those recorded as receiving scheduled toileting and those not. There was also no difference between the two groups in the discrepancy between received and preferred toileting. There was no difference in residents' reports of received toileting between residents scored differently on state-mandated incontinence quality indicators. It appears that while being incontinent mobilized the ritual of documenting a toileting assistance plan, it did not result in the reality of more toileting assistance. This is the ugly face of ritualism – documentation of incontinence history and documented evidence of responding to it as a ritual of comfort. The regulatory state gets comfort while very sick and elderly incontinent citizens suffer extreme discomfort.

More disturbing still, residents who received three to four assists with their toileting per day were more than twice as likely to be able to stand without human assistance as those who received zero assists per day. In other words, it appears that more mobile residents who objectively need less assistance with toileting get more, presumably because they are the easiest ones for staff to assist. Simmons et al. (2002) and Pokrywka et al. (1997) found discrepancies between chart documentation of food intake and direct observations of eating. This is evidence of rituals of comfort that cause the widespread malnutrition in nursing homes:

> Chicago dietary inspector (J. Braithwaite fieldnotes): They think they can solve their problems by designing a fancy sheet [that records percentage of food eaten for each meal]. Paper compliance we call it. They like to show the state that they're doing something. Give them a new documentation and that will get them off our back, they think. But then even the food service supervisor tells us she can't understand why all this food comes back on the trays when the sheets say that they are eating well. But she can't say work out who it is who is not eating their food because the sheets say they are all eating in cases where we've found that they did not eat today.

Bates-Jensen et al. (2003) found that repositioning on a two-hour schedule was documented for 95 per cent of nursing home residents at risk of pressure sores – impressive charting for the state of this ritual of comfort. The observed reality of resident comfort in the study was that 78 per cent of the residents were not moved on a schedule of three hours or less. Cotton (1993: 2338) discussed a study by Joseph Oslander of the University of California at Los Angeles (UCLA) that tested the reality of documentation of two-hourly release of physical restraints and repositioning of residents. Research staff put an invisible fluorescent mark in the centre of knots.

A light can then detect whether the restraint has been untied for repositioning. In the majority of cases the documentation was falsified; the restraint was not released when it was recorded as having been. It follows from this kind of systematic evidence that we should heed the wisdom of the crusty old inspectors who say 'Don't take too seriously the ticks in the boxes they show you. Kick the tyres.'

OTHER FORMS OF RITUALISM

In their nursing-home research Braithwaite et al. (2007) considered many different forms of scientific ritualism. One example was random sampling ritualism that required inspectors to move from purposeful selection of residents for record reviews and observation of treatment to random sampling. The industry was supportive of this 'more scientific' approach when it was introduced because it stopped inspectors from being detectives who sniffed out the most suspicious cases of neglect or abuse. Yet selecting six residents randomly from a population of 60 residents has no statistical power or sampling reliability – different random samples of six will give very different results, especially on rare events like pressure sores or abuse. Random sampling was about giving inspection a patina of legitimacy by following the rituals of science, as opposed to doing good science.

Technological fixes can sometimes be rituals of comfort. There is considerable evidence that electronic screening at airports contributed to reducing hijacking since the 1970s. But when after the shoe-bomber incident the US introduced electronic screening of shoes (abandoned years later) this was an expensive ritual of comfort. A bomb small enough to be concealed in a shoe could be concealed in many places on and in a human body.

Scientific and technological ritualism do not exhaust the infinite variety of ways that regulators and regulatees can obsess about institutionally approved means in ways that fail to secure the supposed ends of a regime. There is no merit in piling on more varieties of ritualism here. In our bigger book on this topic, Toni Makkai, Valerie Braithwaite and I have already done that to the point where we think it is a persuasive claim that in conditions of regulatory capitalism ritualism is a much more difficult problem than either rebellion or retreatism.

TRANSCENDING RITUALISM

Because ritualism can follow many paths that fail to reach governance goals, disparate solutions are needed – perhaps technological for technological ritualism, legal for rule ritualism, and so on. Whatever meandering paths ritualism follows, my hypothesis is that those paths are laid down by a politics of ritualism shaped by the institutional forces of regulatory capitalism. With the example of rule ritualism, we saw that this was embedded in a politics not only of the legal profession, but of industry associations, advocates, the media, the gerontological establishment and of executive government defensivenss. In conditions of regulatory capitalism, all these networks are important. But because they are networked, all are capable of engaging transformative networking and nodal governance to tackle ritualism.

In nursing-home regulation, the most interesting case study was of the leadership of the National Citizens' Coalition for Nursing Home Reform in the US on ritualistic enforcement of restraint rules. At the beginning of our nursing home research in the late 1980s, 42 per cent of residents of US nursing homes were being tied up on a regular basis; by the end of the study in 2006, fewer than 4 per cent of residents nationally were being physically restrained. Enforcement in the 1980s was ritualistic in the following ways. A nursing-home inspector would see a resident in the worst cases with both her wrists and ankles tied to a wheelchair. When the inspector expressed concern, a nurse would produce a physician's order that the resident should be restrained in this way for her own safety. However much the inspector felt the physician was a captive of the home's interests who would sign anything submitted by the home, inspectors felt it was beyond their power to challenge the professional judgement of a doctor when they were only a nurse. This changed after the National Citizens' Coalition ran an Untie the Elderly Campaign on Capitol Hill. The campaign made heroes of restraint-free homes. It showed how these homes always challenged orders to solve a problem with restraint no matter who had signed them. This transformed inspection practice. In the 1990s inspectors started challenging physician's orders to restrain: 'Yes I see the signed order. But I don't see where your staff have done an assessment that there is no alternative way of solving this problem to restraint.' A signed doctor's order simply ceased being accepted as a ritual of comfort. The important empirical conclusion of the Braithwaite et al. (2007) study here, however, was that the defeat of this very micro form of ritualism required a national campaign, an NGO node of governance that networked all the leading stakeholders and critics of the industry into a macro-project of transformation of ritualism.

Transformation through networked governance requires acuity in grasping micro–macro linkages. Braithwaite et al. (2007) found that participatory ritualism was widespread in nursing homes – residents' councils that might discuss where to take the next bus trip, but that did not grapple with any of the big issues driving the quality of care. The National Citizens' Campaign for Nursing Home Reform transcended this silencing of voices at the micro-level by a grass-roots membership that did a lot of talking about the big issues of nursing-home reform at residents' council meetings inside nursing homes. Some of these voices were wheeled out of the nursing home up onto the national stage on Capitol Hill. This theme of NGO facilitation of bubbling up of law reform proposals from below is a topic further explored in the final two chapters of this book.

The other linkage from the national policy stage down to the micro-level that was brilliant about this campaign was learning from master practitioners of restraint-free care at the facility level and learning from the street-level bureaucrats of the regulatory agencies. These obscure local players were put on the national stage as well. So the doubters who thought it was impossible to run a restraint-free nursing home were confronted with nurses who were doing it. Those who thought it was impossible for nurse-inspectors to challenge the authority of physicians who ordered restraint were confronted with the experience of inspectors who were very good at it, who had dramatically reduced restraint levels on their patch. One of the encouraging findings of the Braithwaite et al. (2007) study was that in regulatory conditions that institutionalize ritualism, creative street-level bureaucrats manage to subvert the rituals in order to refocus the regulatory enterprise on achieving the outcomes that matter – better quality of care for the elderly. To take a simple example, they subvert a scientific ritualism that they know is fatuous in requiring that the residents for intensive review be randomly selected; they replace the random resident with one they notice on the initial tour of the facility to have a menacing black eye. That detective work leads them to tackle a physical abuse problem in the nursing home.

The generic transformation strategy in play here is what Christine Parker (2002) called triple-loop learning. The quality improvement committee in an obscure facility in Vermont diagnoses how it needs to change to become restraint-free; over a period of years it pulls off this change (micro-change in the first loop of learning). The national nursing-home chain to which that home belongs and the state or regional inspectorate learns from the restraint-free care of the innovative home (double-loop learning). A national campaign enables learning from the meso-change observable in levels of restraint in that chain and in that state to effect macro-change that delivers continuous reduction in the level of restraint nationally (triple-loop learning). The schema for this process is outlined in Figure 6.1.

Figure 6.1 Triple-loop learning

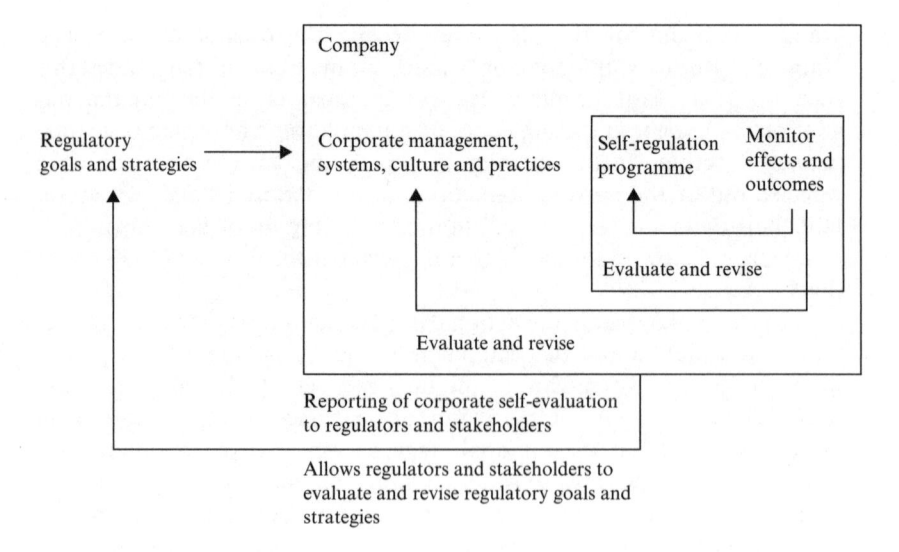

```
Regulatory goals and strategies → Corporate management, systems, culture and practices → Self-regulation programme → Monitor effects and outcomes
                                                                                    ← Evaluate and revise ←
                                  ← Evaluate and revise ←
← Reporting of corporate self-evaluation to regulators and stakeholders
Allows regulators and stakeholders to evaluate and revise regulatory goals and strategies
```

Source: Parker (2002: 278).

THE METAGOVERNANCE OF MARKETS IN THE VIRTUE OF CONTINUOUS IMPROVEMENT

More widely, the conquest of ritualism requires a shift from a blame culture to a learning culture. In the contemporary world with its intense demands for regulatory vigilance, a favourite of politicians to placate the baying wolves of the media is to throw a scapegoat to the pack. Corporate governance systems connive in this as well, as I found in American pharmaceutical multinationals of the late 1970s and early 1980s that had a 'vice-president responsible for going to jail'; after a period of loyal service as a designated scapegoat for the CEO they would be promoted to a safe vice-presidency (Braithwaite 1984). The ritual of blaming someone for failures that are system failures is ritualistic in the sense that it seeks to calm critics by giving them a fall guy to chew on instead of fixing the problem. Air safety regulation is said to be the regulatory domain that has worked hardest at shifting from a blame culture to a learning culture, a shift that has been successful by the measure of declining air travel fatality rates (Wilf-Miron et al. 2003). Instead of being blamed, it is argued that pilots and other staff are rewarded for their contribution to a learning culture when they report near misses.

A learning culture enables continuous improvement. One of the simplest strategies for transcending ritualism is to require regulated organizations to engage in a deliberative process with stakeholders (for example, a quality improvement committee in health care) that defines the most serious problems the organization needs to confront and how to measure improvement. Then the regulatory framework mandates continuous improvement against that self-selected measure. For example, if the weakest link in environmental stewardship is the level of production of waste product X, the self-selected objectives might be both to reduce the amount of X produced each year by a targeted percentage and to increase the reuse of that X which is produced. It is a simple change in the way laws are written to require, in the way Australian nursing-home law does, continuous improvement on a variety of standards. Even if you have achieved a high absolute standard, the law still requires you to do better than you did last year and to prove that you did! With such a reverse onus of proof, obviously no criminal penalties can apply to failure to prove improvement. To create a market in the professional pursuit of continuous improvement, financial penalties in the regulatory pyramid and reputational rewards and prizes in the strengths-based pyramid are all that are needed. In Australia this has created a dynamic aged care continuous improvement consultancy industry of variable but improving competence.

Braithwaite et al. (2007) discuss the problem of continuous improvement ritualism and the counter-moves available to regulators and NGOs to guard against it. In general, these are the strategies being developed in the metaregulatory research tradition (Braithwaite 1982; Grabosky 1995; Parker 2002). This conceives of metaregulation as regulated self-regulation. Metaregulation is a growth industry of the era of regulatory capitalism and part of a wider pattern that the political scientists call metagovernance (Jessop 1998; Sorensen 2006). It has arisen because as public demands for regulation proliferate, direct state monitoring of more and more regulatory outcomes becomes unmanageable. Different kinds of inspectors end up knocking on the firm's door every week of the year. The alternative is for the law to require self-regulation, self-monitoring of the effectiveness of the self-regulation and independent audit of the integrity of those processes. The self-regulatory rules, self-monitoring results and independent audit reports are then all provided to the regulator.

Better still, they are provided on a public website so NGOs and other third parties can check them. Occasionally state regulators and NGOs will target suspicious metaregulatory performance for audit of the independent audit of self-regulatory performance and integrity. Prosecutions can be launched when this integrity is found wanting. Qui tam laws, as discussed in Chapter 3, encourage NGOs and auditors who are competitors to those who did the scrutinized audit to meta-monitor and prosecute privately. Even without qui tam, regimes of requiring independent audit reports that evaluate self-regulatory improvement to be posted on the Internet can foster a market in professional virtue. When one environmental compliance consultant puts up a shoddy, ritualistic report purporting to show continuous improvement in environmental stewardship by a corporate client, competing consultants can anonymously point out that shoddiness to environmental regulators. Indeed they can even make a submission to the corporation that such sloppy monitoring jeopardizes their reputation for integrity in a way that the competitor's own more credible monitoring services could remedy. The Registered Software Project of the Australian Taxation Office is an interesting example in which a certification website allows competitors in the software industry to catch other software producers for offering products that come up with the wrong answer on tax liabilities when tested against ATO-approved test scenarios on the website. Some metaregulatory strategies have outflanked gaming of the law by regulated corporations with dramatic effectiveness (for example, Braithwaite 2005: ch. 5). While it is very early days in this evaluation research literature, it is not unreasonable to say metaregulation has promise as a cure for ritualism.

TRANSCENDING RITUALISM WITH A STRENGTHS-BASED PHILOSOPHY

Another move for confronting ritualism is to shift from Sparrow's (2000) philosophy of 'pick important problems and fix them' to 'pick strengths and expand them'. Chapter 5 provided one illustration of this possibility with the collaboration-strengthening pyramid to share knowledge in new technologies. The philosophy is that the best way to improve is to build out from your strengths; ultimately these strengths will grow to conquer weaknesses or to compensate for them. Another part of the strengths-based philosophy is the belief that human organization is collective. So with staff in an organization, if we build out from everyone's strengths, the chances that the weaknesses of one individual will be covered by the strengths of another will be much improved. Similarly with a team inspection – cultivate the strengths of individuals and compose teams to complement one inspector's weaknesses with another's strengths. A virtue seen in this philosophy by regulators who subscribe to it is that everyone in a regulatory community (Meidinger 1987) is part of a community of care, each helping one another to build their strengths. Whether one is a consumer, a vendor or a regulator, one can share in the integrity, the holism of a strengths-based philosophy. The open-source movements in IT and biotechnology look like promising transformative examples.

More mundanely, the strengths-based approach is also a strategic philosophy of inspection. In any organization there will be friends and enemies of compliance. Using this philosophy, it is more important to know your friends than to know your enemies. What you try to do is 'strengthen the hand of those who are going in the right direction internally'. It has been a recurrent observation in the occupational health and safety literature, for example, that inspectors will often find the safety manager as their ally in a mine or a factory whose management are committed to cutting corners on safety. Once a good relationship has been established with that safety manager, they will often lead the inspector to a problem they have been unable to persuade management to fix (Braithwaite 1985; Hawkins 1984; 2002). The inspector and the safety officer in effect conspire to get that problem written up in the inspector's report, so the safety manager can say to senior management that now they must fix this or they will be exposed to future penalties or civil litigation for failing to solve a problem identified by the state.

Many problems of neglect in the regulation of social care and health care are subtle, nuanced matters of degree, and therefore matters of difficult judgement. I might observe a dining-room scene in a nursing home and pick out a resident who I believe is neglected because they are not receiving enough assistance from the care workers with eating. You might disagree upon observing the same scene. You might think that resident is not eating because you, like the care worker, have noticed a cue from the resident that suggests they have already had enough to eat. While going hungry is a matter of profound importance, it is just plain difficult to judge who is right in this situation. The standard contemporary inspection approach to this dilemma is to follow a certain kind of rule of optimism (Dingwall et al. 1983): if there is doubt about your capacity to prove neglect, ignore it. The strengths-based inspector reframes this problem by a focus on excellence rather than neglect. She spends a lot of time in the dining room. When she sees attentiveness to residents who need assistance with eating, she praises that. Then she might gather all the care assistants together in the dining room at the end of the meal, summarize all the good things she has seen, and ask them how they could improve further. 'Are there any other residents who you think might need the extra assistance that I saw you give Mrs Jones?' Perhaps they will mention Mr Smith, who the inspector is concerned about. If not, she can say, 'What about Mr Smith? He is the only one who I wondered if he needed more help.' Perhaps then the inspector will learn that they are wrong about Mr Smith and perhaps the care workers will learn that they need to build on their strengths to make Mr Smith a beneficiary of them. Whichever way it cuts, the philosophy of the strengths-based inspector is that uncertainty about an important concern is not a reason for doing nothing. The rule of optimism of the enforcement-oriented inspector is the path to neglect. Australian nursing home inspectors are more strengths-based than US and English inspectors. There is evidence from a quantitative study of 410 Australian nursing homes that inspectors who made greater use of praise accomplished higher compliance two years after their inspection (Makkai and Braithwaite 1993).

A key skill of the strengths-based inspector is being a good listener. You cannot build strengths without empowering those with the strength. A mistake I observed many neophyte inspectors in Australia to make when they had a strengths-based philosophy, but executed it badly, was to jump in quickly with communicating expectations on what kind of improvement is desired. More sophisticated practitioners of this philosophy were more patient, encouraging nursing-home staff to tell their own story of how they were building on their strengths, what their plans were for future improvement. Kay Pranis (2001) argues you can tell how powerful a person is by how many listen to their stories. When the President visits a town, many come to listen; when a beggar arrives in town, most try not to listen to what he or she utters. It follows that we can empower people by the simple act of listening to their stories, making their stories the point of reference for the stories we contribute to our conversation with them. Therefore, good strengths-based inspectors are accomplished listeners. Through their listening they help convince staff that yes they do have the power in their own hands to transcend regulatory ritualism and secure real further improvement.

All this goes to the merit of complementing a regulatory enforcement pyramid with a strengths-based pyramid as discussed in Chapter 5. A regulatory pyramid is still needed to keep performance above a floor. But a strengths-based pyramid is best designed to take performance up through a ceiling. In light of the analysis in this chapter, we can reframe the diagnostic, clinical economics of the likes of Joseph Stiglitz, Dani Rodrik and Jeffrey Sachs discussed in Chapter 1 as an alternative to the old neoliberal nostrums of a ritualistic IMF. Instead of afflicting economies with a standard recipe book of solutions, to tick off as a ritual of comfort for the IMF, clinical economics asks national leaders to think diagnostically about what are the strengths in their economy and what are the bottlenecks impeding the flow of those strengths. However enfeebled their economy is, they are empowered to ponder their own story of what are their institutional strengths, and to build out from them.

CONCLUSION

While I have argued that regulatory capitalism creates the conditions for a pandemic of ritualism, it also creates spaces for innovation to transcend it.

This is because regulatory capitalism harnesses the power of markets to innovate. Many markets in vice are markets in the completion of rituals that fail to serve citizens; these can be flipped into markets in virtue (Chapter 2). The virtuous market forces at issue are not only those that increase profits for firms that reduce say workplace injuries or greenhouse gas emissions. They are also professional markets in gatekeeping and in continuous improvement. Increasingly, what we see is markets in environmental stewardship, in compliance systems, in preventive law, forensic accounting, continuous health quality improvement consulting, and the like.

In this chapter we have seen the many paths to goal attainment that innovation can find in order to transcend ritualism – visionary NGO networking to refocus regulatory politics from ritualism to inspiring outcomes, triple-loop learning, harnessing the creativity of master practitioners of street-level inspection, listening and deliberation that empowers reflective practice, continuous improvement, metaregulation, strengths-based regulation, clinical economics.

Empirically, we can identify inspiring instances of all of these things happening. Equally, we can despair at histories of all such modes being crushed before they realize any significant transcendence of ritualism. Both trajectories are amply illustrated in Braithwaite et al. (2007). This takes us back to the insight that we live in an era of regulatory flux, an era of possibilities. Regulatory capitalism surely does bring with it a proliferation of regulatory ritualism, but also a proliferation of new ways of transcending it. Put the other way round, what former British Prime Minister Blair introduced as better regulation included a lot of thoughtful reform but also even more of the audit society and vacuous rituals of comfort to Downing Street. In criminal law, the Blair government gave the community more of the ritual of comfort of prosecuting and incarcerating more criminals for longer when we know building more prisons will not work. At the same time, we saw some genuine innovation in crime prevention and its evaluation and in restorative justice and its evaluation. Social democrat Tony Blair's Britain and conservative John Howard's Australia both provided interesting and different kinds of laboratories of ritualistic regulation and imaginative attempts to transcend it to make outcomes better.

One tradition of research that is an important component of an integrated micro–macro social science that might inform the transcendance of ritualism is the social psychological one Valerie Braithwaite has led (Braithwaite 2008). This has included work on a politics of trust (Braithwaite and Levi 1998) and of hope and governance (Braithwaite, V. 2004) that motivates goal-oriented transformation. That work explores empirically how regulatory actors can flip ritualistic postures of gaming rules and grudging capitulation over to commitment to the noblest aspirations of a regulatory regime. Commitment is the motivational posture that gives birth to visionaries who seek to take environmental stewardship up through ceilings far higher than the standards environmental law has ever contemplated, that seek mines and factories with zero lost-time accidents, nursing homes with zero restraints and that provide *regenerative* care for people in their nineties. The reason that Valerie's motivational postures part of the regulatory puzzle is not at the centre of the present analysis is that this book is one volume in a three-volume series – the first being our more extended treatment of regulatory ritualism (Braithwaite et al. 2007), then this volume that connects this and other themes to the more macro theme of regulatory capitalism, and finally Valerie Braithwaite's (2008) book on defiance in governance that connects both to the more micro theme of motivational posturing. The most meta-ambition of that shared life's work is to use the way regulatory theory grapples with a problem like ritualism to develop a more interdisciplinary and holistic micro–meso– macro social science that works both in solving problems and building strengths.

7. Metagovernance of justice[1]

REGULATORY CAPITALIST PATHWAYS TO JUSTICE

This chapter argues that access to justice cannot be secured by more progressive law – legal aid, public interest law. Max Weber (1954) explained why: as the quantity of law and the size of bureaucracies grows, law as an institution becomes more useful to those with institutional power (and less accessible to others). In the mega-corporate world of the regulatory capitalist era, the more serious the injustice, the more likely large organizations will somewhere be stakeholders in it. Meta-regulatory strategies, regulated self-regulation, then become more productive paths to justice. Christine Parker (1999) has planted the seed of a new debate with the idea of generalizing corporate obligations to prepare equal employment opportunity (EEO) plans, environmental and safety plans. Her more general approach would require large organizations to have a plan continuously to improve access to justice. Is meta-regulatory movement towards restorative and responsive justice for the whole of law possible? Large organizations are already on a trajectory of incipient justice meta regulation,[2] NGOs already in many specific ways demand it. Nudging these developments forward more accountably is a social justice agenda worth consideration.

While the justice of the courts is an important kind of justice, it is argued here that often courts offer inferior justice to restorative justice circles. Access to justice in this book thus only means access to the justice of the courts when that is a good way of securing justice. Access to justice means here access to effective ways of securing justice in a given context. The next section argues that access to justice is a receding ideal in a capitalism dominated by large corporations, which drives law to new layers of complexity. Yet these conditions also create spaces for the growth of responsive regulation, metaregulation and a reinvention of restorative justice. In the previous chapters we have already seen glimpses of this possibility. Compared to the past, large organizations today perpetrate a larger proportion of the injustices that occur in the world. They also have the greatest capacities to prevent injustice, not only within their walls, but up and down their supply chains as well – into the lives of small organizations and families.

Philip Selznick's (1992) notion of responsive law as integrity is conceived as holding the key to access to justice in such an organizational world. The third section of this chapter conceives a marriage of restorative justice and responsive regulation as following from Selznick. Access to justice is best secured by applying the principles of restorative justice and responsive regulation to the delivery of justice itself. The chapter then explains that this assertion does not only apply to limited domains of law, like criminal law, but that it applies to the whole of law. This is because when people go to law, they are inclined to feel injustice. Contested senses of injustice are intrinsic to the meaning of law as an institution. It is argued that conflicts over who is the victim of injustice rarely or never lack important implications for human relationships. Because relationships are hurt by injustice, justice should heal and justice should be relational. It should be restorative of respectful relationships between people.

This is why restorative justice is more likely to be win-win for the disputants, while litigated justice is more likely to be win-lose or lose-lose (especially relationally). However, because some disputes are less relational and more calculative, it is essential to be able to escalate up a responsive regulatory pyramid from restorative justice to deterrence of injustice to incapacitation of injustice. Still, the important point is that often motivation at the base of regulatory pyramids empirically is, and normatively should be, relational. Gerry Stoker (2006) argues that networked governance moves away from both traditional public administration and the new public management in that the motivational force for improvement does not come primarily from rules or incentives, it comes from relationships of mutual respect and shared learning with others. The motivational story is that we work hard in a network such as the social movement for restorative justice itself, not to get rich or because a rule requires it; we work hard to support others in the network who are sharing that journey with us and in the hope of being supported in turn by them.

A paradoxical feature of the argument is then introduced: because the drivers of injustice in the contemporary world are to be found in a Weberian sociology of organizations, the solutions are about flipping organizations to be agents of justice. Organizations can be regulated to do this both by NGOs and the state. Christine Parker's idea is that organizations above a certain size be required to prepare a justice plan. Such a law would require private and public organizations to engage in a process of democratic deliberation with their stakeholders on what are the most important injustices their organization causes. Then it must consider what it is doing to prevent and repair such injustices.

Each year it must consider how it can improve the access to justice it provides next year compared to this year. It must pursue continuous improvement in access to justice and monitor whether citizens affected by the organization are actually getting more just treatment. This might mean women getting more equal employment opportunities, workers fewer injuries, fishermen fewer dead fish in the river, students fairer assessment. Evidence of continuous improvement would have to be reported to an access to justice accreditation agency. Adverse legal consequences would follow from denial of accreditation as an organization that was continuously improving access to justice.

The chapter then considers in a preliminary way how this would work. It argues that it complements many developments in internal corporate compliance, corporate integrity and ethics systems that the private sector are being pressured to introduce by NGOs with increasing success. This leads to a discussion of the role of NGOs with justice agendas in preventing the access to justice accreditation agency from being captured by powerful organizations. Strategies for NGOs to secure the resources to sue the state and corporations for failing to enforce the credibility of the justice plans regime are considered. While the metaregulation of access to justice is a utopian agenda, it is argued that there is a pragmatic democratic politics of how to move toward it. It can be implemented incrementally, and indeed in important ways NGOs are already making this happen.

The final part of the chapter assesses whether such a reform agenda would address certain pathologies of alternative dispute resolution (ADR) that are well documented in the socio-legal literature. It is concluded that the pathologies of ADR and of litigation are not so much achieved by reforming each but by putting restorative justice and litigated justice in fertile interplay. This means covering the pathologies of litigation with the strengths of restorative justice, and the pathologies of restorative justice with the strengths of courts. It is argued that universal access to legal aid to go to court is economically feasible, indeed conducive to economic growth, in a world where there is universal access to restorative justice. Incremental reformers might therefore struggle for ever-increasing access to legal aid and ever-increasing access to restorative justice as complementary rather than competing agendas. Such a struggle is for an access to justice that also has a more productive economy as an outcome.

So it is concluded that a struggle is already under way for a macro-restructuring of justice from being something provided by a market for lawyering to becoming something the self-regulation of large organizations is regulated to provide. My ambition is to render plausible the theory that justice is best secured by applying restorative justice and responsive regulation to the provision of justice itself, and to discuss some major worries about its implausibility. The ambition is also to motivate empirical research to evaluate responsive, restorative and metaregulatory experiments to enable future evidence-based assessment of the approach. I sketch some of the features of such a programme of future empirical research.

THE WIDENING IMPOSSIBILITY OF ACCESS TO JUSTICE

Developed democracies have seen enormous growth in the quantity of law. Australia, for example, has not only seen steep growth in the number of Acts in recent decades, the number of rules per Act, the complexity and length of Acts is also increasing. For the 1990s, the number of pages of law per Commonwealth Government Act was twice the number for the 1980s and three times the quantity for the 1970s (Argy 2003). As in many nations, tax law is probably the most extreme example, which has grown twenty-seven-fold in pages of law since 1970 (Inglis 2003). It is post-1970s rules in commercial areas such as tax and corporations law that account for the largest part of the growth in litigation.[3]

The regulatory capitalism literature, as explained in Chapter 1 and by David Levi-Faur in the Foreword, also documents the rise in the number of state agencies that enforce laws and in the enforcement personnel available to them. Metaregulatory theory asserts that the existence of more law and more public enforcement of it is one factor driving more private enforcement of law. As the quantity of law to be enforced grows, delegation to private regulation that is then publicly monitored becomes a coping strategy. Growth in private enforcement has not all been growth in litigation, or even mainly growth in litigation. Legal systems also coped with the growth of both law and the capability to contest law with massive expansion of ADR during the same post-1970 period that regulatory capitalism rose. Alternative dispute resolution has been an important part of the growing truth of Galanter's (1981) insight that justice occurs in many rooms.

In the era of regulatory capitalism, we have seen that it is not only states that do more steering and less rowing (Osborne and Gaebler 1992). Business firms also do less of their own rowing; they get more things done by contracting out and regulating the performance of contractors. Professions, NGOs, intergovernmental organizations, industry associations and a plethora of hybrid business–NGO organizations also do a lot of regulating. In a world where there is continuous growth in the quantity of law and private regulation and their private and public enforcement, access to justice retreats further beyond the reach of those with limited resources. Of course, where access to justice matters is with those with insufficient resources to fight their own legal battles. Max Weber (1954) revealed to us the most profound reason why as the formality and complexity of law grows, access to justice becomes more impossible for little people (see Sutton and Wild 1978). The more formal and complex the law becomes, the more it favours formally rational organizations such as business corporations that have evolved to govern complexity. Increasingly, individuals and small businesses cannot cope with things such as doing their own tax returns; they contract the services of a tax preparer expert in managing this particular kind of complexity. In most spheres of life, small players cannot afford to contract the services of an organization that is expert in managing formal legal complexity that ordinary people cannot comprehend. Mostly they lump it.

So regulatory capitalism structurally induces expanding spheres of injustice. This is a result of the fact that more of the important things that get done during the era of regulatory capitalism get done through the private and public enforcement of private and public rules and standards. A paradox of regulatory capitalism is that even specific laws designed to fix injustice contribute to this wider structural fact of injustice. We see it with tax law: new rules designed to plug a loophole that is available to the rich but not the poor are later used to open up newly conceived loopholes for the rich (see Chapter 2). Moreover, by increasing the quantity of law, the new rules may make the law more incomprehensible to ordinary folk and more exploitable by formally rational managers of complexity.

A new paradigm seems required. More of the same – writing more laws to favour the poor, more legal aid from experts in managing legal complexity – cannot solve the dilemmas of regulatory capitalism. Social justice advocates might do better to pull their fingers out of a dyke riddled with cracks that constantly open under its own growing weight. Better to pull back from the dyke to build some new protective structures. These will not be structures that give up on a dyke that might collapse under its own weight any day; they will be structures that regulate dyke maintenance. The access to justice project that counts most, this chapter argues, is a meta-regulatory project (Grabosky 1995; Gunningham and Grabosky 1998; Parker 2002; Morgan 2002). It is about the regulation of extant regulatory structures.

The meta-regulatory project I consider is restorative and responsive justice for the whole of law. This chapter will summarize the argument of my 2002 book *Restorative Justice and Responsive Regulation* in its application to all areas of law and will reconceptualize from that work a meta-regulatory strategy for pursuit of justice. It is argued that a restorative and responsive strategy for the whole of law is more than a utopian project to build a better dyke than the one public interest lawyers seek to plug. There is a theory of transition to restorative and responsive justice. In the process of working to build the alternative structures, the meta-regulation of the injustices of the existing structures is got under way. Parker et al. (2004) have argued that, faced with the realities of regulatory capitalism, actors naturally turn to meta-regulation when they are concerned to shape the world.

HOMAGE TO SELZNICK

It would be nice to go further and conclude that there is some sort of sociological imperative for an evolution towards responsive law, as Nonet and Selznick (1978) have done. I am not persuaded that it is descriptively accurate to see an evolution from repressive to autonomous to responsive law; nor am I persuaded that a plausible mechanism exists to drive forward such an evolution. Mine is a more mundane claim that while access to justice through more law of the right kind is sociologically implausible, access to justice through responsive meta-regulation might at least be sociologically and economically feasible. Whether restorative and responsive justice happens or not is about how effectively reform movements struggle for it.

While my theoretical ambitions are not as great as Philip Selznick's, the debt to his bigger ambition is profound, especially on the question of what responsiveness might mean, a matter on which Selznick's 1992 book, *The Moral Commonwealth: Social Theory and the Promise of Community*, has a more sophisticated account than Ayres and Braithwaite's (1992) *Responsive Regulation*. For Selznick (1992: 336), the challenge of responsiveness is the challenge 'to maintain institutional integrity while taking into account new problems, new forces in the environment, new demands and expectations'. Vincent-Jones (2006) has further elaborated the idea of responsiveness in application to the new public contracting. Integrity, according to Selznick, requires authentic communication that connects reason to emotion, not political or commercial spin that dissociates emotional appeal from reason. Reason connected to emotion through practical experience forges integrity as holistic purposiveness.

For Selznick, one of the things that enables such integrity is connecting the private to the public sphere. In this part of Selznick's responsiveness story, I find a rationale for privileging restorative justice at the foundations of responsive regulation. An opportunity for the justice of the people to bubble up into the justice of the law can be institutionalized through direct emotional engagement of stakeholders with particular instances of injustice. This fits with Selznick's (1992: 465) notion that 'responsiveness begins with *outreach* and *empowerment* . . . The vitality of a social order comes from below, that is, from the necessities of cooperation in everyday life' (original emphasis). Responsiveness means having respect for the integrity of practices and the autonomy of groups; response to 'the complex texture of social life' (Selznick 1992: 470). The project of both Tom Paine (Selznick 1992: 505), in the *Rights of Man*, and James Madison is that empowered civic virtue is at least as important to democracy as constitutional checks and balances: 'power should check power, not only in government but in society as a whole' (Selznick 1992: 535). So, for example, business custom shapes responsive business regulatory law and state regulators check abuse of power in business self-regulatory arrangements, and both should have their power checked by the vigilant oversight of NGOs and social movements.

MARRYING RESTORATIVE JUSTICE AND RESPONSIVE REGULATION

Restorative justice is a process to involve, to the extent possible, those who have a stake in an injustice and to collectively identify and address harms, needs, and obligations, in order to heal and put things as right as possible (adapted from Zehr 2002: 37). It is a tradition that has mainly developed in criminal law and transitional justice, as with the South African Truth and Reconciliation Commission. Responsive regulation (Ayres and Braithwaite 1992) is mainly discussed as a business regulatory tradition.

A core idea of restorative justice is that because injustice hurts, justice should heal. Healing, it contends, is most likely when there is undominated deliberation among stakeholders about the consequences of the injustice and what should be done to right the wrong. The core idea of responsive regulation is that regulation (whether by governments or other actors who regulate) should be responsive to the motivational postures of the regulated (Braithwaite, V. 1995), to their customs, their actual conduct and to structural facts about regulated markets.

Like restorative justice, responsive regulation makes the explanatory claim that legally pluralist deliberative institutions that engage multiple stakeholders are most likely to secure the regulatory purposes of such institutions. Like restorative justice, responsive regulation values flexibility, citizen participation in crafting contextually attuned solutions to problems and parsimony in recourse to coercion. Yet deterrence and incapacitation have vital roles in responsive regulation. It advances the paradox that by signalling a willingness to escalate to the levels of deterrence or incapacitation needed to secure a just outcome, we actually reduce the punitiveness of regulation. By signalling (without making threats) a resolve to escalate up an enforcement pyramid until a just outcome is secured, we can actually drive most of the regulatory action down to the base of the enforcement pyramid. In the integration between restorative justice and responsive regulation proposed in this book, this regulatory action at the base of the pyramid is restorative justice. In the worst case, we do need to incapacitate criminals by capturing and incarcerating them, armies by capturing and disarming them, criminal corporations by revoking their licences to operate (or replacing their directors and top management). Signalling the inexorability of this resolve actually empowers more deliberative forms of restorative and deterrent justice. The pyramid connotes a presumption that it will mostly be fairer, cheaper and more effective to try restorative justice before deterrence. But there will be exceptions where this presumption is rebutted after considering restorative justice first and then deciding to escalate immediately to deterrence or incapacitation.

The explanatory theory of the pyramid that accounts for the parsimonious resort to punishment should be complemented by a normative theory of justice. In my colleagues' writing on both restorative justice and responsive regulation, that normative defence of parsimonious punishment with firm upper limits on punishments is a civic republican theory (Braithwaite and Pettit 1990). According to these republican lights, both restorative justice and responsive regulatory institutions should be crafted to maximize freedom as non-domination. Values like forgiveness, that are common ground between the restorative and responsive traditions, are justified in terms of maximizing freedom as non-domination.

Fundamentals of procedural justice are also justified in terms of minimizing domination (Pettit 1997). Again the normative-explanatory theoretical package is that observance of procedural justice constraints is not only normatively required, it increases the effectiveness of restorative and responsive justice in achieving its purposes (see Tyler 1990; Tyler and Dawes 1993; Tyler and Blader 2000; Tyler and Huo 2001). Wars fought in compliance with the Geneva Convention are hypothesized as more likely to secure a just peace; criminal laws enforced without racial discrimination more likely to prevent crime; environmental civil litigation that treats corporate polluters with respect rather than humiliation more likely to restore the environment. In this book I do not seek to prove any of these claims. I simply point out that they follow from the theory of restorative and responsive justice, that they are testable empirical claims and that they show the theory is fertile in making a wide sweep of empirical predictions.

Nor do I make the empirical case that developed Western legal systems are injustice systems that require us to take access to justice seriously as an issue. I simply assert that when legal rights are created, these are systematically and increasingly used by large corporations to avoid basic obligations like the payment of tax, while poor and middle-class people almost never have the resources to enforce such rights in the courts (Johnston 2003). While it is where law is most coercive that we invest most in legal aid for the poor – the criminal injustice system – it is here we find that multimillion dollar corporate tax offenders, insider traders, price-fixers or environmental criminals almost never go to prison. This while most of those who do end up in prison are poor, not employed at the time of their arrest, and most of the women in prison have a history of physical and/or sexual abuse (Braithwaite and Pettit 1990: ch. 9).

THE WHOLE OF LAW HYPOTHESIS

Is there any plausibility to my claim that restorative and responsive justice is relevant across international treaties, tax, trusts and tort? The general claim made about law is that when people go to law, they are likely to feel some sense of injustice. This is because defining what is just is intrinsic to the social meaning of law as an institution. Moreover, if the dispute gets as far as litigation, the litigation process is likely to further sharpen this sense of injustice. Why? Because lawyers are trained to sharpen the story of injustice in their client's claim and to imbue their client with that sharpened story should they end up in the witness box. Because judges and juries like to believe that law is about justice, this sharpening helps win trials.

There is unfortunate fallout, however, when two parties sharpen their competing stories of injustice to stories designed to lead to exactly opposite conclusions in court. The juxtaposition of the claims 'X is unjust' and 'not-X is unjust', the very talking past each other on what are the kinds of injustices most relevant to the legal decision, engenders resentment between litigants. The structured legal failure to acknowledge the injustices suffered by the other causes this resentment to take the form of anger that the other side cannot see a whole range of injustices that lurk in the relationship between the parties. We see this routinely with divorcees who begin the dissolution of their marriage both resolved to be fair. Resolve wilts when the tabling of the first affidavit triggers, through its narrowing of the account of the injustice in dispute, a whole host of resentments about the marriage.

Most of these other injustices are legally irrelevant; the lawyers ignore them during the trial. This strategic suppression of anger often makes anger worse. If we think of a relationship between parties as a bottle with a mix of respectful and resentful emotions in it, litigation pumps some new resentments into the bottle and puts a lid both on articulation of one's own resentments and acknowledgement of the justice claims in the resentments of the other. Restorative justice, in contrast, is a theory about how to open up the bottle so that the reservoir of respect within it is enticed to find expression, acknowledgement of the injustices of the other is encouraged and acknowledgement of one's own hurts is welcomed in a way that creates an opening for the other to respond to the hurt with a gesture of healing.

The claim that our deepest disputes have disturbing relational meanings to litigants may seem implausible in an ostensibly cold and calculative dispute, for example with a revenue authority over tax law. On the contrary, the empirical evidence shows that compliance with tax laws is greatly affected by perceptions of being treated with respect and procedural fairness by officers of the tax authority, believing that the government is distributively fair in the way it defines tax laws, and having an identity as an 'Australian' citizen who thus owes a fair share of tax to the Australian community (Wenzel 2002; 2003; 2004).

Part of the restorative theoretical perspective is that disputes will rarely or never be lacking in important implications for human relationships and will often have their source in problems with human relationships. There is an essentialist claim here that human beings are relational animals. It is therefore hard to understand or resolve their disputes if relationships are excluded as legally irrelevant. A second essentialist assumption is that human beings are storytelling animals. So if disputants are prevented from telling their own story in their own way about the dispute, they will be frustrated in any ambitions they have to heal the relationship problems.

It follows that restorative justice with tort, contract, labour or competition law may not be as conceptually different from restorative justice with criminal law as we might initially assume. Restorative justice is a whole of law issue,[4] which is about widening the agenda of legal disputes to relational rifts that might be healed. In a matter like personal injury tort cases, the relationship issues may be more profound with a family doctor who prescribed a dangerous drug recklessly or a supervisor at work who failed to show due care, than with criminal injury by a stranger. The tensions between winning in court and getting on with restoration may also be more profound:

> In civil practice in the US it is common for the motor vehicle accident traumatic brain injury plaintiff to have any rehabilitation efforts postponed until after the case has been tried/settled. This translates to a patient waiting 4+ years before participating in any programs that look to restoring lost functional/cognitive abilities, 'reprogramming' attitudes and goals into realistic ones, and coordinating such processes with family members, co-workers, and friends.[5]

In cases like traumatic brain injury, the need to involve caregivers and children of the victim in a restorative justice process when their lives are also permanently and devastatingly transformed is generally more profound than in a criminal shooting case for example. Also, the need is greater for priority to be given to professional and family consensus on a restorative health and caregiving plan. The anger a woman directs at a large corporation when she believes it has destroyed her body through leakage of silicone from a breast implant can be greater and more self-destructive for the victim even than the anger a rape victim experiences towards the individual who has defiled her body. This is especially so because of the number of years that pass before a mass tort case may fizz to an unsatisfactory conclusion, such as the corporation disappearing into bankruptcy.

Braithwaite (2002: 240–42) seeks to show how business–business disputes over matters like contracts tend to become individual–individual disputes because there are issues of trust among the individuals who negotiated the contract. Indeed, very often a contract dispute is just a symptom of a deeper dispute over human relationships. If this is true and if it is also true that litigation ignores legally irrelevant relationship issues, then privileging restorative justice at the base of a regulatory pyramid opens up the option of addressing the underlying resentments as a dispute resolution strategy.

Note that this involves a radically different dispute resolution strategy than we normally find with mediation or arbitration positioned as a pre-trial settlement process. In the latter context, mediators and arbitrators tend to want to keep personal resentments out of the process, eschew the strategy of inviting gestures of healing by articulating hurts and keeping control of emotions, and narrow the issues on the table to those that are legally relevant. This is even true of family court mediation, terrain one might have thought where the disputes were most relational.

Braithwaite (2002) identified three characteristics of our deepest disputes that prove of strategic importance to the policy analysis: (1) they are complex in a way that means they would cascade across many areas of law were it not for the fact that lawyers tend to simplify them to the one category of law that courts can most productively (for their clients) digest; (2) our deepest disputes have disturbing relational meanings to litigants and are markers of identity; and (3) legal disputes between two individuals that reach litigation are uncommon and when they do occur they are usually disputes between individuals which are embedded in organizational action.

When disputes get legally or economically serious, organizational actors of wider sway get involved – corporate complainants with the same grievance as the individual, government regulators or industry associations. Private law cases become public law cases when governments cannot afford politically to sit on the sideline. The main exceptions to point (3) are very important ones – family law disputes, disputes between neighbours and crimes perpetrated by individual strangers.

FROM A ZERO-SUM TO MORE OF A WIN-WIN INSTITUTION

The evidence is that participants are less angry following restorative justice conferences than they are following court cases (Strang 2002; Poulson

2003) and that victims suffer less post-traumatic stress (Angel 2005). But on anger, as on a lot of the other destructive effects disputants suffer, the theoretical claim of restorative justice is more than just that there will be less of it. Heather Strang (2002) finds that win-win for victims and offenders[6] is more common in criminal restorative justice conferences than in court, several times more common.

Win-win on emotional healing means that victims get more emotional healing after the hearing and offenders get more emotional healing. Lose-lose, which Strang finds to be more common in cases randomly assigned to court, means that victims suffer increased emotional hurts and offenders also suffer greater hurt. Strang thinks this result may occur because justice is relational. Healing for offenders begets healing for victims and vice versa. And hurt begets hurt. Whereas courtroom justice has a reciprocal negative dynamic of hurt begetting hurt, restorative justice is characterized by healing begetting healing (Zehr 1995). Strang's data are on too small a sample to be definitive in testing this relational hypothesis (n = 240), but they are suggestive that these empirical claims may be correct, especially in relation to emotional healing and hurting.

What is clear in Strang's data is that win-win is more common in restorative justice, and not just on emotional outcomes. What is not so clear is whether this is a relational effect of healing for the victim begetting healing for the offender. It does look like some of this is going on. Or is it more an effect of expanding the agenda of issues in dispute creating a bigger contract zone where win-win is a formal possibility? Widening the agenda, especially to an agenda about relationships, is precisely what restorative justice does. The relational hypothesis and the contract zone hypothesis as to why win-win is more common in restorative justice may therefore be related rather than alternative hypotheses. Finding either plausible depends on being persuaded by stories of how disputes actually play out, persuaded that routinely there are cross-cutting non-legal conflicts entangled with legal ones (see, for example, Braithwaite 2002: 240–42).

A third explanation of higher rates of win-win in restorative justice may be to do with the politics of identity. Adversarialism locks disputants into identities like victim versus gang member, business versus complaining consumer. What restorative justice encourages is the pursuit of shared superordinate identities which are a basis for cooperation – such as school member rather than school bully or victim (Eggins 1999; Morrison 2001). It may be that even restorative justice participants who share no preexisting superordinate identity can discover a kind of shared identity as a group of people who work together to solve the problem that has been placed in the centre of the circle. In these senses, restorative justice tends to be different from settlement mediations ordered by courts when they shy away from widening the agenda of disputes into the (legally irrelevant) arena of human relationships between the disputants, or the arena of shared identities.

The rebuttable empirical claim is that if legally narrowed mediation/arbitration were replaced by restorative justice, we would see more settlement and less litigation. From a longer-term perspective, this may be even more true. We have seen that it is in the nature of disputes between human beings that they are connected to other disputes of a seemingly unrelated kind. Hence, a settlement to a legally narrowed dispute that sweeps deeper underlying disputes off the agenda may plant seeds of resentment that will burst into a broader dispute later. The claims that restorative justice performs better at preventing ongoing feuds and more often delivers a win-win result provide an interpretation for the large number of studies that have consistently found higher levels of satisfaction and perceived justice for disputants in restorative justice processes compared to controls (Latimer et al., 2001; Poulson 2003; Bonta et al. 2006; Sherman and Strang 2007). This client satisfaction will later become important to asserting the feasibility of a metaregulatory transformation of access to justice that people will support.

DETERRENCE, INCAPACITATION AND RELATIONAL DISPUTES

The concern was raised above that disputes like tax litigation may be in the realm of rational calculation so that relational resentments will not be important to their just resolution. Obversely, it can be argued that a rational actor model is irrelevant to, say, a dispute over the custody of a child. Certainly with child custody there is more reason to opt for a justice that is not blind to personal resentments and relationship issues between the contestants than in a tax dispute. But there are actually very often reasons to escalate to deterrent strategies. A parent who believes that the level of access the other party is given to their child is unjust or against the interests of the child can be deterred from compromising an agreement by the threat of a reduction of their own future access. If they abuse a right of access by sexually assaulting a child, prison can incapacitate them from doing so again. Geographical distance can also be used to incapacitate access.

The general claims of the theory here are:

1. Restorative justice is more often useful to securing justice than deterrence and so our presumption should be to opt for restorative justice as a strategy of first resort.

2. Deterrence is more often useful to securing justice than incapacitation and so our presumption should be to opt for deterrence before the last resort of incapacitation.
3. Some injustices are more calculative (for example, tax cheating) and with them we can be more willing to override the presumption in 1.
4. Other injustices are more relational (for example, child custody abuses) and with them we should be more reluctant to override the presumption in 1.
5. Therefore denying ourselves the capacity to be responsive up and down the full enforcement pyramid is contrary to the interests of justice in any serious legal dispute.

It should follow from these propositions that for any serious legal dispute citizens should be guaranteed a right to both restorative justice and to a justice of the courts that might resort to deterrence or incapacitation. As no society currently funds restorative justice programmes at a level to guarantee the first right, and no society funds legal aid at a level to guarantee the second, this seems a wildly utopian prescription.

THE PRAGMATICS OF LEGAL SYSTEM TRANSFORMATION

The key empirical claim towards rendering this prescription less utopian was that the legal world changed dramatically in the course of the twentieth century from one where most legal disputes were between individuals to one where one or both sides to most disputes are organizational actors (corporations, governments, NGOs) (Braithwaite 2002: ch. 8). Moreover, it was argued that even where lawyers would narrow a dispute to that of individual versus individual over a contract, for example, if we allow all the issues that are actually in conflict, we might find it is also about industrial relations, anti-discrimination law, the public law of consumer protection and relationships of trust. That means we continually find that there are organizations as well as individuals implicated in ways that are important to finding a path to a just outcome.

I will not make the case here that organizations are involved in important ways in most of the disputes that go to law in the twenty-first century (in a way that was not true a century ago). If this claim is right, a strategy suggested by Christine Parker (1999; 2002) shows one way to move in the direction of a right to both restorative justice and the justice of the courts for any serious legal dispute. Parker accepts the hypothesis that organizations are implicated in a large proportion of the injustices of the contemporary world:

> People experience domination in the places where they spend their daily lives in the presence of more powerful others – families, schools, workplaces, shops, government departments and community organizations. Because commonplace dominations make up most injustice, it is in these institutional loci that citizens will frequently experience injustice (or be enriched by justice). (Parker 1999: 174)

So what is the implication of our story about legal disputes between individuals ceasing to be the majority of disputes?

It opens up the possibility of the state 'steering rather than rowing' (Osborne and Gaebler 1992) the justice system. We have seen in a variety of other arenas that the regulatory capitalist state has moved away from the direct provision of services (such as health or justice) to the public regulation of the private provision of such services (Majone 1994; Loughlin and Scott 1997; Parker 1999; Teubner 1983). Justice, like health, can never be a perfect fit to the regulatory state paradigm because government itself will always be one of the organizational actors that is a principal site of injustice. In response to this, regulation of one part of the state by another (for example inspectors of prisons – some public, some private) is central to regulatory capitalism scholarship (Hood et al. 1999).

Parker's responsive regulatory idea is that each organization (public or private) above a certain size would be required by law to prepare a justice plan in relation to all the kinds of injustices its activities are likely to touch – injustices to prisoners if it is a prison, to consumers if it is a business, to creditors, shareholders, suppliers, and so on. Every large organization can be required to report annually on the Internet their performance under this plan. For organizations with only 100–1000 employees, reporting might only be required triennially (unless they had experienced special problems with access to justice). The key performance requirement would be continuous improvement in access to justice. The organization would have to demonstrate to independent auditors who examine all disputes touched by its activities that it had improved access to justice compared to the last reporting period.

These access to justice auditors, who would be accredited as independent and competent by an accreditation agency, would examine complaint files, staff, student or customer satisfaction surveys, practical availability of dispute resolution, evidence that disputants were advised of their rights to appeal outcomes to the courts, evidence of disputant satisfaction with the fairness of the dispute resolution they got and evidence of the effectiveness of dispute prevention. The latter is particularly important because it will usually be the case that the most efficient way for an organization to reduce continuously the injustice for which it is responsible will be dispute prevention rather than dispute resolution. The auditors would look for evidence of internal deliberation about what the organization's gravest justice problems are. Then they would look for studies that measure improved performance indicators for the targeted injustices.

It follows that every large organization's justice plan would look different. Universities might prioritize fair assessment and quality of education outcomes for students in their justice plans, transparency to students of how assessment and teaching quality is administered and participation of student representatives in that administration. A multinational mining company might emphasize environmental justice, occupational health and safety, and land rights of indigenous people whose traditional lands are mined. They might prioritize participation of environmental groups, mine workers in remote communities and indigenous elders in their dispute resolution and prevention plans.

An economic argument for the justice plan is that it might shift most of the costs of dispute resolution into the hands of the actors who control dispute prevention. The idea is that the organizational sector of the economy would internalize most of the costs of the injustice externalities they cause. And that the cheapest way for them to internalize the costs of justice would be to prevent injustice. Parker (1999; 2002) and others (Sigler and Murphy 1988; Braithwaite 1993) have written a great deal about what makes for excellence in intra-organizational access to justice, corporate integrity and compliance systems and on the standards that have been set by industry associations, regulatory agencies and voluntary standards bodies around the world on these matters. We will not traverse this research here. The important thing to note is that requiring corporations to develop plans for increasing access to justice sets them a challenge of a kind they have a lot of experience in meeting.

When many dissatisfied patients, workers or shareholders were taking an organization to court, this would trigger heavier regulation of the organization by the access to justice accreditation agency. A second auditor might be sent to observe the organization's dispute resolution processes, to work with the organization to prepare an injustice prevention plan. Implementing the agreed prevention plan would be mandatory – heavy legal penalties would apply when there was a failure to implement. Parker (1999: 190) also recommends that courts impose exemplary damages on organizational defendants that had failed to prevent the litigation by making their access to justice policies work.

A regime of justice plans would to some degree be self-enforcing. For example, firms in a chain of custody for a hazardous chemical – raw material supplier, manufacturer, reprocessor, distributor, retailer – would refuse to do business with a member of the chain which lacked a credible complaints resolution system lest the complaints from environmentalists or harmed consumers came to them instead.

What Parker is advocating in effect is responsive metagovernance of access to justice. Access to justice becomes less something the state provides, more something the state regulates others to provide.[7] Here it is important to note that, as in any responsive regulatory strategy, there is a critical residual role for direct state provision (in this case of access to justice). The key economic idea of Parker's approach is that by making the organizational sector of the economy pay for most of those disputes that are currently pricing the justice system beyond the reach of ordinary people, existing court and legal aid budgets would be freed up for individual–individual disputes.

If we get most commercial litigation out of the courts, resources can be shifted to the family court. The most expensive parts of our present justice system are the tying up of the higher courts with commercial litigation for the rich and the tying up of the prisons system (and the lower, criminal courts) by the poor. A reform programme of restorative criminal justice that reduces the latter cost, and justice plans that reduce the former, might therefore be self-funding. This is a speculative claim. Restorative justice programmes are not cheap, but they are in comparison to running large prison systems, which in a state like California costs more than the entire state university system. And the salaries of restorative justice facilitators are modest in comparison to the fees of commercial litigators and judges. When much of the cost of commercial disputes is shifted to large companies and much of the cost of regulating criminals is shifted from prisons to the compassionate governance and care of relatives and friends, the resources saved would be considerable. These resource savings might fund a quantum increase in legal aid so battered women can be guaranteed quality legal advice when they choose to fight for their rights in the family court. The resource savings of the justice plans model could also guarantee the option of restorative justice circles to battered women – rather than just quick one-on-one mediation in the shadow of a self-represented court appearance. The cost savings at the commercial and criminal ends of the system could also fund more community justice centres that can provide a restorative justice service for neighbourhood disputes and other individual-versus-individual disputes.

The goals of the access to justice accreditation agency under the proposed transformation of the legal system would be to ensure that:

1. Restorative justice becomes available for all genuine (non-vexatious)[8] grievances of injustice. This would be achieved by:
   (a) regulating for access to justice plans in organizations beyond a specified size; and
   (b) government funding for restorative justice programmes to cover grievances beyond the organizational sector.

2. Legal aid is allocated to ensure that any citizen of modest means is legally represented when they confront a serious legal dispute (including all family law and criminal cases) that they cannot or do not wish to resolve through restorative justice.
3. Justice plans and state-subsidized restorative justice programmes safeguard fundamental human rights; they are responsively regulated to continuously improve the quality of justice, including human rights.
4. Annual reports on the Internet chart changes in the patterns of injustice revealed by the accreditation agency's oversight of the private and public provision of access to justice.

Points 3 and 4 are the goals the regulator would have to meet if we are to confront what Braithwaite (2002) concludes the large critical literature on alternative dispute resolution has established as the three major pathologies of ADR – the domestication of injustice as conflict, the privatization of the public and imbalance of power. How this might be accomplished is the challenge for the next section.

CAN RESTORATIVE AND RESPONSIVE JUSTICE CORRECT THE PATHOLOGIES OF ADR?

Critiques of the pathologies of both the courts and ADR tend to be so pessimistic because they are so micro. They lack a macro-sociological imagination. Certainly, most court cases and ADR cases can be pulled apart to reveal imbalances of power. These tend to play out so the case helps the powerful more than the powerless disputant. There is a fallacy of composition in arguing that therefore the sum of all those court and ADR cases increases imbalances of power. Engel and Munger (1996) show that people with disabilities almost never assert their rights in the courts. However, they do ask their workmates, teachers, classmates to respect those rights in the organizations across which they move their wheelchairs. One of the reasons they often get a positive response is that the courts have declared rights of wheelchair access to buildings and like rights. Justice, as Galanter (1981) instructed us, must be seen as occurring in many rooms. While the courtroom is just one of those rooms, the public discourse of rights it articulates has an influence on the private justice systems in the many other rooms where the paraplegic seeks to manoeuvre his or her wheelchair.

What is the macro-sociological challenge of transforming legal institutions into things that reduce imbalances of power? It is revolutionary change in the way the public justice of the courtroom influences the private justice that occurs in other rooms, and vice versa. The vice versa is critically important because commercial interests – of business, the legal profession and the crime control industry (Christie 1993) – dominate the stage in courtrooms. Indigenous, womens' and disabled persons' groups do not dominate the courts. The macro-legal change suggested is (1) to push out of the courts most of the cases those commercial interests are presently pushing into them; (2) to give voice to the interests of less powerful citizens through restorative justice; and (3) to open a communication channel between restorative justice and courtroom justice so the justice of the people influences the justice of the law.

We must also keep open the communication channel from the justice of the courtroom downstairs to the private justice that occurs in so many other rooms. Indeed, we must improve it. Parker (1999: 64) has theorized the macro-challenge as the pursuit of a culture of justice where every potential claimant has a choice of whether to pursue their dispute informally or formally, yet where 'less disputing is necessary because justice is less frequently denied'. But this will always be a romantic ideal unless we regulate organizational provision of access to informal justice so that disputants can always get it, and its quality becomes so high that disputants actually prefer it to the justice of the courts. Once the courts are uncluttered with disputes from the organizational sector, an affordable right to the justice of the courts might become real. Yet the right to restorative justice is what most powerless citizens would actually choose because in most, but not all, cases it would be the superior justice for them (see the evidence in Braithwaite 2002: ch. 3, and in Parker 1999; Poulson 2003; Strang and Sherman 2003).

Put another way, we must reframe the choice between courtroom justice and ADR so it is no longer a debate about where the imbalance of power will be worse. The better ideal to pursue is a macro-restructuring of legal process so that the powerless always have a choice of both and always have access to good legal advice so they can choose the venue where the imbalance of power will be less. Moreover, the macro-challenge is to change the nature of the power-imbalance dynamic between the two. Instead of a woman being dominated in a family law mediation because the alternative is a court in which her partner is legally represented and she is not, that woman can be empowered by a transformed system wherein if she is dominated in the mediation she can walk away from it with assurance that she can fight in court with a lawyer to help her. The ideal is that the most powerless complainants must be able to regulate the other responsively. Restorative justice and responsive regulation are not simply twin capabilities that should be available to the state as dispenser of justice. They should be available to every potential player of the justice game. If our analysis is correct that restorative justice is a powerful tool for securing respect for legal rights, but more powerful if it is backed by the possibility of responsive escalation to litigated justice, then an important way of securing equal protection of rights is to make both restorative justice and responsive regulation as available to the poor as they are to powerful corporations and state regulators.

Braithwaite (2002) perhaps is utopian in arguing that in a domain like family law simply improving existing mediation programmes by making them more like restorative justice circles would make much difference. After all, in many societies mediation already helps divert about 95 per cent of divorces to settlement. Simply because most people prefer conferenced outcomes to litigated outcomes after the event, this does not mean that, up front, resentful people will prefer the peace of reconciliation to the vindication of adjudication (if they win). Availability of a restorative justice option may do little to increase a 95 per cent settlement outcome already being achieved in a field like family law.

But it may make the settlements more satisfactory than those delivered by traditional family court mediation. If various members of the divorcees' extended families or friendship network are driving demands for vindication, resources or custody in the dispute, then it may be better to have them in the settlement circle. Without their presence, according to restorative justice theory, settlements are more likely to unravel. Moreover, those relatives and friends may be able to offer the practical help and support, with childcare for example, to make agreements work well. Finally, self-representing disputants in a restorative justice circle may not be able to call on a lawyer to resist the domination of a domineering spouse, but may choose to have cousin Mary sit beside her precisely because cousin Mary is so effectively assertive in speaking up on her behalf. Or she may choose to have publicly funded battered women's advocates present if fear of battering is an issue for her.

This is not to deny that there will be situations where disputants will wisely choose one-on-one mediation over the presence of a phalanx of relatives when they are likely to be more destructive than constructive. In a domain as important as family law, we need a range of different types of mediated, conferenced and trial paths, where there is competition between state-supplied and NGO-supplied ADR options. Evidence on how procedurally fair the justice is, on what percentage of disputants got what they wanted, should be collected and fed back to new disputants to inform their choices of which path to take. If there are many evaluated paths to settlement, the competition will improve the quality of both restorative justice and courtroom justice. If there are: (1) many ADR paths, (2) simplified, accessible data on when they produce good outcomes for men and women, and (3) helpful pathfinders to open gates to those ADR programmes, then gatekeeping to the court can be less coercive. There should be no need to make pre-trial mediation compulsory when there is both gate-opening to genuine choice and well-communicated evidence on the efficacy of the plurality of options.

NGO REGULATION OF ADR

Equal access to restorative justice and the courts (through legal aid) is not enough however. The organizational sector of the economy will still have organization on their side; regulatory capture will remain endemic. The remedy to this is organization of citizen groups – a consumer movement to stand behind consumers, an indigenous rights movement to stand behind indigenous people, a welfare rights movement to stand with claimants, a tenants' union to stand behind renters, and so on. An important part of the function of these NGOs is simply to be a countervailing lobby against the power of corporate interests. Corporate interests will attempt to capture, corrupt or politically influence the access to justice accreditation agency when it impacts upon their interests. When that happens, lobbying from a citizen group that exercises a countervailing power, putting the regulator in the middle, is needed if we are to mute power imbalance (Ayres and Braithwaite 1992: ch. 3).

Non-governmental organizations have a particularly important role in overcoming the pathology of privatized ADR, of depoliticizing disputes that should be in the public arena, that should be given a collective as opposed to an individualized quality. If NGOs are resource-poor, they should be eligible for legal aid. They must have standing to sue. Chapter 3 argued that wider availability of qui tam would widen standing and legal resources for NGOs. With a little resourcing they can then transform private troubles into public issues. They can do this through aggregating individual claims into high-profile class actions. They can do it by jumping in to defend a restorative justice settlement that is appealed to the courts by a more powerful actor in the system. They can do it by appealing a restorative justice settlement to the courts to establish a legal guideline that protects against domination. They can do it by monitoring the monitoring of patterns in disputes by the access to justice accreditation agency. Guarding the guardians of access to justice. NGOs need more resources to do this – from qui tam, tax deductible citizen donations, foundations, and government funding. One option is a tax *credit* (as opposed to a deduction or a check-off to pay extra taxes) that would give all citizens a right to issue checks to their favoured NGOs up to a value of say $500 from the taxes they pay (Braithwaite 1998: 364).

Depending on how well resourced they are, NGOs can also play a role in responding to invitations from less powerful or articulate citizens for support in restorative justice circles. This is particularly important in an arena like nursing-home regulation where on one side of the circle you have a well-resourced business, doctors and other health-care professionals and on the other residents who are old and sick, often unable to voice their concerns audibly and unable to sustain their attention on the negotiation.

It is hard for most advocacy NGOs to do a lot of this, however, unless they are given funding specially for this purpose. Volunteer nursing-home visitors can nevertheless be effective advocates with a little training. The first line of defence against this kind of imbalance of power is auditors of organizational justice plans collecting interview data on whether circle participants felt disadvantaged or dominated because of their age, sex or disability, on whether circle facilitators achieve a plural balance of supporters on both sides of a dispute. For a discussion of how circles might be designed to generate reduced imbalances of power compared to one on one mediation, and how they often fail to do so, see Braithwaite (2002: ch. 5).

REGULATING THE JUSTICE OF ADR THAT ALREADY EXISTS

Alternative dispute resolution is already widespread in both the organizational sector and in civil society generally. Power imbalance in those programmes is also widespread. Privatized, corporatized ADR is where making the private more public is imperative, where we must be on guard against victims of injustice being rendered quiescent by domination. So we need regulation of access to justice not only to expand and regulate new restorative justice options, but also to regulate the quality of this large quantum of organizational ADR that already exists. We need regulators who get out and discover what is happening in some of those programmes, who blow the whistle on them so appropriate NGOs get concerned and take up their concerns to be exposed to the justice of the courts; or NGOs that simply counter quiescence by speaking truth to power.

The ideal, as articulated by Parker (1999; 2002) and Braithwaite and Parker (1999), is for the justice of the law, particularly fundamental human rights, to filter down into restorative justice and for the justice of the people given voice in restorative deliberation to percolate up into the justice of the law. Advocacy groups that are politicized in their capacity to see a private trouble that should be turned into a public issue are the critical mediators for opening up both these channels of communication. It is hard to see a simple mechanical solution to the filtering down of law to the people and the percolating up of the people's justice into law.

It requires informal brokers. In Parker's (2002) work on how the justice of the law finds its way into corporate self-regulation, compliance professionals, like health and safety managers, are those brokers. They are also among the brokers who take private sector managerial innovations into the law to ultimately become legal mandates through epistemic communities of health and safety professionals. The brokerage function is even messier with taking reform ideas from restorative justice circles deliberating on a specific injustice into reform of the law – in that it requires the agency of a plethora of NGOs concerned about many different types of injustices. Yet when we live in a world of networked governance where it is nodes of governance that grasp together networks of influence to effect change, restorative justice circles can count among those nodes (see Castells 1996; Shearing and Wood 2003; Wood and Shearing 2007). This is why advocacy of a radical strategy for better funding NGOs seems an important part of a reform agenda for metaregulation of justice. If this seems romantic radicalism, remember that NGO strength is naturally growing as a response to the opportunities that networked governance provides them, especially in developing countries (Braithwaite and Drahos 2000: 497–501; Kaldor 2003).

Our conclusion is not quite that restorative justice can deal with the three main pathologies of ADR better than mediation. Aspects of the microdesign and the value-framing of restorative justice as justice surely do help with the domestication of injustice as conflict, the privatization of the public and the imbalance of power. However, the main conclusion is that these pathologies of ADR are not mainly addressed by measures internal to ADR design, but by the way ADR is articulated to a macro-restructuring of access to justice, where justice is no longer seen as something that falls out of a market for lawyering (with a bit of *pro bono* on the side). Rather, in conditions of regulatory capitalism, we can begin to see justice as a responsive regulatory accomplishment.

You get justice on this view by applying restorative justice and responsive regulation to the provision of justice itself. Justice is most unlikely to fall out of a system where we simply rely on lawyers to be trained in law schools to be ethical and then paid to be the guardians of justice. Equally, justice is unlikely to be a product of a market for commercial arbitration and other forms of ADR that constitute simply a competing professionalism to law. Many ADR advocates think it will. In this they are being starry eyed, self-serving, or both. We can only transform our legal system from an injustice to a justice system if we reinstitutionalize justice with a framework of justice values (I would urge responsive republican values) that perhaps should be given a constitutional status (Braithwaite, J. 1995) and a set of responsive processes to regulate for justice, for ensuring that all the professional guardians of justice are guarded, for preventing ordinary citizens from being crowded out of the courts by those who pay the piper. Otherwise the tune becomes a lament for citizen justice corrupted as corporatized justice.

CERTAINTY FOR BUSINESS?

One of the paradoxes of corporatized justice, however, is that constant corporate game-playing in the courts is actually not the best way to deliver the macro-certainty in the law that is in the interests of the economy and business as a whole (McBarnet and Whelan 1999). The complex uncertainty of the domains of law most dominated by commercial legal work – corporations and tax – are adequate demonstrations of that. The text of these laws gets longer every year and further beyond the comprehension of business people. That is the price of the courts becoming captured as a stage for the most creative legal entrepreneurs.

Under responsive regulation of access to justice, organizations would have a right to test uncertain laws in the courts, even an obligation to do so in circumstances where such uncertainty is blocking the access to justice they would be required to provide. However, organizations that persistently opt for legal gamesmanship in the courts to evade the spirit of the law would increase the risk of failing to demonstrate to the accredited access to justice auditor that they have improved access to justice. This may escalate the regulatory oversight to which they are subject, shorten their audit cycle, expose them to exemplary damages when they lose cases in the courts, or to be named in reports to the legislature as a firm that has failed to improve access to justice. If this responsive regulation worked in reducing the appeal of the entrepreneurs of legal obfuscation, business leaders would spend less time in court, more time running their businesses according to laws that might be more certain. Certainty might improve because law would mostly move up from the good faith operation of private justice systems to the public courts because there genuinely was an issue of law that needed to be clarified.

In general business people who meet face to face with their suppliers, competitors or customers want to keep life simple and respect their relationships, by complying with the principles of fair play in the law (Collins 1999). If the other side is captured by a legal entrepreneur who advises them of a way of getting around the law, however, they tend to get angry and hire their own legal mouthpiece to do likewise. Often in that circumstance, the business later realizes that litigation was not in their interests. An empirical literature on business disputing going back to Macaulay's (1963) classic demonstrates that this is so. What is also true, however, is that it is not in the interests of business to have a legal *system* where the law is continually made more complex by other business people engaging in this kind of disputing. Business has a profound interest in the kind of culture of justice Parker advocates – a culture where it is poor form in the world of business relationships to be someone who seeks business advantage by corrupting the spirit of a just law. Notwithstanding the rise and rise of commercial ADR, business is far from realizing that collective interest in legal certainty and a business culture of justice they can rely on to be shared by those they do deals with. As Hugh Collins (1999) points out, one reason for this is that private law is insufficiently open to continual reconfiguration to absorb changing business expectations. Business gets more certainty when legal doctrine is continuously and contextually returned to business expectations.

Parker's (1999; 2002) two-channel communication – top-down from the courts to business restorative justice and bottom-up from business restorative justice to the courts – would increase business demand and legal responsiveness for principle-based law, as opposed to complex and detailed rule-based law. If the law is to be a comprehensible guide to business people who sort out disputes face to face, complex rules that can only be mediated through lawyers is not as useful as simple principles. Tax may be an exception where big business has a macro-interest in a hopelessly complex law as well as a micro-interest in exploiting and adding to that complexity in specific disputes. It is the macro-complexity in the law that makes it possible for big business to iteratively play for the area of the law left grey after each round of law reform (see Chapter 2). This enables many large corporations to pay only as much tax as they want to pay (which often means none). Although a more principle-based tax law may not be in the interests of large businesses and very wealthy individuals, it is clearly in the public interest. In some domains, big business has joined with negotiated justice. The US and Australia have shown a lead with the notion of Advanced Pricing Agreements, whereby the tax authority reaches a product by product agreement on how prices on international intra-corporate sales will be set for the purpose of transfer pricing. The tax authority gets a guaranteed tax take from intra-corporate sales and the company is spared audits on this matter. To make restorative justice and responsive regulation work well in an area like this, however, two things are needed: a formidable capacity of the tax authority to audit and contest the transfer prices of multinationals who stay out of Advance Pricing Agreements, and a willingness of the courts to respond to such challenges with a principle-based approach to the interpretation of tax law.

Recent evidence suggests that one reason the Australian Taxation Office has been able to increase corporate tax revenue at three times the growth rate of GDP for more than a decade, while the US corporate tax collections as a percentage of GDP constantly fall, is the deployment of a responsive metaregulatory strategy (Braithwaite 2005). Australia's innovative metaregulation of profit shifting by transfer pricing has netted a billion dollars in extra tax for each million dollars spent on putting new target companies into the metaregulatory programme. There may be many areas of law where businesses will continue to pursue self-interest by exploiting an uncertainty that is against their collective interests. Tax may be the exception where business in some ways has a collective interest in an uncertain law. All the more reason why ordinary people should push for a structural transformation of the law that makes the wealthy pay their fair share of public provision.

GETTING STARTED

The programme proposed for transforming the legal system would involve a revolution. Before this can happen, perhaps we need more of a crisis of confidence, more and nastier lawyer jokes, a deeper cost-of-justice crisis, a deeper collapse of the integrity of the tax system. But reformers can and are getting on with the job of bottom-up restorative justice programmes in many corners of the justice systems of dozens of countries (Braithwaite 2002: ch. 1). States can and are getting on with the job of meta-regulation for tax system integrity (Braithwaite 2005). Numerous companies are developing the sophistication and fairness of their internal justice systems and relying more heavily on restorative justice. Standards Australia and comparable organizations have developed complaints handling and compliance system standards (AS4269; AS3806) for the private sector that are now being used by the courts and by regulators. Parker (1999: 189) commends the example of the (former) Australian Affirmative Action Agency's strategy of paving the way for a new regime of enforced self-regulation by persuading lead companies to trial new affirmative action programmes that can provide models for companies less confident of tackling a new access to justice challenge (Braithwaite 1993).

So her idea is that the gradualist path to more radical change would involve a reforming state persuading lead companies and public sector bureaucracies to develop wide-ranging justice plans appropriate to their business. She adduces some persuasive empirical evidence that this would not be so difficult to do because it is in fact good business to give superior justice to customers than competitors do, it is good business to attract ethical investors (Margolis and Walsh 2001; Orlitzky et al. 2003), to hold and motivate excellent employees by treating them (and other stakeholders) justly. It is good business to be ready and able to restructure in response to a competitive environment by virtue of the trust built through just policies. Finally, it is good business to be able to keep environmental and other NGOs at bay who might threaten the firm's legitimacy.

Parker believes the lead firms increasingly do show that improving justice improves business. In time, the idea of mandating justice plans should therefore not seem so threatening to business; and, indeed, organizations that had already invested in them would press for others to be required to do so. In many domains of business regulation, such as pollution control (see Porter 1990; Porter and van der Linde 1995a; 1995b; 1995c), we have seen this dynamic now – new forms of regulation that are bitterly resisted by most businesses are embraced by the innovative few, who then show they are good for business in sophisticated markets. In deploying their management creativity to deliver the desired regulatory outcome, they discover innovative ways of doing so that had never occurred to state regulators. Parker (1999: 188) notes that: 'Lawyers and political philosophers are disinclined to think of the challenge of justice as a challenge of management creativity.' But we can actually get on with the task of creating simultaneously more efficient and just strategies of guaranteeing justice by talking to the innovators who might show the way at the cutting edge (the healing edge) of the organizational sector of the economy. In addition, we can educate the next generation of business and governmental leaders to an understanding of access to restorative justice by giving them direct experience of participating in restorative justice programmes in schools that succeed in dealing with problems such as bullying (Morrison 2007). This step is also now being taken in thousands of schools around the world.

The argument is that real improvement in access to justice requires major structural change to the legal process so that there is both greatly expanded access to restorative justice and greatly expanded access to legal aid in the courts. The idea is that if there is quality in how the expansion of informal justice is done, demand upon the expanded access to legal aid will be modest and affordable. Research by Blankenburg (1994; see also Parker 1999: 77), comparing litigation in the Netherlands and the neighbouring German state of Northrhine-Westphalia, shows that the analysis may hold up even when the revolutionary structural difference advocated is only partially in place. The Netherlands has much greater access of citizens to legal aid than Northrhine-Westphalia and more activist consumer organizations that are more willing to pursue legal complaints. Yet the latter has a litigation rate 13 to 20 times higher than in the Netherlands. After eliminating a variety of other possible explanations for this difference, Blankenburg concludes that people litigate less in the Netherlands even though it is easier for them to do so because pre-court ADR is much more satisfactorily available in the Netherlands. It follows that while radical structural change to the legal process is advocated in this chapter, this is not a case where no positive change can ever occur until the full revolutionary transformation is enacted. As long as the partial change is structurally significant, there is every reason to hope that the partial improvement in access to justice will be significant.

The best way to get started towards transforming the legal system from an injustice to a justice system is to participate in building the social movements we have found to be crucial to making decent transformation possible. These include all the social movements with an agenda of legal advocacy, of public interest law, to ameliorate the dominations less powerful actors experience in the society – the gay and lesbian rights movement, indigenous rights, consumer, environmental, animal rights, children's and aged care advocacy, the women's movement and so on. In addition, of course, there is the work of building and enriching the social movement for restorative justice itself. All these social movements matter on the analysis herein not only because of their direct contribution to a richer democracy, but also because they are the key brokers of law's currently feeble contribution to democratization. Social movements that confront injustice, according to Parker's (2002) analysis, broker the permeability of the justice of the law to the justice of the people and broker the permeability of the justice of the people to the justice of the law.

One interim metaregulatory strategy for strengthening anti-domination NGOs is to reconfigure ethical investment or social responsibility ratings processes away from technocratic box-ticking and towards deliberative NGO assessments. Under the Reputex ratings system before it was revised in 2004, an NGO like Greenpeace was one of 19 'research groups' who provided social responsibility ratings of the top 100 companies operating in Australia on a variety of environmental criteria (Reputation Measurement 2003). Others like Diversity@Work and trade unions rated equal employment opportunity and occupational health and safety criteria. Fifty criteria were rated by 19 groups, mostly NGOs, though some like the Australian Shareholders' Association and the Australian Institute of Management were rather pro-business NGOs.

The ways of getting started with metaregulation for access to justice are many. Those of us in jobs can start in the organizations where we work; children and those with children can start in their schools. One of the pragmatic appeals of the strategy is that the first mover to improve any particular kind of access to justice can be a private organization that uses the improvement as a competitive tool or as moral leadership, a state organization that requires it as a matter of regulation, or an NGO that demands it as a matter of politics from below. Metaregulatory strategy is about ratcheting-up incrementally the reigning in of injustice. The metaregulatory institutional design is to push NGO, state and corporate ratchets in series – so when one justice ratchet moves up a click there are knock-on effects on the other ratchets (Braithwaite and Drahos 2000: 282, 611–29).

SUMMARIZING THE CHALLENGE OF ACCESS TO JUSTICE

The transition to regulatory capitalism has been associated with a rise in the importance of ADR across the legal system driven by quite a long list of structural shifts (Braithwaite 2002):

- global competition with national court systems for commercial disputing business from arbitrators and mediators
- a crisis of the cost-efficiency of formal legalism in managing the risks of time-space compression manifest in developments such as derivatives trading across the globe (space compression) that accumulate profits or losses at a velocity not seen before (time compression)
- a shift towards responsive regulation by business regulatory agencies
- a privatization of security and compliance auditing in 'risk society' fostering a privatization of dispute resolution and dispute prevention
- declining citizen trust in the courts and lawyers
- the growth of mediation as a quasi-profession
- pursuit of efficiency via the new case management by the courts themselves.

This means that a restorative and responsive transformation of the entire legal system is not as utopian as it first seems; it goes with the grain of these structural and cultural shifts and can even be defended in neoliberal discourses that resonate in many corridors of corporate and state power. Yet it is not clear whether the growth in ADR has been good or bad from the perspective of restorative justice values. Informed by the feminist critique of ADR, there are three key restorative justice concerns: the domestication of injustice as conflict, the institutionalization of imbalance of power and the privatization of what should be matters of public concern. On the latter there is also a worry about the expansion of public coercion into domains that should be private – ADR net-widening for juvenile offenders, or video cameras in workers' washrooms to detect and confront drug abuse.

The moral neutrality, the non-judgementalism of mediation professionalism provides it with no normative basis for concluding what should be private issues and what should be public concerns. Restorative justice, which values non-domination, fairness and justice rather than neutrality, can develop the value framework for resolving these judgements in a principled way. Non-domination and deliberation itself seem the most useful values for guiding what should be public or private. Public accountability of restorative justice in terms of these values is needed to guard against the domestication of injustice as mere conflict (Roche 2003; Braithwaite 2006a). Restorative justice values reconciliation, healing and forgiveness; these values cannot be realized through restorative injustice. Truth is valued before reconciliation, justice before healing, responsibility before forgiveness.

Of course, non-domination as a value also requires restorative justice to be on guard against imbalance of power. Braithwaite (2002: ch. 5) contends that restorative justice processes that engage a wide plurality of stakeholders in the circle are structurally more able to remedy imbalances of power than mediations that only engage two principals to a conflict (see also Roche 2003). However, the more fundamental shift needed is one where ADR with an imbalance of power is not coerced because a disputant cannot afford a lawyer. And litigation that involves an imbalance of power has the alternative of guaranteed access to restorative justice, preferably to competing restorative justice models. The deepest source of the imbalance of power in our contemporary legal system is that the rich have effective access to both litigation and ADR, while the poor are forced to accept one or the other. The indigenous criminal defendant is forced to accept the white man's court (while the corporate criminal can opt for ADR). The woman in a family law dispute is forced to accept ADR. The structural inequality in the availability of options means that a wealthy man can dominate in the family law ADR because he can go to court with the support of competent counsel and his wife cannot; the white-collar criminal can get criminal proceedings dropped in exchange for offers of compensation to victims and organizational reform; the unemployed offender cannot. A universal guarantee to rich and poor of access to both court and restorative justice for any serious claim of injustice seems a utopian structural shift.

THE METAREGULATORY RESPONSE TO THE CHALLENGE

Parker (1999) has shown one way universal access to both restorative justice and the justice of the courtroom might be fiscally possible. It is possible because in the era of regulatory capitalism most serious disputes involve large organizations on one side or the other. The fact that we have become an organizational society is the source of our worsening access-to-justice problem. Harnessing organization is also the direction for a solution to that problem. Growing organizational power is the driver of contemporary injustice – from local employment discrimination, to global warming, to Guantanamo Bay. For most disputes that appear to be conflicts between individuals, organizations are actually the big players, the drivers behind the disputes. So giving more individuals legal aid lawyers responds to the surface appearance of the access to justice problem.

It is the organizational-driver–organizational-solution analysis that leads us to metaregulation – regulating organizations to self-regulate injustice prevention and provision of access to justice when their injustice prevention fails. Doubtless we can apply our imagination to a metaregulatory paradigm shift in a variety of ways. But the most developed proposal before us for now is Christine Parker's. Her idea of responsively metaregulating large organizations to continuously improve justice plans could cause the organizational sector of the economy to internalize most of the current public costs of civil disputing.

This huge cost shift could increase the competitiveness of economies for three reasons. First, most of the internalization of the costs of disputing in a risk society would be dealt with by dispute prevention rather than by dispute resolution. Second, where commercial dispute resolution was necessary, it would be rational to institutionalize win-win restorative justice options more than the win-lose and lose-lose options which Strang's (2002) data suggests to be more common in adversarial justice. Third, courtroom commercial law that was driven by the need to solve the problems thrown up by justice plans would be more principle-based, less costly, than the proliferation of complex rules driven by legalism. Because thickets of rule complexity built up by adversarial legalism ultimately cause a collapse in the certainty of commercial law, a move toward principle-based law ironically can increase the legal certainty required for efficient capitalism (Braithwaite 2005; McBarnet and Whelan 1999; Anderson and Kagan 2000).

More important than the economic efficiency argument, a rule of law that grows from the impulses bubbled up from the restorative justice of the people, a legal system where the justice of the law has a conduit for filtering down to the justice of the people and vice versa, will be a more democratic rule of law than one shaped by legal entrepreneurs who work only in the service of the powerful (Parker 1999). The most crucial determinant of the quality of justice in societies is neither the quality of their state justice system nor the quality of the culture of justice in private dispute resolution; it is the relationship between the two. When citizens are imbued with a culture of justice learned in part from a principled law that filters down to them (and that law is shaped by the principles that bubble up from their indigenous deliberation of disputes), when weaknesses of indigenous disputing can be remedied by legal enforcement of rights, then justice has the deepest meaning. It is not that the 'balance' between restorative justice and state justice has been got right, it is that the one is constantly enriching and checking the other. The appendix to this chapter gives some empirical content to how bubbling up and filtering down of justice can work.

We know that in many domains, restorative justice routinely backfires (Braithwaite 2002) and we know that court cases also routinely do more harm than good. So we should expect a lot of joint failure from joint access to circles and court. Even in advance of a thorough evaluation research agenda on the innovations proposed by the theory, we can identify domains where its claims would be utterly false. At one extreme are wrongs that matter, but where both restorative justice and litigated justice would be overkill for regulating them. Library fines will continue to be a good idea, and suspension of rights to use the library the way to deal with failure to pay them. At the other extreme, some of the biggest injustices in the world – for example, genocide in Rwanda – require armed force against those perpetrating them. In between, all manner of contingencies about the way the world works, are sure to continue to make, for example, no-fault insurance systems more effective for compensating victims of traffic accidents than either restorative circles or litigation.

Even with a longer list of qualifications and exclusions, it remains plausible that once the state had been relieved of the burden of funding most of the commercial litigation that dominates its civil dockets, most of its criminal litigation and prison beds, it would have the resources to guarantee restorative justice to all individuals who want it, legal aid to all of modest means who are not satisfied with their restorative justice. Corporate justice plans might plausibly save the economy the resources to fund an access to justice accreditation agency to hold both private justice plans and publicly funded restorative justice programmes accountable for continuous improvement in equality of access to superior justice. Annual reports debated in the legislature on changes in the patterns of injustice revealed by the accreditation agency's oversight of the private and public provision of justice might turn more private troubles into public issues. Public funding for advocacy groups to monitor the accreditation agency and directly monitor justice providers that fail to guard against the domination of the groups they represent might control a lot of capture.

Comparative empirical research on which funding models for NGOs extant in different societies deliver more vibrant NGO capability for metaregulated capitalism is one in a long list of types of research needed to develop and refine the theory herein. Another is the kind of critical empirical work Parker herself is undertaking, evaluating specific innovations in metaregulation (Parker 2002; Parker et al. 2004; see also Braithwaite 2005), access to justice (Parker 1999), responsive regulation (Nielsen and Parker 2005) and restorative justice (Parker 2004), research of the likes of Strang (2002), Sherman (2003), Ahmed et al. (2001), Murphy (2004), Morrison (2007) and Braithwaite (2003) that explores the underlying emotional and micro-dynamics of these processes, of Gunningham and Grabosky (1998) and Haines (1997; 2005a; 2005b) that explore mismatches in their macro-institutional dynamics, of Braithwaite et al. (2005) that aspire to test their limits in international arenas of injustice, of Levi-Faur and Jacint Jordana themselves in developing an empirical understanding of the global spread of regulatory capitalism, and critical empirical investigation of how democratic accountability works in the execution of restorative and responsive justice (Fisse and Braithwaite 1993; Roche 2003; Yeung 2004; Braithwaite 2006a).

While metagovernance of justice is a radically transformative agenda, all its elements are susceptible to incremental democratic experimentalism (Dorf and Sabel 1998). Both competitive forces and collaborative evidence-based public administration can be harnessed to drive innovation in restorative and responsive justice. A talented international community of law and society researchers is already driving forward this R&D agenda. Hence the hope and the vision that the impoverished ADR on our horizon today could one day be richer.

APPENDIX

Justice of the People

In practice, what do we mean by the republican ideal of the justice of the people bubbling up into the justice of the law and the justice of the law filtering down into the justice of the people?[9]

A story of reconciliation being retold following a restorative justice conference over an egregious act of discrimination against a female assistant professor in a university might have dual effects on the rippling of justice. On the one hand, it becomes an occasion to filter down the justice of university EEO policies into departmental politics. On the other, the story of how the injustice was inadequately addressed by a lip-service EEO regime, becomes an occasion for a university-wide, or even wider, politics of transformation on gender justice. That is the model of restorative storytelling as a fulcrum for checking abuses of power from above and from below. Crucial to this possibility is the insight that culturally resonant narratives can do what mute EEO policies cannot on those occasions when a big enough splash is created at one node of governance to cause ripples to spread across the whole pond of an organization or society.

Declan Roche (2003: 214) and Kathleen Daly (2004: 506) have challenged Braithwaite and Parker's (1999) 'bubbling up' conception of restorative justice as a vehicle of democratic impulses. Roche argues that 'the real instrument of change of formal law is formal law itself . . . [because] the law works as a self-referential system of communication . . .'. First, Braithwaite and Parker's (1999) normative push is precisely about rendering formal law less self-referential. Second, the contested empirical idea of autopoiesis (Teubner 1987) that law is overwhelmingly self-referential is simply less true in the 'Age of Statutes' (Calabresi 1983), when less law is made by judges reading old legal texts, and more by reading new statutes. The legal content of many of those new statutes *does* come from democratic impulses from below. Third, we will argue a little later that democratic impulses to change policies of executive governments are often more important than those that change formal law. But first we consider more fully the second point, that the normative push for statutory reform *could* come from below more often, more democratically and more deliberatively per vehicle of restorative justice. This is the point, for example, of Braithwaite and Parker's (1999) illustration of how Australian insurance law and policy changed following a press conference to publicize the outcome of a series of restorative conferences concerning exploitation of rural indigenous consumers by major insurance companies (see further Parker 2004).

Another example comes from Braithwaite et al.'s (2007) study of nursing home regulation. They found exit conferences at the end of nursing home inspections in the 1980s in the US to be quite restorative and multipartite (staff, residents, relatives, management, proprietors, church representatives for church-run homes, advocacy groups, inspectors, and sometimes other kinds of participants), commonly 15–20 in number, sitting down together to discuss the problems detected in the inspection and movement towards a 'plan of correction'. Two decades on, exit conferences are much less restorative, having succumbed to 'adversarial legalism' (Kagan 1991). Particularly important during the 1980s was the role of advocates in these processes. A September 1991 survey of 520 facilities in 40 states found representatives of the ombudsman to be present at a quarter of exit conferences; residents from the facility were present in half, while attorneys were present in only 2.5 per cent (American Association of Homes for the Aging 1991). Most of the ombudsmen were trained community volunteers and some of the state and local area ombudsman programmes were contracted to advocacy organizations, such as Citizens for Better Care in Michigan, that were prominent in national nursing-home politics.

When I interviewed leaders of the Oklahoma Ombudsman programme,

I was told that their 250 volunteer advocates were trained that 'Part of the Ombudsman's role is to monitor development of the law.' This meant Oklahoma state and federal law; concrete examples of ombudsmen influencing both were provided. A facilitating linkage of volunteer ombudsmen (many of them retirees) in Oklahoma was to the Silver Haired Legislature, convened from time to time by the American Association of Retired Persons, to define an elderly issues agenda for legislators that sometimes touched on nursing-home law. Bubbling up was facilitated by linkage of a volunteer ombudsman in a remote rural community in Oklahoma to networking meetings of the state Ombudsman programme, and linkage in turn of state Ombudsman programmes to the National Association of State Long-Term Care Ombudsman Programs and the National Citizens' Coalition for Nursing Home Reform (NCCNHR). Braithwaite et al. (2007) show that the latter organization, partly in collaboration with the former, led the transformation of US nursing-home law in the 1980s and 1990s. State ombudsmen counted among many of the leading activists of the Nader-initiated NCCNHR. The highwater-mark of its influence was 24 April 1987, National Nursing Home Residents' Day, when NCCNHR convened most of the major nursing-home interest groups, including some industry groups, to discuss and settle which of a wide-ranging raft of law reforms each interest group would sign on to as a consensus position. This long list of consensus reforms then became the blueprint for the most sweeping set of national nursing-home law reforms in US history.

Let us now consider how democratic impulses to change policies of executive governments are often more important than those that change formal law. I recently challenged British advocates on restorative justice in schools with our failure to define the institutional mechanisms for private troubles to bubble up to become public issues. Belinda Hopkins, the author of *Just Schools* (Hopkins 2004), replied that restorative justice advocates were seeking, not very successfully to date, to seduce British educational policy to an explicit way of bubbling up specific personal narratives into national policy. This mechanism was the constant revision of National Practice Guidelines on Restorative Justice in Schools (Restorative Justice Consortium Principles, 2005)[10] adapted for restorative justice in school settings in light of bottom-up experience. She explained that in conferences, workshops and around the table in drawing up these guidelines and principles 'personal narratives from professional experiences are shared and help to make the strong case for policy review and change'. Her claim was that ordinary peoples' stories do 'inform the debate and influence decision making'. However, this was mainly 'bad news' stories, for example involving domestic violence or school bullying not being responded to punitively and bad outcomes befalling victims (even suicide in one influential school bullying case) that had limited the roll-out of restorative justice in a democratically responsive way that she did not always agree with. This led me to recall my own experience as a member of a committee that debated and drafted the 2004 Australian Capital Territory Restorative Justice Act. Many aspects of that law were drafted in response to specific stories of real cases in the experience of those around the table.

This could, of course, be taken further. General principles in something like the British National Practice Guidelines document could be illustrated by personal stories of ordinary citizens that have shaped their drafting. This indeed is an interesting translation of the old idea that corporate cultures can be a story book (more than a rule book – Shearing and Ericson 1991) into the more democratically ambitious idea that the networked governance of national institutions can be guided by a story book. Many leading corporations, such as 3M, have come to the conclusion that an excess of abstraction in corporate policies is a problem. So policies and plans are brought to life by stories intended to create the desired kinds of sensibilities among employees:

> Stories are central to human intelligence and memory. Cognitive scientist William Calvin describes how we gradually acquire the ability to formulate plans through the stories we hear in childhood. From stories, a child learns to 'imagine a course of action, imagine its effects on others, and decide whether or not to do it'... Cognitive scientists have established that lists, in contrast, are remarkably hard to remember... (Shaw et al. 1998)

Iris Young has been an influential thinker about the link between narrative and justice. Storytelling, for Young, can be 'an important bridge between the mute experience of being wronged and political arguments about justice' (Young 2000: 72). Human beings tend to make sense of their experience of injustice through an architecture of narrative. Just as psychotherapy can be a form of narrative repair when people cannot construct an adaptive story about their worries, restorative justice can be about restorying lives in disarray because of a crime. They are renarrated as the lives of people who have survived, transcended or repaired injustice (Zehr 1995; Pranis 2001; Neimeyer and Tschudi 2003). As a general matter, the non-narrative processing of human experience might be somewhat exceptional (Neimeyer and Levitt 2001). Courtrooms and law books can undermine real worlds of justice because they too ruthlessly crush narratives about new injustices (with old abstractions). Narratives are meaning-making; they can give new meaning to justice itself.

A restorative institution such as a Truth and Reconciliation Commission (there have been 25 now) makes it easier to understand how a justice institution can turn the private troubles of victims into public issues (but see Stanley

2005 on the suppressed recognition of women's truth in the East Timor Commission, for example). Public Commission hearings in which victims confront perpetrators attract more attention than the average court case. The stature of a leader like Nelson Mandela resides in his legacy of restorying South Africa as a nation that has transcended an unjust institution. Whatever their race, all South Africans begin to share the identity that they have all been victims of apartheid, all impoverished by it to something less human.

Let us try to better understand what is democratically at issue in our bubbling-up–filtering-down of legitimacy by sticking with the school example. Whole-school programmes with a restorative ideology are taking hold in education systems of the Anglophone world much more rapidly than restorative justice is taking hold in criminal justice systems. These school programmes first seek to filter the justice of rights down into the justice of the school community. Classroom by classroom, whole-school programmes initiate conversations among administrators, teachers, students, parents and other community members such as janitors and counsellors about what is acceptable and what is not. This engenders a rights culture intended to secure the rights of children and staff alike to be safe against bullying, for example. Democratic deliberation in local sites like classrooms teaches and affirms commitment to rights enshrined in the law and builds commitment to intervene in say playground bullying when these rights are threatened. System-wide education policies to nurture and resource whole-school restorative programmes systemically foster that filtering down of the justice of the law into a popular culture of rights in schools.

That is the filtering-down side. The bubbling-up side at the micro-level of the school has been documented in cases in the literature of, for example, school conferences dealing with incidents of sexual harassment or sexual assault. One case describes the reversal from blaming the victim as a girl who was 'asking for it' in the anti-rights culture of an Australian school (Braithwaite and Daly 1994; Braithwaite 2002: 66–70). In the outcome of that conference, the responsible boy and his friends agreed to go out into the school to spread the message that this girl was not responsible for what happened to her. The boys were responsible, and the boys attending the conference accepted an obligation to confront and change the patriarchal culture of that school which was disrespecting of girls' bodies. On my account, what is happening here is that justice impulses from below, from dominated teenage girls, bubble up through the agency of remorseful boys to transform the private justice system of one school.

The next step is to constitute justice story books, as in the conversation with Belinda Hopkins on national guidelines for restorative justice in schools, that create a path for local stories to bubble up to influence system-wide justice. These can be stories more oriented to learning how to secure victim rights or the rights of alleged perpetrators, children's rights or those of parents or teachers.

Legalists will of course say that school justice systems or corporate justice systems (as at 3M) are a far cry from state legal systems. The restorative justice theorist finds that an overstated reaction at three levels. First, there is the legal pluralist response that justice occurs in many rooms (Galanter 1981), where courtrooms in a sense do best by justice through overseeing (checking and balancing) the justice-making that occurs in those many rooms. Second, the restorative justice theorist says we are not born just; we are not born democratic. We have to learn to be democratic citizens who will do justice well in courtrooms and other rooms later in life as complainants, witnesses, jurors, lawyers, journalists reporting the case, and in other roles. Enriching justice experiences in school are important to us learning to be just, in particular to learning to make human rights active cultural accomplishments as opposed to passive legal restraints.

Third, state justice is itself not mainly transacted in courtrooms. It is lawyerly myopia to see it that way. The empirical evidence is that 'the process is the punishment', that police and prosecutors exact more punishment outside courtrooms than inside them (Feeley 1979). So when (as in cases discussed by Roche 2003) a mother complains about excessive use of force against her son during arrest, or discrimination against her son by his arrest while the police treated other perpetrators more leniently, this is not a marginal issue. It is a story at the heart of how we would want the justice of the people to bubble up into the justice of law enforcement.

In my experience as a Commissioner with Australia's national competition and consumer protection regulator, I chaired conferences that discussed allegedly illegal conduct by major corporations in which they complained about the fairness of how we as the regulator treated them in our enforcement work. I would take these concerns back to meetings of the full Commission to discuss whether the complaints justified a need to revise our policies and procedures. There were other cases where such complaints about unfair process through such channels were ignored and were revisited by the corporation attacking us in the media. Such bubbling up of checks and balances about pre-trial justice is absolutely fundamental to the quality of a justice system and therefore its legitimacy in the eyes of citizens. Post-trial, rather intra-trial, we should also look forward to the day when a judge sends a case to a restorative justice conference not only for a recommendation on sentence, but on any injustices that should be repaired in the context of this trial. We should look forward to the day when such a conference returns to the judge with some advice on how he or she might have handled the case with more propriety or sensitivity, or why an apology from him or her to a witness might be in order.

Two centuries ago in Jeffersonian America democracy was close to the people. Electors may never have met the Governor or the President, but mostly knew the mayor or a local legislator they elected to vote in the capital. Today the debates that matter most – to go to war, increase taxes, make a key appointment – happen in the executive offices of the capital. Deliberation on the floor of chambers that are open to citizens – legislatures and town meetings – count less and less as decision-making nodes. Disputes over specific injustices that affect citizens, nevertheless, continue to be heard in chambers that are no less open to ordinary citizens than they used to be. Restorative justice is partly about reconceiving the judicial branch of governance more than the legislative branch as a site where deliberative democracy can be reinvigorated, where ordinary stakeholders can be given a more genuine say (a theme we return to in Chapter 8). When people have been a victim of injustice, whether as a victim of crime, of a consumer rip-off or of school bullying, there is more edge to their desire for participation than there is to participate in neighbourhood watch or consumer or school policy-making. The restorative justice circle in a school to confront a playground assault thus becomes an opportunity for young citizens to acquire a taste for becoming deliberatively democratic.

NOTES

1. The research in this chapter was supported by an Australian Research Council Discovery Grant on Meta-Regulation with Nicola Lacey, Christine Parker and Colin Scott. I thank these three colleagues for their comments on the paper and to participants at seminars at Yale, University of California Berkeley and Chicago-Kent College of Law.
2. They are regulated to have environmental compliance groups, OHS compliance groups, tax compliance groups, securities law compliance groups and so on. The justice plans proposal discussed in this chapter would not be as expensive as it might first seem as it would consolidate these numerous already existing metaregulations of injustice.
3. The most dramatic growth in a single locus of litigation has been the use by business litigants of the 1974 Trade Practices Act, Australia's competition and consumer protection law. Globally, growth in the quantity of the latter kind of law has also been from a zero base in most countries, substantial and even more recent than in Australia. Most of the world's nations now have competition laws and competition enforcement agencies. Most have acquired them since 1990 (CUTS 2003; Jordana and Levi-Faur 2003).
4. I am thankful to Angus Corbett via Christine Parker for this characterization.
5. Personal communication with US plaintiff lawyer L. Virginia McCorkle.
6. Win-win here means that both victims and offenders feel that they were better off after than they were before the adjudication. Obviously, in an adjudicated criminal case it is likely that both sides will feel they are losers compared with the situation where the crime never occurred.
7. Note the whole package is for metagovernance, not just for metaregulation, because it involves governing the providing, distributing and regulating for justice. In the first instance, justice is not something to provide; it is something to do. But once injustice has been done or alleged, access to justice is something to provide according to Parker.

8. Even for vexatious grievances, it is generally best to sort them out so the vexatiousness does not lead to other injustices.
9. This appendix is adapted from different parts of Braithwaite et al. (2007).
10. The UK also has more general principles (Restorative Justice Consortium 2005) that were also developed collaboratively by practitioners, partly on a foundation of sharing crime narratives.

8. Is regulatory capitalism a good thing?

IMAGINING CAPITALISM WITHOUT THE REGULATION

Is regulatory capitalism a good thing? For a civic republican like this writer who approaches such a question by asking if it increases freedom as non-domination (Pettit 1997), the answer is it is a decidedly mixed bag. It generates more dynamic, globalizing markets than classical liberalism might ever have accomplished. Laissez-faire would have been quite incapable of allowing the securitization of the world and the consequent growth of competitive global corporations. Without non-Chicago antitrust, as argued in Chapter 1, this would not have happened. Without the escalated regulation of securities markets, without the increasingly metaregulatory prudential governance of banks and other financial institutions, key economies would have struggled to emerge from crashes, these markets would have disintegrated under the weight of their own venality and communism might have triumphed over capitalism. The same can be said about the welfare state of provider state capitalism that ameliorated, and continues to ameliorate, the inegalitarian excess of laissez-faire.

The paradox is that because regulatory institutions, institutions of state provision of infrastructure and redistribution, have succeeded in generating more dynamic markets of increasingly global reach, not only is this creating greater swags of wealth, it is also creating bigger swells of crisis. No sooner does the world feel that it has done rather well in coping with the crisis of the closing of the ozone hole, than it is overwhelmed by the much larger crisis of global warming sending waves crashing into the birthplace of capitalism in the low country of the Netherlands.

The fundamental reason for this, according to our analysis, is that more vibrant capitalism fostered by more enabling metagovernance of competition has a logic of simultaneously engendering more vibrant markets in vice and in virtue. State provision of infrastructure, the legacy of the provider state economy, is part of this accomplishment. So today we have Microsoft generating great wealth and innovation yet manoeuvring to close off the intellectual commons in worrying ways, and nuclear power firms much more effectively metaregulating their safety than they did in the 1970s and 1980s becoming one possible alternative to fossil fuel capitalism, yet harbouring within it a market in the vice of selling nuclear materials both to terrorists and to rogue states who secretly develop weapons of mass destruction. Neither information technology, nor biotechnology nor nuclear technology would be where they are today without the germinal statist infrastructure investment of the US Department of Defence and the contributions of state-funded university and non-university scientists from many other nations, particularly the UK and Germany.

AMORAL MARKETS

Markets do not make moral judgements. If they work more efficiently, they will more efficiently produce bads as well as goods. Multinational pharmaceutical companies globalized the production and distribution of heroin (Braithwaite and Drahos 2002) just as they did for drugs that can conquer HIV-AIDS. The globalization of disease is itself a result of the conquest of the world by commerce, of the way capitalism has enabled sea and air transportation networks to carry disease everywhere. While it is possible for remote villages in Melanesia still to pretty much opt out of the global market economy and survive happily with their traditional gift economy, and while this path to cultural and economic diversity should be enabled and protected, it is not possible for the states in which they live to opt out. As soon as they have a capital served by international airlines, AIDS will fly in; as soon as they are served by international shipping, rats will run in. If they fail to demand action from richer nations, global warming will sink more of their secluded island paradises. For most of us there is no opt-out option. Regulatory capitalism is a fact of how capitalism has evolved. If we do not govern it, the markets in vice it engenders will afflict us with unspeakable misery.

While markets do not make moral judgements, regulatory institutions should and do. Drug regulatory regimes make the call that the market in heroin is a market in vice, the market in HIV-AIDS drugs a market in virtue. Competition policy and international trade institutions make the judgement that the global patent regime is over-regulating the latter market with overly expansive monopoly rights that make these drugs unaffordable for Africa and New Guinea. Of course, corporate self-regulatory institutions make moral judgements too. They can and sometimes do choose to forgo their hard-won monopoly rights for the benefit of the poor. Not very often though, and only when they are put under withering reputational pressure from NGOs and pro-poor social movement politics. Because ordinary citizens grasp this, they lend financial and political support to such participatory politics. This creates a proliferation of NGOs, expanding especially rapidly in the poorest nations, as part of the reality of networked governance of the globe.

NODAL SOCIAL DEMOCRATIC POLITICS

Sadly, regulatory capitalism creates ever greater wealth in a way that is distributed ever more unequally. Africa and New Guinea fall further behind. The gap between poor African Americans and white Americans widens. The reason is that productive innovation is always ahead of redistributive innovation, through the tax system for example. And markets in vice are always one step ahead of regulatory institutions. Regulatory institutions cannot respond to vices that markets have yet to invent, so they play catch-up, though as we saw in Chapter 2, B-grade economies can prepare themselves for the next wave of market abuse by watching closely the waves of abuse crashing over A-grade economies today.

Derivatives markets we also saw in Chapter 2 come in forms that are markets in virtue and other forms that are markets in vice. In both their good and bad versions these markets have accumulated staggering wealth in the hands of the super-rich, who are cocooned in financially engineered shelters from obligations to pay their share to the provider state. This has profoundly eroded the legacy of the New Deal in America. Large corporations that pay no tax have at the same time been beneficiaries of profligate corporate welfare in the form of subsidies, R&D grants and the like. The US state has ceased being an institution to redistribute wealth from the super-rich to the rest of the society through its tax and welfare systems as it did up till the era of regulatory capitalism. Today it redistributes wealth from the rest of the society to the super-rich (Braithwaite 2005).

This means that the old-fashioned social democratic politics that gave birth to the New Deal is as relevant today as ever. Versions of republicanism that conceive it as about political equality as an ideal, but not economic equality (for example, Sunstein 1988), therefore do not have much more appeal than liberalism. Philosophers' debates about what level of inequality is or is not morally acceptable are unimportant in the context of a social system called capitalism that will always drive already unacceptable levels of inequality to ever higher levels unless checked by redistributive politics. Nowhere ever in the history of capitalism has accomplished a level of redistribution that has triggered even the beginnings of a debate among social democrats that perhaps this was too much equality. Too much equality is something that might happen in some philosophically possible world, but never in any sociologically existing world of regulatory capitalism.

We can say the same thing about equality between men and women, rich countries and poor ones, the disabled and the able bodied, and so forth with other comparatively disadvantaged groups. If freedom as non-domination is your ideal, poverty and disadvantage makes freedom impossible; choices for the poor are dominated and constrained by those with the economic power to push them around (Pettit 1997). As the social democrat plays catch-up with the latest power plays, the financial engineering to escape obligations to the poor, the stock market fiddles, the tax shelters, the monopolization of the intellectual commons, he or she need not worry about being too successful in any future sociologically possible world of regulatory capitalism.

Indeed, our social democrat will not be very successful at all if he or she is an old-style social democrat still infatuated with the politics of the welfare state. The statist politics of provider capitalism no longer delivers social democratic objectives. Markets are too innovative into new vices, too internationally footloose, for statist regulation/redistribution to be capable of saving civic republican ideals. Nor can non-domination be effectively pursued through a single social democratic party or through a single set of NGOs such as the trade union movement. Non-domination requires social democrats to be networked with the women's movement, human rights NGOs, green NGOs, indigenous rights groups, development NGOs, the National Citizens Coalition for Nursing Home Reform (Chapter 6) and on and on.

If that sounds like a politics of infinite complexity, we should remember the pragmatics of the nodal governance tradition discussed in Chapter 4. Because a network society is more fluid, complex and indeterminate than older structures of government such as parties and ministries, understanding how governance unfolds is more challenging. This challenge has increased the appeal of nodal governance as a way of thinking about possibilities for strategic regulatory action. The question becomes what are the nodes where networks can be organized, where the levers at the disposal of one network can be tied in to the levers available to another network, or a number of them. A node is a place where resources, ideas, deliberative capability and leadership are available to make networked governance buzz. These nodes are the focus of attention in this theoretical tradition because synoptic understanding of how whole networks and sets of networks operate is beyond our grasp. What we may be able to grasp is whether there are effects when nodal governance is mobilized to bind networks together. This is an old idea in Eastern philosophy. Sima Qian around 89 BC quotes the following exchange with Confucius:

'Do you think me a learned, well-read man?'
'Certainly,' replied Zi-gong. 'Aren't you?'
'Not at all,' said Confucius. 'I have simply grasped one thread which links up the rest.' (Quoted in Castells 1996: 1)

Each strand of a web of controls that seeks to govern some persons or some phenomenon may be weak and we may have a dim understanding of this complex web of governance. Yet, if we learn to pull the right strand at the right time we might find that the entire fabric of the web of controls tightens to become quite strong. Obversely, we can learn that if we pull the wrong strand at the wrong time, the entire fabric of control can unravel. From a republican point of view, we should be interested in how to cause the unravelling of webs of control that dominate citizens in an arbitrary way and how to secure webs of control that prevent domination. This will be accomplished by strategic deliberation at strategic nodes of networked governance.

WHITHER DEMOCRACY?

Republicans like Pettit (1997) do not see democracy narrowly as the means whereby a society as a whole asserts its collective will – its autonomous will as opposed to that of a dictator or colonial overlord. Pettit sees this as an important side of democracy – the side that makes it important to have referenda at times and to elect the legislatures that enact the laws that protect against arbitrary exercise of power. This is the (indirect) 'authorial' role that democracy requires the people to have. Pettit also emphasizes the 'editorial' role of the people that he describes as the 'contestatory' side of democracy. For Pettit, contestability is more important than consent in preventing exercises of power that are arbitrary (Pettit 1997: 184–5). For contestation to be possible, decision-making must be open enough for there to be potential for public reason to contest it and there must be many channels of contestation – writing to a Member of Parliament, complaint to an ombudsman, judicial appeals, rights to take to the streets in protest, and so on. Because Pettit rejects democracy as a purely electoral ideal, he disagrees with handwringers who see in every global decision-making forum an erosion of national electoral sovereignty. If a global institution, say a UN human rights agency, effectively contests a national form of domination, then that national polity has more channels open for public reason to contest its power. Hence, democracy may be enlarged rather than reduced by it.

Petitt's republicanism is in better shape than a unidimensional electoral conception of nationally sovereign democracy for application to a world of networked governance. You cannot elect a network; you cannot have written constitutions for all the nodes of governance that matter. We cannot ensure that networked power is a product of popular will. Yet Sorensen and Torfing (2006) point out that post-liberal theorists of democracy see possibilities for governance networks as functionally organized supplements to territorially organized representative democracy that add flexibility and plurality (Rhodes 1997), yet can be metagoverned by a representative democracy (Jessop 1998). They see possibilities for networks as venues where sub-elites can challenge dominant elites (Etzioni-Halevy 1993; Bogason and Musso 2006), as vertical bridges of top-down representative democracy to more participatory civil society governance (Hirst 1994) and as pluralizers of discursive contestation in democracies (Dryzek 2000). The contestatory dimension of democracy is more useful for a world of nodal governance of networks. We can ensure that networked power is required to survive popular contestation by setting up multiple nodes of popular contestation at strategic intersections of networks.

Before challenging the supremacy of electoral democracy with contestatory democracy, Pettit (1997) is rather dismissive of the feasibility of the ideal of direct deliberative democracy. We are no longer in the village, the New England town or ancient Athens. The scale and institutional complexity of a mass society with a sophisticated division of labour means that direct participatory democracy, even in the most important domains of governance, is for Pettit an unlikely ideal.

Just as the realities of plurally networked governance make electoral democracy a less serviceable ideal than contestatory democracy, so the realities of nodal governance should cause us to return to a rediscovered serviceability of deliberative democracy at the nodes that count. It is the contestatory ideal that accounts for the importance of democratic citizens joining together at a node of governance to contest networked power that they believe oppresses them. Once those citizens are assembled at that place, even if it is in cyberspace, deliberative democracy is the ideal that can most fruitfully be deployed to enrich freedom as non-domination. I presume here that giving direct democratic voice to people affected by a decision is the best way to respect the autonomy and empower the public reason of citizens wherever it is institutionally feasible and affordable to do so.

CONTESTATORY CITIZENSHIP, DELIBERATIVE DENIZENSHIP

Clifford Shearing and Jennifer Wood (2003) have resurrected a distinction between citizens (in the discourse of state governance) and denizens (of nodal governance). Denizen is a pre-Westphalian term that has disappeared from the latest edition of the *Online Oxford English Dictionary* (http://dictionary.oed.com) but is still there to be found in the previous edition. For Shearing and Wood (2003), a denizen is a habitual, even if temporary, visitor to a place, who has rights and responsibilities in the governance that occurs in that place. This is consistent with a 1655 attribution of the *Online OED* that 'The Charter of London . . . is the birth-right of its own Denisons, not Strangers.' Denizens were often frequent travellers to a place where they were not native-born. Genoan merchants who frequented the Genoan Guild in Bruges or London would be described as denizens of those places. So the *OED* refers from 1632 to 'An authenticke Bull, charter or patent of denizonship or borgeousship of Rome.' But by 1871, the triumph of Westphalianism seems to have devalued the currency of denizenship: 'Denizenship is a mongrel state, not worth preserving when the process of obtaining naturalization is so simple.'

Consider national and nodal governance of armed conflict. Citizens of Israel who are concerned about their state's conduct in Palestine can mobilize electoral democracy, voting against their current national leadership. They can engage with contestatory democracy by attending peace rallies, signing petitions, and so on. Or they can strategically engage with the networked governance of armed conflict by initiating or joining a node of second track diplomacy in Geneva which has key participants from the crucial networks of stakeholders in the conflict. As that node of governance develops an alternative peace plan to the US state's Roadmap, the number of participants around the table in Geneva is sufficiently small for the democracy of the node to be directly deliberative. Contestatory democracy from citizens of Israel can take them to the node of second-track diplomacy; deliberative democracy can inform their participation in the public reasoning at that node. When that node delivers up a draft peace plan, contestatory democrats will come out to criticize the plan from many directions. Then good democratic practice involves inviting those critics into a widened circle of democratic deliberation at the node. In summary, we have three stages of contestatory citizenship with deliberative denizenship:

1. In a world of networked governance, democratic citizenship contests domination most effectively at strategic nodes of deliberative governance.
2. The decisions of that node of deliberative governance should be contested by citizens who did not participate in it.
3. The circle of deliberation should be widened by inviting in the most vigorous and contentious contestors.

None of the revisionism of contestatory citizenship and deliberative denizenship denies the importance of electoral democracy. Indeed, in a world of pluralized governance, we need electoral democracy at many levels – city government, state government, European Union, United Nations, annual meetings of corporations to elect directors, annual meetings of NGOs and professional associations to elect office-holders. It is just that in a world of networked governance, perfect electoral democracy at all these levels would be a thin set of reeds to protect us against domination. Pluralized electoral democracy still leaves us with a shallow democracy unless we also invest in the kind of contestatory democracy of citizens advocated by Pettit (1997), complemented by deliberative democracy of denizens at strategic nodes of governance, as advanced by Shearing and Wood (2003). A rich democracy gives us frequent opportunities to *vote* for people who represent our interests, many nodes of governance that give us an opportunity to *contest* power and *deliberate* in our own voice at that node of governance. Controlling domination does not require that we all spend our evenings in meetings, just that enough of us assume the responsibilities of denizenship when we see injustices that are not being righted. It requires a learning democracy where enough of us learn to care to engage, learn to be democratic through early experiences of deliberation in schools and families, and learn how to convene nodes of governance at the strategic intersections of networks that can regulate abuse.

The evidence-based denizenship of the social movement for restorative justice illustrates how statist governance working on its own is not very effective in responding justly and effectively to a problem like crime. In contemporary conditions the effective governance of security is networked. Among its requirements is that denizens of a place forge nodes of governance that work to prevent the niches of criminal opportunities that emerge in that place. I have argued in this book that there is evidence that deliberative denizenship sometimes works to secure our property and our persons from violence. This is a pragmatic participatory politics favoured by growing ranks of hard-headed state police, not a deliberative democracy confined to romantic dreamers of radical politics. But it is not enough. We also need a state with awesome powers to shoot at, interrogate and incarcerate those who threaten our security. Here the classic form of Pettit's (1997) republicanism comes into its own. Pettit gives an account of why such frightening state powers are tolerable, but only if they are contested by active citizens of a democracy and only if their exercise is non-arbitrary, constrained by a rule of law. A state with a Guantanamo Bay and extraordinary rendition of terrorist suspects to offshore torture cannot be a republic.

Yes, freedom as non-domination requires contestatory citizenship. But what we have learned from a restorative and responsive approach to street crime and corporate social responsibility (Chapter 7), nursing-home regulation (Chapter 6) and peace-building (Chapter 4), is that it also requires deliberative denizenship. Let us assume that Castells (1996) is right – that while states still matter a lot, governance is becoming less statist, more networked, across the spectrum of all issues of public concern. If so, deliberative denizenship that seizes opportunities for nodal governance will become increasingly central to institutions of republican governance. An emergent role for contestatory citizenship will then be to contest down to the decisions of the denizens of places as well as up to the rules and rulers of states.

A combination of nodal governance of networks from below and metagovernance of networks by institutions of representative democracy such as courts can provide superior accountability and superior transparency than either approach alone. The superiority comes from covering the weaknesses of hierarchical accountability with the strengths of horizontal accountability and vice versa. A republic nurtures a creative tension among electoral accountability, accountability to the rule of law, contestatory accountability and directly deliberative accountability of each to every other in circles of denizens. Accountability is accomplished by circles of widening circles of deliberative accountability (for the details see Braithwaite 2006b) bubbling up the justice of the people into the justice of the state. Meanwhile the state takes responsibility for educating its citizens to a rights culture that filters the justice of the law down to the justice of the people.

All nodes of separated private, public or hybrid governance need enough autonomy so that they cannot be dominated by other nodes of governance. Equally, each needs enough capacity to check abuse of power by other nodes so that a multiplicity of separated powers can network to check any node of power from dominating all the others. But of course, as Chapters 5 and 6 argued, it is more important that they influence one another with strength-building pyramids than with regulatory pyramids. The participatory nature of deliberative denizenship is a better vehicle for capacity building and adult learning than non-conversational voting. Responsiveness and integrity (Selznick 1992; Vincent-Jones 2006) is enabled by a society with a strong state, strong markets and strong civil society, where the strengths of each institution enable the governance capabilities of the other institutions (Braithwaite 1998).

If we believe that democracy is fundamentally an attribute of states, when we live in a tyrannous state or a 'failed state', we are disabled from building democracy – we are simply shot when we try to or we waste our breath demanding state responses that it does not have the capacity to provide. But when our vision of democracy is messy – of circles of deliberative circles – there are many kinds of circles we can join that we believe actually matter in building democracy. Democracy is, then, not something we lobby for as a distant utopia when the tyrant is replaced by free elections; democracy is something we start building as soon as we join the NGO, practise responsively as a lawyer, establish business self-regulatory responses to demands from green groups, deliberate about working conditions with our employees or employers, educate our children to be democratic citizens, or participate in politically serious global inter-cultural conversations on the Internet.

DEMOCRATICALLY EXPERIMENTAL REGULATORY CAPITALISM

Chapter 2 argued that we need to understand that because the crises of regulatory capitalism are cyclical, with lead economies sometimes one cycle ahead of laggard economies, the laggards have more data and more time for crafting governance responses to markets in vice. Not all the advantages of regulatory capitalism accrue to the strong. Weapons of the weak exist. One is qui tam (Chapter 3). A more general one is for the weak to enrol the strong to their projects at strategic nodes of governance. There is a general reason for this to be more possible than social democratic pessimists assume. It is that wherever there is a market in vice, there is likely to be a market in virtue under conditions of regulatory capitalism. We saw in Chapter 2 that just as there is a market for aggressive tax planning professionals, there is also a lot of demand for the services of 'honest, low-fuss' tax advisers. Just as there are firms whose business model is to close off the intellectual commons, there are other firms with open source business models that open it up. There is a niche for firms who cut corners on greenhouse gas emissions and a niche for firms who increase their profits by innovating in new greenhouse gas reduction technologies. A paradox of metagovernance is that by enabling more vibrant markets, metagovernance of competition enables more innovative vice, and by mandating private markets in the regulation of self-regulation metagovernance creates professional markets in virtue (such as markets in environmental compliance professionalism).

We saw in Chapter 2 that there are some generic strategies for flipping markets in vice to markets in virtue. There are some general strategies for transcending the regulatory ritualism that is a particular pathology of the era of regulatory capitalism (Chapter 6). There are responsive regulatory strategies of general import for responding to regulatory capture and corruption. When the weak cannot defeat the strong, they can still mobilize private governance that builds out from the islands of civility that persist in the most corrupt and war-torn societies in the world (Kaldor 1999). Of course, this cuts both ways; Al-Qaeda can network their weapons of the weak out from islands of incivility that crush freedom. For the metagovernance tradition, the most promising ways of regulating islands of incivility are from islands of civility rather than through central state coercion. They are from mosques that build non-violent capacities that help Muslim young people to flourish democratically, for example. While this means rejecting a state-led war on terror in favour of nodal leadership, there is still a place for state coercion in the rear rather than at the vanguard of governance, as a last resort at the peak of a counter-terrorism regulatory pyramid.

Globally, regulatory capitalism, with all the momentum it creates for markets in vice and virtue, is something we cannot decide not to have. But we can decide to be democratic citizens who engage with debates on what are the bads and what are the goods that capitalism engineers. We can decide to be activists who join networked governance to do something about what we see as the bads. We can decide to be empirical regulatory researchers who test whether the strategies of the activists have the good effects they hope for. It is perhaps a good thing to do all three if we have the energy and the talent. A participatory, evidence-based social democracy will not necessarily save the stock market from itself, nor the polar bears from global warming, nor guarantee human rights and access to justice, nor free us from domination. Yet at the end of this journey, it still seems a good thing to try to make regulatory capitalism work with a bit more justice and efficiency.

References

Ahmed, E., N. Harris, J. Braithwaite and V. Braithwaite (2001), *Shame Management through Reintegration*, Melbourne: Cambridge University Press.

Amann, E. and W. Baer (2006), 'From the developmental to the regulatory state: the transformation of the government's impact on the Brazilian economy', in E. Amann (ed.), *Regulating Development*, Cheltenham, UK and Northampton, MA, USA: Edward Elgar.

American Association of Homes for the Aging (1991), 'ANHA questionnaire on OBRA surveys', Washington, DC: American Association of Homes for the Aging.

Anderson, C.L. and R.A. Kagan (2000), 'Adversarial legalism and transaction costs: the industrial flight hypothesis revisited', *International Review of Law and Economics*, **20** (1), 1–19.

Angel, C. (2005), 'Crime victims meet their offenders: testing the impact of restorative justice conferences on victims' post-traumatic stress symptoms', PhD dissertation, University of Pennsylvania.

Argy, S. (2003), *Mechanisms for Improving the Quality of Regulations: Australia in an International Context*, Canberra: Productivity Commission.

Askanase, E.S. (2003), 'Qui tam and the False Claims Act: criminal punishment in civil disguise', *Defense Counsel Journal*, **70**, 472–84.

Australian Securities and Investment Commission (ASIC) (2003), *Compliance with Advice and Disclosure Obligations: ASIC Report on Primary Production Schemes*, Sydney: Australian Securities and Investments Commission.

Ayling, J., P. Grabosky and C. Shearing (2006), 'Harnessing resources for networked policing', in J. Fleming and J.D. Wood (eds), *Fighting Crime Together: The Challenges of Policing and Security Networks*, Sydney: UNSW Press.

Ayres, I. and J. Braithwaite (1992), *Responsive Regulation: Transcending the Deregulation Debate*, New York: Oxford University Press.

Baldwin, R. and K. Hawkins (1984), 'Discretionary justice: Davis reconsidered', *Public Law*, **1984**, 570–99.

Baldwin, R., C. Scott and C. Hood (1998), *A Reader on Regulation*, Oxford: Oxford University Press.

Bankman, J. (1999), 'The new corporate tax shelters market', *Tax Notes*, **83**, 1775.
Banner, S. (1997), 'What causes new securities regulation? 200 years of evidence', *Washington University Law Quarterly*, **75** (2), 849–53.
Barton, B. (2006), 'The theoretical context of regulation', in B. Barton, L.K. Barrera-Hernandez, A.R. Lucas and A. Rønne (eds), *Regulating Energy and Natural Resources*, Oxford: Oxford University Press, pp. 11–33.
Bates-Jensen, B.M., M. Cadogan, D. Osterweil, L. Levy-Storms, J. Jorge, N. Al-Samarrai, V. Grbic and J.F. Schnelle (2003), 'The minimum data set pressure ulcer indicator: does it reflect differences in care processes related to pressure ulcer prevention and treatment in nursing homes?', *Journal of the American Geriatrics Society*, **51** (9), 1203–12.
Beck, U. (1992), *Risk Society: Towards a New Modernity*, Beverly Hills, CA: Sage.
Becker, G.S. and G.J. Stigler (1974), 'Law enforcement, malfeasance and compensation of enforcers', *Journal of Legal Studies*, **3**, 1–17.
Benkler, Y. (2004), 'Commons-based strategies and the problem of patents', *Science*, **305**, 1110–12.
Benkler, Y. (2006), *The Wealth of Networks: How Social Production Transforms Markets and Freedom*, New Haven, CT: Yale University Press.
Berle, A. and G. Means (1932), *The Modern Corporation and Private Property*, New York: Macmillan.
Bernstein, M.H. (1955), *Regulating Business by Independent Commission*, Princeton, NJ: Princeton University Press.
Bevir, M. and R. Rhodes (2003), *Interpreting British Governance*, London: Routledge.
Bikhchandani, S. and S. Sharma (2000), *Herd Behavior in Financial Markets: A Review*, Washington, DC: International Monetary Fund.
Black, J. (1997), *Rules and Regulators*, Oxford: Oxford University Press.
Black, J. (1998), 'Talking about regulation', *Public Law*, **1998**, 77–105.
Black, J. (2002), 'Critical reflections on regulation', *Australian Journal of Legal Philosophy*, **27**, 1–36.
Black, W. (2005), *The Best Way to Rob a Bank Is to Own One*, Austin, TX: University of Texas Press.
Blackstone, W. (1769), *Commentaries on the Laws of England, Vol. 4*, reprinted (1966), London: Dawsons.
Blankenburg, E. (1994), 'The infrastructure for avoiding civil litigation: comparing cultures of legal behavior in the Netherlands and West Germany', *Law and Society Review*, **28** (4), 789–808.
Bogason, P. and J.A. Musso (2006), 'The democratic prospects of network governance', *American Review of Public Administration*, **36** (1), 3–18.

Bonta, J., R. Jesseman, T. Rugge and R. Cormier (2006), 'Restorative justice and recidivism: promises made, promises kept?', in D. Sullivan and L. Tifft (eds), *Handbook of Restorative Justice: A Global Perspective*, London: Routledge, pp. 108–20.

Bourdieu, P. (1998), 'The essence of neoliberalism', *Le Monde Diplomatique*, December, 1–6.

Bradbury, N. (2002), 'Face the facts on transport safety', *Railwatch*, November, 6–7.

Braithwaite, J. (1982), 'Enforced self-regulation: a new strategy for corporate crime control', *Michigan Law Review*, **80**, 1466–507.

Braithwaite, J. (1984), *Corporate Crime in the Pharmaceutical Industry*, London: Routledge & Kegan Paul.

Braithwaite, J. (1985), *To Punish or Persuade: Enforcement of Coal Mine Safety*, Albany, NY: State University of New York Press.

Braithwaite, J. (1995), 'Community values and Australian jurisprudence', *Sydney Law Review*, **17**, 351–72.

Braithwaite, J. (1997), 'On speaking softly and carrying sticks: neglected dimensions of republican separation of powers', *University of Toronto Law Journal*, **47**, 1–57.

Braithwaite, J. (1998), 'Institutionalizing distrust, enculturating trust', in V. Braithwaite and M. Levi (eds), *Trust and Governance*, New York: Russell Sage Foundation.

Braithwaite, J. (2002), *Restorative Justice and Responsive Regulation*, New York: Oxford University Press.

Braithwaite, J. (2004), 'Methods of power for development: weapons of the weak, weapons of the strong', *Michigan Journal of International Law*, **26** (1), 298–330.

Braithwaite, J. (2005), *Markets in Vice, Markets in Virtue*, New York and Sydney: Oxford and Federation Press.

Braithwaite, J. (2006a), 'Responsive regulation and developing economies', *World Development*, **34** (5), 884–98.

Braithwaite, J. (2006b), 'Accountability and responsibility through restorative justice', in M. Dowdle (ed.), *Public Accountability: Designs, Dilemmas and Experiences*, Cambridge: Cambridge University Press.

Braithwaite, J. and V. Braithwaite (1995), 'The politics of legalism: rules versus standards in nursing-home regulation', *Social and Legal Studies*, **4**, 307–41.

Braithwaite, J. and K. Daly (1994), 'Masculinities, violence and communitarian control', in T. Newburn and E.A. Stanko (eds), *Just Boys Doing Business*, London and New York: Routledge.

Braithwaite, J. and P. Drahos (2000), *Global Business Regulation*, Melbourne: Cambridge University Press.

Braithwaite, J. and P. Drahos (2002), 'Zero tolerance, naming and shaming: is there a case for it with crimes of the powerful?', *Australian and New Zealand Journal of Criminology*, **35**, 269–88.

Braithwaite, J. and C. Parker (1999), 'Restorative justice is republican justice', in L. Walgrave and G. Bazemore (eds), *Restoring Juvenile Justice: An Exploration of the Restorative Justice Paradigm for Reforming Juvenile Justice*, Monsey, NY: Criminal Justice Press.

Braithwaite, J. and P. Pettit (1990), *Not Just Deserts: A Republican Theory of Criminal Justice*, Oxford: Oxford University Press.

Braithwaite, J., H. Charlesworth and L. Dunn (2005), 'Peacebuilding and responsive governance project: discussion draft', Regulatory Institutions Network, Australian National University, Canberra, http://peacebuilding.anu.edu.au/_documents/Discussion_Draft.pdf (accessed 15 October 2007).

Braithwaite, J., T. Makkai and V. Braithwaite (2007), *Regulating Aged Care: Ritualism and the New Pyramid*, Cheltenham, UK and Northampton, MA, US: Edward Elgar.

Braithwaite, V. (1993), 'The Australian government's affirmative action legislation: achieving social change through human resource management', *Law and Policy*, **15**, 327–54.

Braithwaite, V. (1995), 'Games of engagement: postures within the regulatory community', *Law and Policy*, **17**, 225–55.

Braithwaite, V. (ed.) (2003), *Taxing Democracy: Understanding Tax Avoidance and Evasion*, Aldershot: Ashgate.

Braithwaite, V. (2004), 'Preface to special issue on hope, power and governance: collective hope', *Annals of the American Academy of Political and Social Science*, **592**, 6–17.

Braithwaite, V. (2008), *Defiance in Taxation and Governance*, Cheltenham, UK and Northampton, MA, US: Edward Elgar.

Braithwaite, V. and M. Levi (eds) (1998), *Trust and Governance*, New York: Russell Sage Foundation.

Brennan, G. and P. Pettit (2004), *The Economy of Esteem: An Essay on Civil and Political Society*, Oxford: Oxford University Press.

Bucy, P.H. (2002a), 'Private justice', *Southern California Law Review*, **76** (1), 1–160.

Bucy, P.H. (2002b), 'Information as a commodity in the regulatory world', *Houston Law Review*, **39** (4), 905–78.

Bucy, P.H. (2004a), 'Games and stories: game theory and the civil False Claims Act', *Florida State University Law Review*, **31** (3), 603–706.

Bucy, P.H. (2004b), 'Game theory and the civil False Claims Act: iterated games and close-knit groups', *Loyola University Chicago Law Journal*, **35** (4), 1021–47.

Bucy, P.H. (2004c), 'White collar criminal law in comparative perspective: the Sarbanes–Oxley Act of 2002', *Buffalo Criminal Law Review*, **8**, 277–322.

Busch, P.-O., H. Jorgens and K. Tews (2005), 'The global diffusion of regulatory instruments: the making of a new international environmental regime', *Annals of the American Academy of Political and Social Science*, **598**, 146–67.

Calabresi, G. (1983), *A Common Law for the Age of Statutes*, Cambridge, MA: Harvard University Press.

Calavita, K., H.N. Pontell and R.H. Tillman (1997), *Big Money: Fraud and Politics in the Savings and Loans Crisis*, Berkeley and Los Angeles, CA: University of California Press.

Canellos, P.C. and E.D. Kleinbard (2002), *Disclosing Book-Tax Differences*, www.tax.org/readingsintaxpolicy.nsf/ (accessed January 2005).

Cashore, B., G. Auld and D. Newsom (2004), *Governing Through Markets: Forest Certification and the Emergence of Non-State Authority*, New Haven, CT: Yale University Press.

Castells, M. (1996), *The Information Age: Economy. Society and Culture, Volume 1: The Rise of The Network Society*, Oxford: Blackwell.

Castells, M. (2000), *The Information Age: Economy. Society and Culture, Volume III: End of Millennium*, Oxford: Blackwell.

Castles, F.G. (2004), *The Future of the Welfare State: Crisis Myths and Crisis Realities*, Cambridge: Cambridge University Press.

Caulfield, T., E. Eisiendel, J. Merz and D. Nicol (2006), 'Trust, patents and public perceptions: the governance of controversial biotechnology research', *Nature Biotechnology*, **24** (11), 1352–4.

Chandler, A.D. Jr (1977), *The Visible Hand: The Managerial Revolution in American Business*, Cambridge, MA: Belknap Press.

Chandler, A.D. Jr (1990), *Scale and Scope: The Dynamics of Industrial Capitalism*, Cambridge, MA: Belknap Press.

Chanock, M. (2005), 'Customary law, sustainable development and the failing state', in P. Orebech, F. Bosselman, J. Bjarup, D. Callies, M. Chanock and H. Petersen (eds), *The Role of Customary Law in Sustainable Development*, Cambridge: Cambridge University Press.

Chomsky, N. (1999), *Profit Over People*, New York: Seven Stories Press.

Christie, N. (1993), *Crime Control as Industry: Towards Gulags, Western Style?* London: Routledge.

Clarke, M. (1986), *Regulating the City: Competition, Scandal and Reform*, Milton Keynes: Open University Press.

Clarke, T. (2004), 'Cycles of crisis and regulation: the enduring agency and stewardship problems of corporate governance', *Corporate Governance*, **12** (2), 153–61.

Clegg, S. (1989), *Frameworks of Power*, London: Sage.
Coffee, J.C. Jr (1981), 'No soul to damn, no body to kick: an unscandalized essay on the problem of corporate punishment', *Michigan Law Review*, **79**, 413–24.
Coffee, J.C. Jr (2006), *Gatekeepers: The Professions and Corporate Governance*, Oxford: Oxford University Press.
Coffee, J.C. Jr (2007), 'Law and the market: the impact of enforcement', Columbia Law and Economics Working Paper No. 304, http://ssrn.com/abstract=967482 (accessed 15 October 2007).
Coleman, J.S. (1982), *The Asymmetric Society*, Syracuse, NY: Syracuse University Press.
Collins, H. (1999), *Regulating Contracts*, New York: Oxford University Press.
Cooter, R. and N. Garoupa (2000), 'The virtuous circle of distrust: a mechanism to deter bribes and other cooperative crimes', Berkeley Program in Law and Economics, Working Paper Series, University of California, Berkeley.
Cotton, P. (1993), 'Nursing home research focus on outcomes may mean playing catch-up with regulation', *Journal of the American Medical Association*, **269** (18), 2337–8.
Cotterrell, R. (1999), *Emile Durkheim: Law in a Moral Domain*, Palo Alto, CA: Stanford University Press.
Crumplar, T. (1975), 'An alternative to public and victim enforcement of the federal securities and antitrust laws: Citizen enforcement', *Harvard Journal on Legislation*, **13**, 76–124.
CUTS Centre for Competition, Investment and Economic Regulation (2003) 'The role of international cooperation in building an effective competition regime', *CUTS Newsletter*, no. 6/2003, 1.
Daly, K. (2004), 'Pile it on: more texts on restorative justice', *Theoretical Criminology*, **8** (4), 499–507.
Day, P. and R. Klein (1987), 'Residential care for the elderly: a billion pound experiment in policy making', *Public Money*, March, 19–24.
Delmer, D.P., C. Nottenburg, G.G. Graff and A.B. Bennett (2003), 'Intellectual property for international development in agriculture', *Plant Physiology*, **133** (4), 1666–70.
Denis, D.J., P. Hanouna and A. Sarin (2005), 'Is there a dark side to incentive compensation?', http://ssrn.com/abstract=695583.
Dennis, C. (2004), 'Biologists launch open source movement', *Nature*, **431** (7008), 494.
Department of Justice (2003), 'Justice Department civil fraud recoveries total $2.1 million for FY 2003; False Claims Act recoveries exceed $12 billion since 1986', www.usdoj.gov/opa/pr/2003/November/o3_civ_613.htm (accessed 28 July 2004).

Dickson, P.G.M. (1993), *The Financial Revolution in England: A Study in the Development of Public Credit, 1688–1756*, Brookfield, VT: Gregg Revivals.

Dingwell, R., J. Eekelaar and T. Murray (1983), *The Protection of Children: State Intervention and Family Life*, Oxford: Basil Blackwell.

Dodge, C., A. Karolyi and R. Stulz (2004), 'Why are foreign firms listed in the U.S. worth more?', *Journal of Financial Economics*, **71** (2), 205–38.

Dorf, M. and C. Sabel (1998), 'A constitution of democratic experimentalism', *Columbia Law Review*, **98**, 267–473.

Downes, A. (1972), 'Up and down with ecology – the "Issue-Attention Cycle"', *Public Interest*, **28**, 38–50.

Drahos, P. (2000), 'Indigenous knowledge, intellectual property and biopiracy: is a global biocollecting society the answer?', *European Intellectual Property Review*, **22**, 245–50.

Drahos, P. (2001), 'BITS and BIPS: bilateralism in intellectual property', *Journal of World Intellectual Property*, **4** (2001), 791–808.

Drahos, P. (2004a), 'Towards an international framework for the protection of traditional group knowledge and practice', draft paper prepared for the Commonwealth Secretariat.

Drahos, P. (2004b), 'Intellectual property and pharmaceutical markets: a nodal governance approach', *Temple Law Review*, **77**, 401–24.

Drahos, P. (2004c), 'Securing the future of intellectual property: intellectual property owners and their nodally co-ordinated enforcement pyramid', *Case Western Reserve Journal of International Law*, **36**, 1–25.

Drahos, P. (2006b), 'Governance of the European patent system: a separation of powers approach', paper presented at Scientific and Technological Options Assessment Committee's Workshop on Policy Options for the European Patent System, European Parliament, Brussels, 9 November.

Drahos, P. (2007), 'Doing deals with Al Capone: paying protection money for intellectual property in the global knowledge economy', in P.K. Yu (ed.), *Intellectual Property and Information Wealth: Issues and Practices in the Digital Age*, Westport, CT: Praeger.

Drahos, P., with J. Braithwaite (2002), *Information Feudalism*, London: Earthscan.

Drexl, J. (2005), 'The critical role of competition law in preserving public goods in conflict with intellectual property rights', in K.E. Maskus and J.H. Reichman (eds), *International Public Goods and Transfer of Technology Under a Globalized Intellectual Property Regime*, Cambridge: Cambridge University Press.

Dryzek, J. (2000), *Deliberative Democracy and Beyond: Liberals, Critics, Contestations*, Oxford: Oxford University Press.

Dudley, S. and M. Warren, (2005), *Regulators' Budget Continues to Rise:*

An Analysis of the U.S. Budget for Fiscal Years 2004 and 2005, St Louis, MO: Weidenbaum Center, Washington University, http://wc.wustl.edu/Reg_Report/RegBudgetFinal.pdf (accessed 15 October 2007).

Dupont, B. (2006), 'Mapping security networks: from metaphorical concept to empirical model', in J. Fleming and J. Wood (eds), *Fighting Crime Together: The Challenges of Policing and Security Networks*, Sydney: UNSW Press.

Durkheim, E. (1930), *De la Division du Travail Social*, 2nd edn, Paris: PUF.

Ebersole, T.J., M.N. Guthrie and J.A. Goldstein (2005), 'Patent pools and standard setting in diagnostic genetics', *Nature Biotechnology*, **23** (8), 937–8.

Eckstein, H. (1975), 'Case study and theory in political science', in F. Greenstein and N. Polsby (eds), *Handbook of Political Science, Vol. 7: Strategies of Enquiry*, Reading, MA: Addison-Wesley.

Eggins, R.A. (1999), 'Social identity and social conflict: negotiating the path to resolution', unpublished PhD dissertation, Australian National University.

Engel, D. and F. Munger (1996), 'Rights, remembrance and the reconciliation of difference', *Law and Society Review*, **30**, 7–53.

Ernst & Young (1999), *Australian Biotechnology Report*, Canberra: AGPS.

Etzioni-Halevy, E. (1993), *The Elite Connection: Problems and Potential of Western Democracy*, Cambridge: Polity Press.

European Technology Assessment Group (2007), *Intellectual Property Rights – Policy Options for the Improvement of the European Patent System*, Copenhagen: Danish Board of Technology.

Federal Trade Commission (2003), *To Promote Innovation: The Proper Balance of Competition and Patent Law and Policy*, Washington, DC: Federal Trade Commission.

Feeley, M.M. (1979), *The Process Is the Punishment: Handling Cases in a Lower Criminal Court*, New York: Russell Sage Foundation.

Feld, L.P. and B.A. Frey (2007), 'Tax compliance as the result of a psychological tax contract: the role of incentives and responsive regulation', *Law and Policy*, **29** (1), 102–21.

Fink, C. (2005), 'Comment I: competition law as a means of containing intellectual property rights', in K.M. Maskus and J.H. Reichman (eds), *International Public Goods and Transfer of Technology Under a Globalized Intellectual Property Regime*, Cambridge: Cambridge University Press, pp. 770–73.

Fischer, R.W. (1973), 'Qui tam action: The role of the private citizen in law enforcement', *UCLA Law Review*, **20**, 778–803.

Fisse, B. and J. Braithwaite (1983), *The Impact of Publicity on Corporate Offenders*, New York: State University of New York Press.

Fisse, B. and J. Braithwaite (1993), *Corporations, Crime and Accountability*, Cambridge: Cambridge University Press.

Forsyth, M. (2007), 'A bird that flies with two wings: the *kastom* and state justice systems in Vanuatu', PhD dissertation, Regulatory Institutions Network, Australian National University.

Foster, L. and E. Havian (2000), 'Environment is new target for old fraud law', *BNA Toxics Law Reporter*, 14 September.

Fox, E.M. (2005), 'Can antitrust policy protect the global commons from the excesses of IPRs?', in K.M. Maskus and J.H. Reichman (eds), *International Public Goods and Transfer of Technology Under a Globalized Intellectual Property Regime*, Cambridge: Cambridge University Press, pp. 758–69.

Freeman, J. (2003), 'Extending public law norms through privatisation', *Harvard Law Review*, **116**, 1285–91.

Frey, S. (2004), 'Victim protection in criminal proceedings: the victim's rights to information, participation and protection in criminal proceedings', Work Product of the 123rd International Senior Seminar, Fuchu, Tokyo: United Nations Asian and Far East Institute for the Prevention of Crime.

Freyer, T. (1992), *Regulating Big Business Antitrust in Great Britain and America, 1880–1990*, Cambridge: Cambridge University Press.

Freyer, T. (2006), *Antitrust and Global Capitalism, 1930–2004*, Cambridge: Cambridge University Press.

Friedman, D. (1996), 'Beyond the tort/crime distinction', *Boston University Law Review*, **76**, 103–12.

Fukuyama, F. (1989), 'End of history', *National Interest*, Summer.

Fukuyama, F. (2004), *State-building: Governance and World Order in the 21st Century*, Ithaca, NY: Cornell University Press.

Galanter, M. (1981), 'Justice in many rooms', in M. Cappelletti (ed.), *Access to Justice and the Welfare State*, Alphen aan den Rijn: Sijthoff.

Garland, D. (2001), *The Culture of Control: Crime and Social Order in Contemporary Society*, Oxford: Oxford University Press.

Gilardi, F. (2005), 'The institutional foundations of regulatory capitalism: the diffusion of independent regulatory agencies in Western Europe', *Annals of the American Academy of Political and Social Science*, **598**, 84–101.

Gitter, D. (2007), 'Resolving the open source paradox in biotechnology: a proposal for a revised open source policy for publicly funded genomic databases', *Houston Law Review*, **43**, 1475–522.

Glasbeek, H. (2002), *Wealth by Stealth: Corporate Crime, Corporate Law, and the Perversion of Democracy*, Toronto: Between the Lines.

Grabosky, P.N. (1994), 'Green markets: environmental regulation by the private sector', *Law and Policy*, **16**, 419–48.

Grabosky, P.N. (1995), 'Using non-governmental resources to foster regulatory compliance', *Governance*, **8** (4), 527–50.

Graff, G. and D. Zilberman (2001), 'Towards an intellectual property clearinghouse for agricultural biotechnology', *Intellectual Property Strategy Today*, 3, http://www.biodevelopments.org/ip/ipst3n.pdf (accessed 15 October 2007).

Grasmick, H.G. and R.J. Bursik Jr (1990), 'Conscience, significant others, and rational choice: extending the deterrence model', *Law and Society Review*, **24** (3), 837–61.

Grasmick, H.G. and W.J. Scott (1982), 'Tax evasion and mechanisms of social control: a comparison with grand and petty theft', *Journal of Economic Psychology*, **2**, 213–30.

Grundfest, J.A. (2002), 'Punctuated equilibria in the evolution of United States securities regulation', *Stanford Journal of Law, Business and Finance*, **8** (1), 1–8.

Guillen, M. (2001), 'Is globalization civilizing, destructive or feeble? A critique of five key debates in the social science literature', *Annual Review of Sociology*, **27**, 235–60.

Gunningham, N. (1990), 'Moving the goalposts: financial market regulation and the crash of October 1987', *Law and Social Inquiry*, **15**, 1–48.

Gunningham, N. and P. Grabosky (1998), *Smart Regulation: Designing Environmental Policy*, Oxford: Clarendon Press.

Gunningham, N. and D. Sinclair (2002), *Leaders and Laggards: Next-Generation Environmental Regulation*, Sheffield: Greenleaf.

Gunningham, N., R.A. Kagan and D. Thornton (2003), *Shades of Green: Business, Regulation and Environment*, Stanford, CA: Stanford University Press.

Gurr, T.R., P. Grabosky and R.C. Hula (1977), *The Politics of Crime and Conflict*, Beverly Hills, CA: Sage.

Haines, F. (1997), *Corporate Regulation: Beyond 'Punish or Persuade'*, Oxford: Clarendon Press.

Haines, F. (2005a), 'Tracking the regulation debate', *Australian and New Zealand Journal of Criminology*, **38**, 141–7.

Haines, F. (2005b), *Globalization and Regulatory Character*, Aldershot: Ashgate.

Hall, P.A. and D. Soskice (eds) (2001), *Varieties of Capitalism: The Institutional Foundations of Comparative Advantage*, Oxford: Oxford University Press.

Hannah, L. (1991), 'Mergers, cartels and concentration: legal factors in the US and European experience', in G.H. Burgess Jr (ed.), *Antitrust and Regulation*, Aldershot, UK and Brookfield, US: Edward Elgar.

Hardin, G. (1968), 'The tragedy of the commons', *Science*, **162**, 1243–8.

Harding, R.W. (1997), *Private Prisons and Public Accountability*, Buckingham: Open University Press.

Hawkins, K. (1984), *Environment and Enforcement: Regulation and the Social Definition of Pollution*, Oxford: Clarendon.

Hawkins, K. (2002), *Law as Last Resort: Prosecution Decision-Making in a Regulatory Agency*, Oxford: Oxford University Press.

Hayek, F.A. Von (1944), *The Road to Serfdom*, London: Routledge.

Heft, L. (2002), 'Opening space for collaboration and communication with open space technology', www.openingspace.net/papers (accessed 1 January 2007).

Heller, M.A. and R.S. Eisenberg (1998), 'Can patents deter innovation? The anticommons in biomedical research', *Science*, **280** (5364), 698–701.

Hirst, P. (1994), *Associative Democracy: New Forms of Economic and Social Governance*, Cambridge: Polity Press.

Hood, C. (1986), 'Privatizing UK tax law enforcement?', *Public Administration*, **64**, 319–33.

Hood, C., C. Scott, O. James, G. Jones and T. Travers (1999), *Regulation Inside Government: Waste-Watchers, Quality Police and Sleaze-Busters*, Oxford: Oxford University Press.

Hopkins, B. (2004), *Just Schools: A Whole School Approach to Restorative Justice*, London: Jessica Kingsley.

Hopkins, M.M., S. Mahdi, S.M. Thomas and P. Patel (2006), *The Patenting of Human DNA: Global Trends in Public and Private Sector Activity (The PATGEN Project)*, European Commission 6th Framework Programme.

Hope, J. (2007), *Biobazaar: The Open Source Revolution and Biotechnology*, Cambridge, MA: Harvard University Press.

Inglis, M. (2003), 'Why we urgently need a proper, working systemic model for the Australian federal tax system', paper to Centre for Tax System Integrity, September 2003, Australian National University, Canberra.

Israel, J. (1995), *The Dutch Republic: Its Rise, Greatness and Fall, 1477–1806*, Oxford: Clarendon Press.

Janis, M.D. (2005), '"Minimal" standards for patent-related antitrust law under TRIPS', in K.M. Maskus and J.H. Reichman (eds), *International Public Goods and Transfer of Technology Under a Globalized Intellectual Property Regime*, Cambridge: Cambridge University Press.

Jayaraman, K.S., S. Louët, K. Powell, J. Ransom, C. Sheridan, B. Vastag and E. Waltz (2006), 'Who's who in biotech', *Nature Biotechnology*, **24**, 291–300.

Jayasuriya, K. (2001), 'Globalization and the changing architecture of the state: the politics of the regulatory state and the politics of negative co-ordination', *Journal of European Public Policy*, **8** (1), 101–23.

Jessop, B. (1998), *The Rise of Governance and the Risk of Failure: The Case of Economic Development*, Oxford: Basil Blackwell.

Johnston, D.C. (2003), *Perfectly Legal*, New York: Portfolio.

Johnston, L.D. and C.D. Shearing (2003), *Governing Security: Explorations in Policing and Justice*, London: Routledge.

Jordana, J. and D. Levi-Faur (2003), 'The rise of the regulatory state in Latin America: a study of the diffusion of regulatory reforms across countries and sectors', paper presented to the Annual Meeting of the American Political Science Association, 28 August.

Jordana, J. and D. Levi-Faur (eds) (2004), *The Politics of Regulation: Examining Regulatory Institutions and Instruments in the Governance Age*, Cheltenham, UK and Northampton, MA, USA: Edward Elgar.

Kagan, R.A. (1991), 'Adversarial legalism and American government', *Journal of Policy Analysis and Management*, **10** (3), 369–406.

Kaldor, M. (1999), *New and Old Wars: Organized Violence in a Global Era*, Cambridge: Polity Press.

Kaldor, M. (2003), *Global Civil Society*, Cambridge: Polity.

Kapczynski, A., S. Chaifetz, Z. Katz and Y. Benkler (2005), 'Addressing global health inequities: an open licensing approach for university innovations', *Berkeley Technology Law Journal*, **20**, 1031–114.

Keinan, Y. (2001), 'An analytic approach to corporate tax shelter legislation', New York University Law School student paper, New York.

Kilcullen, D. (2005), 'Countering global insurgency', **28** (4) *Journal of Strategic Studies*, **28**, 597–617.

Kinsey, K.A. (1986), 'Theories and models of tax cheating', *Criminal Justice Abstracts*, September, 402–25.

Kleinbard, E.D. (1999), 'Corporate tax shelters and corporate tax management', *The Tax Executive*, **51**, 231–43.

Klepper, S. and D. Nagin (1989), 'The role of tax preparers in tax compliance', *Policy Sciences*, **22**, 167–94.

Klepper, S., M. Mazur and D. Nagin (1991), 'Expert intermediaries and legal compliance: the case of tax preparers', *Journal of Law and Economics*, **34**, 205–29.

Kraakman, R.H. (1986), 'Gatekeepers: the anatomy of a third-party enforcement Strategy', *Journal of Law and Economics and Organization*, **2**, 53–104.

Krattiger, A.F. (2004), 'Financing the bioindustry and facilitating biotechnology transfer', *IP Strategy Today*, **8**, 1.

Kryder, R.D., S.P. Kowalski and A.F. Krattiger (2000), 'The intellectual and technical property components of pro-vitamin A rice (GoldenRice™): a preliminary freedom-to-operate review', *ISAAA Briefs* No. 20, ISAAA, Ithaca, NY.

La Porta, R., F. Lopez-de-Silanes and A. Shleifer (2006), 'What works in securities laws?', *Journal of Finance*, **61** (1), 1–32.

La Porta, R., F. Lopez-de-Silanes, A. Shleifer and R. Vishny (1998), 'Law and Finance', *Journal of Political Economy*, **106**, 1113–55.

Lazer, D. (2005), 'Regulatory capitalism as a networked order: the international system as an informational network', *Annals of the American Academy of Political and Social Science*, **598**, 52–66.

Levi-Faur, D. (2005a), 'The global diffusion of regulatory capitalism', *Annals of the American Academy of Political and Social Science*, **598**, 12–32.

Levi-Faur, D. (2005b), 'Regulatory capitalism: the dynamics of change beyond telecoms and electricity', *Governance*, **19** (3), 497–525.

Levi-Faur, D. (ed.) (2006), 'Varieties of regulatory capitalism', *Governance*, **19** (3), 363–6.

Levi-Faur, D., J. Jordana and F. Gilardi (2005), 'Regulatory revolution by surprise: on the citadels of regulatory capitalism and the rise of regulocracy', paper presented to 3rd ECPR Conference, Budapest, 8–10 September.

Lipsky, M. (1980), *Street-Level Bureaucracy: Dilemmas of the Individual in Public Services*, New York: Russell Sage Foundation.

Loughlin, M. and C. Scott (1997), 'The regulatory state', in P. Dunleavy, I. Holliday and G. Peele (eds), *Developments in British Politics 5*, London: Macmillan.

Macaulay, S. (1963), 'Non-contractual relations in business: a preliminary study', *American Sociological Review*, **28**, 55–69.

Macdonagh, O. (1961), *A Pattern of Government Growth: The Passenger Acts and Their Enforcement*, London: Macgibbon and Kee.

Macdonald, S. (2004), 'When means become ends: considering the impact of patent strategy on innovation', *Information Economics and Policy*, **16** (1), 135–58.

Majone, G. (1994), 'The rise of the regulatory state in Europe', *West European Politics*, **17**, 77–101.

Makkai, T. and J. Braithwaite (1993), 'Praise, pride and corporate compliance', *International Journal of the Sociology of Law*, **21**, 73–91.

Mandich, G. (1960), 'Venetian origins of inventors' rights', *Journal of the Patent Office Society*, **42**, 378, 380.

March, J.G. and Johan P. Olsen (1995), *Democratic Governance*, New York: Free Press.

Margolis, J.D. and J.P., Walsh (2001), *People and Profits? The Search for a Link Between a Company's Social and Financial Performance*, Hillsdale, NJ: Erlbaum.

Martin, R.L. (2003), *The Responsibility Virus*, New York: Prentice-Hall.

Maurer, S., A. Rai and A. Sali (2004), 'Finding cures for tropical disease:

is open source the answer?', *Public Library of Science: Medicine*, **1** (3), e56.
Maxwell, J.W. and C.S. Decker (2006), 'Voluntary environmental investment and responsive regulation', *Environmental and Resource Economics*, **33**, 425–39.
McBarnet, D. and C. Whelan (1999), *Creative Accounting and the Cross-Eyed Javelin Thrower*, Chichester: Wiley.
McCraw, T.K. (1984), *Prophets of Regulation*, Cambridge: Harvard University Press.
Meidinger, E. (1987), 'Regulatory culture: a theoretical outline', *Law and Policy*, **9**, 355–86.
Meidinger, E. (2006), 'The administrative law of global private-public regulation: the case of forestry', *European Journal of International Law*, **17**, 47–87.
Merges, R. and R. Nelson (1990), 'On the complex economics of patent scope', *Columbia Law Review*, **90**, 839.
Merton, R.K. (1968), *Social Theory and Social Structure*, New York: Free Press.
Meseguer, C. (2005), 'Policy learning, policy diffusion, and the making of a new order', *Annals of the American Academy of Political and Social Science*, **598**, 67–83.
Metcalfe, L. (1994), 'The weakest links: building organisational networks for multi-level regulation', in Organisation for Economic Co-operation and Development, *Regulatory Co-operation for an Interdependent World*, Paris: OECD.
Michaels, T. (1999), 'General public licence for plant germplasm', paper presented at meeting of the Department of Plant Agriculture Crop Science Division, University of Guelph, Canada.
Midwinter, A. and N. McGarvey (2001), 'In search of the regulatory state: evidence from Scotland', *Public Administration*, **79** (4), 825–49.
Moffet, J., F. Bregha and M.J. Middelkoop (2004), 'Responsible care: a case study of a voluntary environmental initiative', in K. Webb (ed.), *Voluntary Codes: Private Governance, the Public Interest and Innovation*, Carleton, ON: Carleton Research Unit on Innovation, Science and Environment, pp. 177–208.
Montesquieu, C. de Secondat (1989), *The Spirit of the Laws*, trans. and ed. A.M. Cohler and B.C. Miller, Cambridge: Cambridge University Press.
Moran, M. (2003), *The British Regulatory State: High Modernism and Hyper-Innovation*, Oxford: Oxford University Press.
Morgan, B. (2002), *Social Citizenship in the Shadow of Competition: The Bureaucratic Politics of Regulatory Justification*, Aldershot: Ashgate.

Morrison, B. (2001), 'Affect, identity and the self: a field theory of restorative process', manuscript held at the Centre for Restorative Justice, Australian National University.

Morrison, B. (2007), *Restoring Safe School Communities*, Sydney: Federation Press.

Muller, M.M. (2002), *The New Regulatory State in Germany*, Birmingham: Birmingham University Press.

Murphy, K. (2004), 'The role of trust in nurturing compliance: a study of accused tax avoiders', *Law and Human Behavior*, **28**, 187–209.

Murray, F. and S. Stern (2005), 'Do formal intellectual property rights hinder the free flow of scientific knowledge? An empirical test of the anticommons hypothesis', *NBER Working Paper 11465*, Cambridge, MA: National Bureau of Economic Research.

Neimeyer, R.A. and H. Levitt (2001), 'Coping and coherence: a narrative perspective on resilience', in R.C. Snyder (ed.), *Coping with Stress: Effective People and Processes*, New York: Oxford University Press.

Neimeyer, R.A. and F. Tschudi (2003), 'Community and coherence: narrative contributions to the psychology of conflict and loss', in G.D. Fineman, T.E. McVay and O.J. Flanagan (eds), *Narrative and Consciousness: Literature, Psychology, and the Brain*, New York: Oxford University Press.

Neocleous, M. (1998), 'Policing and pin-making: Adam Smith, police and the state of prosperity', *Policing and Society*, **8** (4), 425–29.

New York State Bar Association, Section on Taxation (1999), 'Comments on the administration's corporate tax shelter proposals', *Tax Notes*, 10 May, 879–901.

Nicol, D. and J. Hope (2006), 'Cooperative strategies for facilitating use of patented inventions in biotechnology', *Law in Context*, **24** (1), 85–112.

Nicol, D. and J. Nielsen (2003), 'Patents and medical biotechnology: an empirical analysis of issues facing the Australian industry', *Occasional Paper No. 6*, Hobart: Centre for Law and Genetics.

Nicol, D. and J. Nielsen (2005), 'Australian medical biotechnology: navigating a complex patent landscape', *European Intellectual Property Review*, **27** (9), 313–18.

Nielsen, V. (2006), 'Are regulators responsive?', *Law and Policy*, **28** (3), 395–416.

Nielsen, Vibeke and Christine Parker (2005), 'The ACCC Compliance and Enforcement Project: preliminary findings from a survey of Australian business', Canberra: Regulatory Institutions Network, Australian National University.

Nonet, P. and P. Selznick (1978), *Law and Society in Transition: Toward Responsive Law*, New York: Harper Torchbooks.

Noveck, B. (2006), 'Peer to patent: collective intelligence and intellectual property reform', *Harvard Journal of Law and Technology*, **20**, 123.

Nussbaum, M. (1995), 'Human capabilities: female human beings', in M.C. Nussbaum and J. Glover (eds), *Women, Culture, and Development*, Oxford: Clarendon Press.

O'Brien, J. (2004), 'Ethics, probity and the changing governance of Wall Street: cure or remission?', *Public Integrity*, **7**, 43–56.

O'Brien, J. (2005), 'Redesigning financial regulation: Eliot Spitzer, state-federal relations and the battle for corporate control', in J. O'Brien (ed.), *Governing the Corporation: Regulation and Corporate Governance in an Age of Scandal and Global Markets*, Chichester: John Wiley.

O'Brien, J. (2006), 'Securing corporate accountability or bypassing justice? The efficacy and pitfalls of pre-trial diversion', *Australian Journal of Corporate Law*, **19**, 1–21.

O'Brien, J. (2007), *Redesigning Financial Regulation: The Politics of Enforcement*, Chichester: John Wiley.

Organisation for Economic Co-operation and Development (OECD) (2002), *Genetic Inventions, Intellectual Property Rights and Licensing Practices: Evidence and Policies*, Berlin: OECD.

Orlitzky, M., F.L. Schmidt and S.L. Rynes (2003), 'Corporate social and financial performance: a meta-analysis', *Organization Studies*, **24**, 403–41.

Osborne, D. and T. Gaebler (1992), *Reinventing Government: How the Entrepreneurial Spirit is Transforming the Public Sector*, Reading, MA: Addison-Wesley.

Ostrom, E., J. Burger, C.B. Field, R.B. Norgaard and D. Policansky (1999), 'Revisiting the common: local lessons, global challenges', *Science*, **284**, 278–82.

Packer, G. (2006), 'Knowing the enemy: can social scientists redefine the "war on terror"?', *The New Yorker*, 18 December, 60–69.

Parker, C. (1999), *Just Lawyers*, Oxford: Oxford University Press.

Parker, C. (2002), *The Open Corporation*, Melbourne: Cambridge University Press.

Parker, C. (2004), 'Restorative justice in business regulation? The Australian Competition and Consumer Commission's use of enforceable undertakings', *Modern Law Review*, **67**, 209–46.

Parker, C. (2006), 'The "compliance trap": the moral message in responsive regulatory enforcement', *Law and Society Review*, **40** (3), 591–622.

Parker, C., C. Scott, N. Lacey and J. Braithwaite (eds) (2004), *Regulating Law*, Oxford: Oxford University Press.

Partnoy, F. (1997), 'Financial derivatives and the costs of regulatory arbitrage', *Journal of Corporation Law*, **22**, 211–56.

Partnoy, F. (2000), 'Why markets crash and what law can do about it', *University of Pittsburgh Law Review*, **61**, 741–817.

Partnoy, F. (2003), *Infectious Greed: How Deceit and Greed Corrupted the Financial Markets*, London: Profile Books.

Pasquino, P. (1991), 'Theatrum politicum: the genealogy of capital – police and the state of prosperity', in G. Burchell, C. Gordon and P.M. Miller (eds), *The Foucault Effect: Studies in Governmentality*, Hemel Hempstead: Harvester Wheatsheaf.

Paternoster, R. and S. Simpson (1996), 'Sanction threats and appeals to morality: testing a rational choice model of corporate crime', *Law and Society Review*, **30**, 549–83.

Paulson Report (2006), *Interim Report of the Committee on Capital Markets Regulation*, 30 November, Washington, DC: Committee on Capital Markets Regulation.

Pearce, F. and S. Tombs (1997), 'Hazard, law and class: contextualizing the regulation of corporate crime', *Social and Legal Studies*, **6**, 79–107.

Peng, L. and A. Roell (2004), 'Executive pay, earnings manipulation and shareholder litigation', http://ssrn.com/abstract=488148 (accessed 15 October 2007).

Peters, M. (1999), 'Neoliberalism', *Encyclopaedia of Philosophy of Education*, www.vusst.hr/ENCYCLOPAEDIA/ (accessed 15 October 2007).

Pettit, P. (1997), *Republicanism*, Oxford: Clarendon Press.

Phillips & Cohen LLP (2006), 'Qui tam statistics, 1986–2006', www.phillipsandcohen.com/CM/FalseClaimsAct/quisat_f.asp (accessed 24 January 2007).

Pokrywka, H.S., K.H. Koffler, R. Rensburg, J. Roth, M. Tayback and J.E. Wright (1997), 'Accuracy of patient care staff in estimating and documenting meal intake of nursing home residents', *Journal of the American Geriatric Society*, **45**, 1223–7.

Polanyi, K. (1957), *The Great Transformation*, Boston, MA: Beacon Press.

Pontell, H. (1978), 'Deterrence: theory versus practice', *Criminology*, **16**, 3–22.

Porter, M. (1990), *The Competitive Advantage of Nations*, New York: Macmillan.

Porter, M. and C. van der Linde (1995a), 'Green *and* competitive: ending the stalemate', *Harvard Business Review*, September–October, 120–34.

Porter, M. and C. van der Linde (1995b), 'Reply to Portney's critique of Porter and van der Linde (1995) "Green *and* competitive: ending the stalemate"', *Harvard Business Review*, November–December, 206–8.

Porter, M. and C. van der Linde (1995c), 'Toward a new conception of the environment-competitiveness relationship', *Journal of Economic Perspectives*, **9** (4), 98–118.

Post, D.L. (2005), 'Standards and regulatory capitalism: the diffusion of food safety standards in developing countries', *Annals of the American Academy of Political and Social Science*, **598**, 168–83.

Potrykus, I. (2001), 'Golden rice and beyond', *Plant Physiology*, **125** (3), 1157–61.

Poulson, B. (2003), 'A third voice: a review of empirical research on the psychological outcomes of restorative justice', *Utah Law Review*, **2003** (1), 167–204.

Power, M. (1997), *The Audit Society: Rituals of Verification*, Oxford: Oxford University Press.

Pranis, K. (2001), 'Restorative justice, social justice and the empowerment of marginalized populations', in G. Bazemore and M. Schiff (eds), *Restorative Community Justice: Repairing Harm and Transforming Communities*, Cincinnati, OH: Anderson, pp. 287–306.

Ramo, J.C. (2004), *The Beijing Consensus*, London: Foreign Policy Centre.

Ramsay, I. (2006), 'Consumer law, regulatory capitalism and the "new learning" in regulation', *Sydney Law Review*, **28**, 9–36.

Rawlings, G. (2007), 'Taxes and transnational treaties: responsive regulation and the reassertion of offshore sovereignty', *Law and Policy*, **29** (1), 51–66.

Rees, J. (1994), *Hostages of Each Other: The Transformation of Nuclear Safety Since Three Mile Island*, Chicago and London: University of Chicago Press.

Reichman, H. and C. Hasenzahl (2003), 'Non-voluntary licensing of patented inventions: historical perspective, legal framework under TRIPS, and an overview of the practice in Canada and the USA', *UNCTAD/ ICTSD Project on IPRs and Sustainable Development*, http://www.ictsd.org/pubs/ictsd_series/iprs/CS_reichman_hasenzahl.pdf. (accessed 15 October 2007).

Reputation Measurement (2003), *RepuTex Report 2003*, Melbourne: Reputation Measurement.

Restorative Justice Consortium (2005), *National Practice Guidelines for Restorative Practitioners*, London: Home Office.

Restorative Justice Consortium Principles (2005), *Statement of Restorative Justice Principles as Applied in a School Setting*, Restorative Justice Consortium: London.

Rhodes, R.A.W. (1997), *Understanding Governance*, Buckingham and Philadelphia: Open University Press.

Ribstein, L.C. (2003), 'Bubble laws', *Houston Law Review*, **40** (1), 77–97.

Robb, J. (2005), 'The open-source war', *New York Times*, 15 October, A35.

Roche, D. (2003), *Accountability in Restorative Justice*, Oxford: Oxford University Press.

Rodrik, D. (2004), 'Rethinking growth policies in the developing world',

draft of the Luca d'Agliano Lecture in Development Economics, 8 October 2004, Torino, Italy, http://ksghome.harvard.edu/~drodrik/Luca_d_Agliano_Lecture_Oct_2004.pdf (accessed 15 October 2007).
Rose, N. and P. Miller (1992), 'Political power beyond the state: problematics of government', *British Journal of Sociology*, **43** (2), 173–205.
Rosoff, S.E., H.N. Pontell and R.H. Tillman (2002), *Profit Without Honor: White-Collar Crime and the Looting of America*, Upper Saddle River, NJ: Prentice-Hall.
Sachs, J.D. (2005), *The End of Poverty: How We Can Make It Happen in Our Lifetime*, London: Penguin Books.
Sackman, S. and M. Coltman (1996), 'Legal aspects of a global securities market', in F. Oditah (ed.), *The Future for the Global Securities Market: Legal and Regulatory Aspects*, Oxford: Clarendon Press.
Sakurai, Y. and V. Braithwaite (2003), 'Taxpayers' perceptions of practitioners: finding one who is effective and does the right thing', Canberra: Centre for Tax System Integrity, Australian National University.
Schepel, H. (2005), *The Constitution of Private Governance*, Oxford: Hart.
Scherer, F.M. (2000), *Competition Policy, Domestic and International*, Cheltenham, UK and Northampton, MA, USA: Edward Elgar.
Schnelle, J.F., M.P. Cadogan, J. Yoshii, N.R. Al-Samarrai, D. Osterweil, B.M. Bates-Jensen and S.F. Simmons (2003), 'The minimum data set urinary incontinence quality indicators: do they reflect differences in care processes related to incontinence?', *Medical Care*, **41** (8), 909–22.
Scholz, J.T. (1998), 'Trust, taxes and compliance', in V. Braithwaite and M. Levi (eds), *Trust and Governance*, New York: Russell Sage Foundation.
Schuck, P.H. (1979), 'Litigation, bargaining and regulation', *Regulation*, **3**, 26–34.
Schwartz, R.D. and S. Orleans (1967), 'On legal sanctions', *University of Chicago Law Review*, **34**, 274–300.
Scotchmer, S. (1991), 'Standing on the shoulders of giants: cumulative research and the patent law', *Journal of Economic Perspectives*, **5**, 29–41.
Scott, C. (2004), 'Regulation in the age of governance: the rise of the post regulatory state', in J. Jordana and D. Levi-Faur (eds), *The Politics of Regulation: Institutions and Regulatory Reforms for the Age of Governance*, Cheltenham, UK and Northampton, MA, USA: Edward Elgar, pp. 145–74.
Scott, W.J. and H.G. Grasmick (1981), 'Deterrence and income tax cheating: testing interaction hypotheses in utilitarian theories', *Journal of Applied Behavioural Science*, **17**, 395–408.
Selznick, P. (1992), *The Moral Commonwealth: Social Theory and the Promise of Community*, Berkeley, CA: University of California Press.

Sen, A. (1992), *Inequality Reexamined*, Cambridge, MA: Harvard University Press.

Shaw, G., R. Brown and P. Bromiley (1998), 'Strategic stories: how 3M is rewriting business planning', *Harvard Business Review*, May–June, 41–54.

Shearing, C. (2001), 'Punishment and the changing face of governance', *Punishment and Society*, **3** (2), 203–20.

Shearing, C. and R.V. Ericson (1991), 'Towards a configurative conception of action', *British Journal of Sociology*, **42**, 481–506.

Shearing, C. and J. Wood (2003), 'Nodal governance, democracy and the new "denizens"', *Journal of Law and Society*, **30** (3), 400–19.

Sherman, L. (2003), 'Reason for emotion: reinventing justice with theories, innovations, and research. The American Society of Criminology, 2002 Presidential Address', Criminology, **41**, 1–38.

Sherman, L.W. and H. Strang (2007), *Restorative Justice: The Evidence*, London: The Smith Institute.

Sigler, J.A. and J.E. Murphy (1988), *Interactive Corporate Compliance: An Alternative to Regulatory Compulsion*, New York: Quorum Books.

Simmons, R.F., S. Babineau, E. Garcia and J.F. Schnelle (2002), 'Quality assessment in nursing homes by systematic direct observation: feeding assistance', *Journals of Gerontology Series A: Biological Sciences and Medical Sciences*, **57**, M665–M671.

Simon, J.H.M., E. Claassen, C.E. Correa and A.D.M.E. Osterhaus (2005), 'Managing Severe Acute Respiratory Syndrome (SARS) intellectual property rights: the possible role of patent pooling', *Bulletin of the World Health Organization*, **83**, 707–10.

Sims, T.S. (2002), 'Corporate returns: beyond disclosure', *Tax Notes*, 29 July, 735–7.

Singer, P.W. (2002), 'Corporate warriors: the rise and ramifications of the privatised military industry', *International Security*, **26**, 186–220.

Skeel, D. (2005), *Icarus in the Boardroom: The Fundamental Flaws in Corporate America and Where they Came From*, New York: Oxford University Press.

Skocpol, T. (2003), *Diminished Democracy: From Membership to Management in American Civic Life*, Norman, OK: University of Oklahoma Press.

Smith, A. (1762), *Lectures on Jurisprudence*, reprinted in R.L. Meek, D.D. Raphael and P.G. Stein (eds) (1978), *Lectures on Jurisprudence*, Oxford: Clarendon Press.

Sparrow, M. (2000), *The Regulatory Craft: Controlling Risks, Managing Problems and Managing Compliance*, Washington, DC: The Brookings Institution.

Slaughter, A.-M. (2004), *A New World Order*, Princeton, NJ: Princeton University Press.

Sorensen, E. (2006), 'Metagovernance: the changing role of politicians in processes of democratic governance', *American Review of Public Administration*, **36** (1), 98–114.

Sorensen, E. and J. Torfing (2006), 'The democratic anchorage of governance networks', *Scandinavian Political Studies*, **28** (3), 195–218.

Stiglitz, J.E. (2002), *Globalization and Its Discontents*, New York: W.W. Norton.

Stiglitz, J.E. (2003), 'The ruin of Russia', *Guardian*, 9 April, http://education.guardian.co.uk/higher/artsandhumanities/story/0,,932848,00.html (accessed 15 October 2007).

Stiglitz, J.E. (2004), *The Roaring Nineties: Why We're Paying the Price for the Greediest Decade in History*, London: Penguin Books.

Stoker, G. (2006), 'Public value management: a new narrative for networked governance?', *American Review of Public Administration*, **36** (1), 41–57.

Strang, H. (2002), *Repair or Revenge: Victims and Restorative Justice*, Oxford: Oxford University Press.

Strang, H. and L.W. Sherman (2003), 'Repairing the harm: victims and restorative justice', *Utah Law Review*, **2003** (1), 15–42.

Stanley, E. (2005), 'Truth commissions and the recognition of state crime', *British Journal of Criminology*, **45**, 582–97.

Stratton, S. (2002), 'Closing the credibility gap by disclosing corporate returns', *The Insurance Tax Review*, **23**, 220–21.

Sulston, J. and G. Ferry (2002), *The Common Thread*, London: Random House.

Sunstein, C. (1988), 'Beyond the republican revival', *Yale Law Journal*, **97**, 1539–90.

Sutton, A. and R. Wild (1978), 'Corporate crime and social structure', in P.R. Wilson and J. Braithwaite (eds), *Two Faces of Deviance: Crimes of the Powerless and Powerful*, Brisbane: University of Queensland Press, pp. 177–98.

Tanzi, V. (2000), 'Globalization, technological developments, and the work of fiscal termites', *International Monetary Fund WP/00/181*, Washington, DC: International Monetary Fund.

Tellis-Nayak, V., J.A. Day and D.J. Ward (1988), *Nursing Home Exemplars of Quality*, Springfield, IL: Charles C. Thomas.

Teubner, G. (1983), 'Substantive and reflexive elements in modern law', *Law and Society Review*, **17**, 239–86.

Teubner, G. (1987), 'Juridification: concepts, aspects, limits, solutions', in G. Teubner (ed.), *Juridification of Social Spheres: A Comparative Analysis of the Areas of Labor, Corporate, Antitrust and Social Welfare Law*, Berlin: Walter de Gruyter, pp. 3–48.

Tombs, S. (2002), 'Understanding regulation', *Social and Legal Studies*, **11**, 113–33.

Tomlins, C.L. (1993), *Law, Labor, and Ideology in the Early American Republic*, New York: Cambridge University Press.

Tramontozzi, P.N. and K.W. Chilton (1989), *US Regulatory Agencies Under Reagan, 1960–1988*, St Louis, MO: Center for the Study of American Business, Washington University.

Tyler, T. (1990), *Why People Obey the Law*, New Haven, CT: Yale University Press.

Tyler, T. and S. Blader (2000), *Cooperation in Groups: Procedural Justice, Social Identity, and Behavioral Engagement*, Philadelphia, PA: Psychology Press.

Tyler, T. and R.M. Dawes (1993), 'Fairness in groups: comparing the self-interest and social identity perspectives', in B.A. Mellers and J. Baron (eds), *Psychological Perspectives on Justice: Theory and Applications*, Cambridge: Cambridge University Press, pp. 87–108.

Tyler, T. and Y.J. Huo (2001), *Trust and the Rule of Law: A Law-Abidingness Model of Social Control*, New York: Russell Sage Foundation.

Ullrich, H. (2005), 'Expansionist intellectual property protection and reductionist competition rules: a TRIPS perspective', in K.M. Maskus and J.H. Reichman (eds), *International Public Goods and Transfer of Technology Under a Globalized Intellectual Property Regime*, Cambridge: Cambridge University Press, pp. 726–57.

Van Overwalle, G., E. Van Zimmern, B. Verbeure and G. Matthijs (2006), 'Models for facilitating access to patents on genetic inventions', *Nature Review Genetics*, **7**, 143–7.

Van Zimmern, E., B. Verbeure, G. Matthijs and G. Van Overwalle (2006), 'A clearing house for diagnostic testing: the solution to ensure access to and use of patented genetic inventions?', *Bulletin of the World Health Organization*, **84**, 352–60.

Verbeure, B., E. van Zimmerman, G. Matthijs and G. Van Overwalle (2006), 'Patent pools and diagnostic testing', *Trends in Biotechnology*, **24** (3), 115–20.

Vincent-Jones, P. (2002), 'Value and purpose in government: central-local relations in regulatory perspective', *Journal of Law and Society*, **29**, 27–39.

Vincent-Jones, P. (2006), *The New Public Contracting*, Oxford: Oxford University Press.

Vogel, S.K. (1996), *Freer Markets, More Rules: Regulatory Reform in Advanced Industrial Societies*, Ithaca, NY and London: Cornell University Press.

Walby, S. (1999), 'The new regulatory state: the social powers of the European Union', *British Journal of Sociology*, **50** (1), 118–38.
Waller, V. (2007), 'The challenge of institutional integrity in responsive regulation: field inspections by the Australian Taxation Office', *Law and Policy*, **29** (1), 67–83.
Walsh, J., A. Arora and W.M. Cohen (2003a), 'Working through the patent problem', *Science*, **299**, 1021.
Walsh, J., A. Arora and W.M. Cohen (2003b), 'Effects of research tool patents and licensing on biomedical innovation', in W.M. Cohen and S.A. Merrill (eds), *Patents in the Knowledge-Based Economy*, Washington, DC: National Academies Press, pp. 285–340.
Wardak, A. (2004), 'Building a post-war justice system in Afghanistan', *Crime, Law and Social Change*, **41**, 319–41.
Way, C.R. (2005), 'Political insecurity and the diffusion of financial market regulation', *Annals of the American Academy of Political and Social Science*, **598**, 125–45.
Weber, M. (1954), *On Law in Economy and Society*, New York: Clarion.
Weiss, L. (2005), 'Infrastructural power, economic transformation, and globalization', in J.A. Hall and R. Schroeder (eds), *An Anatomy of Power: the Social Theory of Michael Mann*, Cambridge: Cambridge University Press.
Wenzel, M. (2002), 'The impact of outcome orientation and justice concerns on tax compliance: the role of taxpayers' identity', *Journal of Applied Psychology*, **8**, 629–45.
Wenzel, M. (2003), 'Tax compliance and the psychology of justice: mapping the field', in V. Braithwaite (ed.), *Taxing Democracy: Understanding Tax Avoidance and Evasion*, Aldershot: Ashgate, pp. 41–70.
Wenzel, M. (2004), 'Social identification as a determinant of concerns about individual, group, and inclusive-level justice', *Social Psychology Quarterly*, **67**, 70–87.
Wickerson, J., N. Reddon and M. Khan (2001), 'Using tax return data to assess the "tax performance" of large Australian companies: an "effective tax rate" perspective, 1991/92 to 1997/98', in M. Walpole and C. Evans (eds), *Tax Administration in the 21st Century*, St Leonards, NSW: Prospect Media, pp. 265–86.
Wilf-Miron, R., Z. Lewenhoff, Z. Benyamini and A. Aviram (2003), 'From aviation to medicine: applying concepts of aviation safety to risk management in ambulatory care', *Quality and Safety in Health Care*, **12**, 35–9.
Wood, J. and C. Shearing (2007), *Imagining Security*, Portland, OR: Willan.
World Bank (1993), *The East Asian Miracle: Economic Growth and Public Policy*, Washington, DC: World Bank.
Yeager, P. (forthcoming), *Markets, Morality and Mischief*, New York: Oxford University Press.

Yeung, K. (2004), *Securing Compliance: A Principled Approach*, Oxford: Hart.

Yin, G. (2001), 'Getting serious about corporate tax shelters: taking a lesson from history', *Southern Methodist University Law Review*, **54**, 209–37.

Young, I.M. (2000), *Inclusion and Democracy*, Oxford: Oxford University Press.

Zehr, H. (1995), *Changing Lenses: A New Focus for Criminal Justice*, Scottsdale, PA: Herald Press.

Zehr, H. (2002), *The Little Book of Restorative Justice*, Intercourse, PA: Good Books.

Index

accountability 108, 140, 142, 186
   types of 205
   virtuous circle of 68–9
accounting firms 25, 29, 50, 51; *see also* Arthur Andersen
Advanced Pricing Agreements 181; *see also* transfer pricing
adversarialism 168, 187, 190
advocacy groups 178, 188; *see also* consumer movement; social movements
Affirmative Action Agency (Australia) 182
Afghanistan 81
African Union 25
airlines, regulation of 25
alternative dispute resolution 159, 160, 178–80, 181
   commercial
   feminist critique of 185
   and imbalance of power 186
   and NGOs 177–8
   pathologies of 174–7, 179
American Association of Retired Persons 191
American Disabilities Act 64
anger 165, 180
antitrust laws 18–20, 28, 31, 44, 197
arbitrage, international 47
armed conflict, governance of 203
Arthur Andersen 34–5, 45, 53, 69
Asian financial crisis 6, 7, 10
audit committees 56
auditing 56, 82, 140, 151, 185
Australia 7, 11, 155
   Advanced Pricing Agreements 181
   Affirmative Action Agency 182
   aggressive tax planning 43, 46–8, 55–6, 60
   Australian Capital Territory Restorative Justice Act 192
   CLERP 9 corporate law reform 35
   Cooperative Research Centres 124, 126
   corporate regulation 34–5
   free trade agreement with the US 133
   General Anti-Avoidance provision 46, 48
   HIH insurance company 34–5
   legal opinions on tax shelters 47, 50, 54
   National Health and Medical Research Council 124
   patent law 136
   price-fixing by petrol stations 71–2
   private prisons 20–21
   Tax Integrity Continuous Improvement Review 56–7
   Trade Practices Act 1974 195
Australian Capital Territory Restorative Justice Act 192
Australian Federal Police 100, 104
Australian Institute of Management 184
Australian Performers Rights Association 109
Australian Securities and Investments Commission 56
Australian Shareholders' Association 184
Australian Tax Office 46–7
   corporate tax collection 7, 31, 181
   Registered Software Project 152
   Transfer Pricing Record Review and Improvement Project 52, 56
autonomy 205
Avocats sans Frontiers 81
Award for the Advancement of Free Software 125
Ayres, Ian 76, 87, 89, 162

Bank of England 17
Bankman, Joseph 48, 58

233

banks 17, 25, 96, 197
Banner, S. 33
Basle Committee 25
Bates-Jensen, B.M. 146
Becker, G.S. 79
Benkler, Y. 110
Berle, A. 36, 40
Bernstein, Marver 34, 62
Bevir, M. 1
Beyer, Peter 122, 126
Bhopal 22, 83
BHP-Billiton 81, 83
BioForge 120
Biological Innovation for Open Society 120
BIOS 139
biotechnology 110, 118, 130
  agricultural 111, 119, 121
  obstacles to innovation 113–14
  patents on 120, 127, 152
Black, Julia 29
Blackstone, W. 13
Blair, Tony 5, 11, 155
blame, culture of 63, 150
Blankenburg, E. 183
bonds 17
boom and bust cycles 33–6, 41, 88
Bourdieu, P. 4, 8
Braithwaite, John ix, 16, 19, 23, 45, 133, 190
  flipping markets in vice to markets in virtue 52–7, 59
  justice 70, 78, 178
  Markets in Vice, Markets in Virtue 43
  nursing homes, regulation of 144, 145–6, 147
  pyramids 76, 89
  regulatory ritualism 141, 151
  responsive regulation 87, 162
  restorative justice 76, 167, 176, 186
Braithwaite, Valerie xiii, 144, 145–6, 147, 155–6
bribery 56; *see also* corruption
Britain 11, 155
  antitrust laws 19
  corporate regulation 44
  Liberal Party 15–16
  Monopolies Act 1948 19
  privatization 9

  regulation of nursing homes 9, 96, 134
  Restrictive Trade Practices Act 1956 19
British South Africa Company 17
Brown, Gordon 11
Bucy, Pamela 64–6, 69–71, 74, 79, 81, 85–6
Buffett, Warren 133
Bush administration 7, 10
Bush, George W. 11
business, certainty for 180–82, 183
business ethics 93
business models and intellectual property 109–39
  niches for 118–19
  non-monopolistic 112–15, 120
  open source 206
business regulation xii, 13–14, 16–18

CAMBIA 120–21, 133, 139
Campbell Collaboration 28
Canada, General Public Licence for plant germplasm 120
Canellos, P.C. 55, 80
capitalism
  Confucian 6
  crony 6, 80
  globalization of 18–20
  managerial 36–7
  mega-corporate 18–20, 20–23
  out of control 36–41
  provider capitalism 23–4
  regulatory capitalism, see regulatory capitalism
  without regulation 197–8
cartels 19; *see also* monopolies
Cashore, B. 95
Castells, M. 3, 205
certainty 180–82
certification programmes 123
Chandler, Alfred Jr 18, 19, 28
chemical pharmaceuticals industry 22
  self-regulation 22, 94–5, 96
China 6, 133
Chomsky, Noam 4
Ciba-Geigy 131
Citizens for Better Care (US) 190
citizenship, contestatory 202–6, 207
Civil Rights Act 1964 (US) 64

civil society 1, 62, 81, 91, 202
Clark, Helen 11, 29
Clarke, M. 30
class actions 177
clearing houses 114, 119, 121–2, 125
CLERP 9 corporate law reform (Australia) 35
Clinton, Bill 5
coal mine safety 73
coercion 93, 107, 163, 207
Coffee, J.C. Jr 41
Coglianese, Cary xi
collaboration 3
collaboration-strengthening pyramid 115–26, 129, 152
Collins, Hugh 181
Common Informers Act of 1951 (UK) 66
communication 78, 181
community networks 61
community of care 152
community of shared fate 22–3, 95, 97
community service obligations 140
competition 185
competition law enforcement 131
competition policy xii, 50, 59, 60, 62, 198
compliance professionals 179
compliance systems 43, 52, 90, 92, 153
compulsory licensing 132
constables 13; *see also* police
consumer movement 177
Consumer Product Safety Act (US) 64
Consumer Product Safety Commission (US) 70
consumers, market power of 95
contagion 46, 48, 49, 50, 53
  reverse contagion 48, 49
contingency fees 54, 60, 86
continuous improvement 3, 60, 150–52, 155, 158–9, 171
contract, freedom of 19
Cooperative Research Centres programme (Australia) 124, 126
Cooter, R. 82–3
copyleft licences 139
Copyright Agency Limited 109
copyright licensing 112–13
Corbett, Angus 195
corporate governance 150

corporate integrity and ethics systems 159
corporate law reform 34–5, 44
corporate social responsibility 57, 130, 184, 205
corporate tax collection 7, 23–4, 31, 181, 199
corporate tax shelters 47, 51; *see also* tax planning
corporations 1–2, 16–18, 29, 34–5, 94
  and access to justice 177
  accumulation of political power in 21–2
  audit committees 56
  benefits of compliance 57
  capacity-building obligations 95–6
  cultures of 192
  disclosure 55, 60
  justice plans 182, 188, 194
  political contributions 34
  public tax returns 82
  self-regulation 179
corporatization 4, 16, 18, 23–4, 28, 30, 64
corruption 82–3, 206
Cotton, P. 146
Council of Economic Advisors (US) 6
crashes 35–6; *see also* boom and bust cycles
creative accounting 51
Creative Commons 120
credit ratings 23, 25, 29, 39, 57
criminal law, restorative justice and 77–8
criminality, white-collar 48

Daly, Kathleen 190
Day, Patricia 9
de-escalation 106
Delaware Declaration of Rights 30
democracy 81, 162, 191, 195, 205–6
  and contestability 201, 202, 203
  electoral 204
  nodal social democratic politics 199–201
  social democracy 207
  theories of 202
Denis, D.J. 36
denizenship, deliberative 202–6
deregulation 5, 8–12, 47, 48, 87

derivatives 37–40, 47, 62, 199
deterrence 93, 169–70
deterrence trap 90
developing countries 19, 28, 80–84, 133, 138
disclosure 55, 60
discretion 142, 143, 144
disputes
 characteristics of 167, 169
 cost of resolution of 172
 and large organizations 186
 prevention of 171
 relational meanings of 165–6, 169–70
 see also alternative dispute resolution
Diversity@Work 184
documentation ritualism 145–7
Dodge, C. 41
domination 171, 175, 178, 186, 204
Dorf, M. 2, 3, 28
Douglas, Michael 7, 34, 63, 69
Drahos, Peter 23
 globalization 16, 19
 intellectual property rights 114, 125, 133, 135, 139
 networked escalation 84, 96
Dunn, Leah 100
Dupont 108
Durkheim 26

East India Company 17
East Timor Commission 192–3
economics, Chicago School 5, 6–7, 10, 28, 31, 88, 197
economy
 dual economy 94
 of esteem 126
 information economy 4, 60
 knowledge economy 109–39
 liberal economy 14–15, 27
 market economies 4
 networked economy 2
 police economy 4, 11, 12–14, 27
 provider state economy 4, 15–16, 24, 27, 171
 Soviet economy 3, 5
Electronic Communications Privacy Act (US) 64
empowerment 154, 155, 162, 175

enforcement 40–41, 53, 61, 64–86
 risk of under-enforcement 71, 92
 of tax law 45, 48–9, 53–4, 69–70, 79
enforcement pyramid 76, 84, 154, 163–4, 170
Engel, D. 174
England 17
 Common Informers Act of 1951 66
 qui tam suits 66
 see also Britain
Enron 33, 34, 38, 51, 69, 79
entrepreneurs 36, 44, 55, 79–80, 119
 legal 65, 81, 180
environmental lawsuits, private 65, 74
Environmental Protection Agency (US) 9
epistemic communities 68
equality 199–200
Equitable Access Licence 120
Ernst & Young 127
Ericson, R.V. 107
escalation 76, 78, 89, 90, 99–100, 117, 129
 networked escalation 84, 94–7, 97–8
ethical obligations 58, 60, 93
European Commission 112–13, 131
European Union 25, 111, 122, 133

Fair Labour Association 83
fairness 52, 180, 186, 194
 procedural 52, 92, 176
False Claims Act (US) 64–6, 70–71, 73
 amendments to 66–7, 69, 82
 dual-plaintiff design 70
 treble damages 72, 74
family court 173, 176
Farm Foundation 121
Federal Aviation Administration (US) 83–4
Federal Bureau of Investigation (US) 38
Federal Trade Commission (US) 16, 34
feudalism 11, 27
financial instruments, trade in 37–40, 47
financial regulation, cyclical 35–6
Food and Drug Administration (US) 16, 34, 70
Forest Stewardship Council 8, 29, 95
Forsyth, M. 28

Foster, L. 73
Fox, Eleanor 31
fraud 36, 67
Free Software Foundation 125
free trade agreements 83, 111, 132, 133
freedom as non-domination 85, 91, 164, 186, 197, 200, 204–5
Freeman, Jody 7
Freyer, T. 19, 31
Friedman, Milton 6, 8, 25, 28, 66
Fukuyama, F. 6, 10

G-20 group of developing countries 133
Gaebler, T. 9
Galanter, M. 160, 174
Garoupa, N. 82–3
Gates, Bill 112, 125, 133
Gates Foundation 124, 133
Germany 19, 76, 183
Giannini Foundation 121
Giuliani, Rudolf 9, 34, 35
Glaxo 133
globalization 19, 28, 45, 48–9, 197
GNR 100–104, 105–6
Golden Rice 119, 122–3
Golden Rice Humanitarian Board 119, 122
Gorbachev, Mikhail 5–6, 29
Gorsuch, Anne 9
governance 7, 20, 26; *see also* metagovernance; networked governance; nodal governance
Grabosky, P.N. 8
Graff, Greg 119, 121
Grange (Granger movement) 33
Grassley, Charles E. 66, 79, 82
Greenpeace 184
Grant, James 44
Guarda Nacional Republicana (Portugal), *see* GNR

Haines, F. 94
Hall, P.A. 28
Havian, E. 73
Hayek, Frederick von 3, 5, 27–8
Health Management Organizations 124
HIH insurance company (Australia) 34–5
Hood, Christopher 30, 79

Hope, Janet 109–39
Hopkins, Belinda 191, 193–4
Howard, John 7, 11, 155
Hudson Bay Company 17
Human Genome Project 120
human rights 20, 26, 174, 178

identity, politics of 168
India 81, 133
Indonesia 6, 80
industry associations, regulation by 23
information 10, 46, 112–15
information economy 4, 60, 109–39
information technology 64
injustice 161, 163, 165, 172, 184
innovation 109, 110–12, 113, 115, 199
  promotion of 117, 127
  and regulatory ritualism 154
inside information 65, 79
inspection, strategic 153
integrity 48, 56–7, 70, 157, 162, 205
  of the tax system 182
intellectual property rights xii, 110–12
  blocking rights 111
  certification programmes 123
  clearing houses 114, 119, 121–2
  and foundations 132–3
  and indigenous knowledge 125, 139
  licensing 114, 118, 132
  mainstreaming intervention 124
  open-source licensing of patents 121
  patents and 114, 118, 119, 122–3, 127
  pyramid to regulate monopolization of 127–37
  reform of the law 133–4
  research clusters 124–5
  rewards for innovation 125–6
  standards bodies 123
interdependence 26, 85
interest group equilibria 35–6
Internal Revenue Service (US) 38, 71
International Civil Aviation Organization 25
International Haplotype Mapping Project 120
International Labour Organization 83
international law 136–7
International Maritime Organization 27

International Monetary Fund 5–7, 10, 17, 25, 154
  good governance agenda 20, 26
International Telecommunication Union 25
Internet 119–20, 151–2, 171, 174
Interstate Commerce Commission (US) 16
investment, market-information-enhancing 119
issue-attention cycle 32, 36

Jefferson, Thomas 30
joint-stock companies 44
Jordana, Jacint vii, xi, xii, 1, 9–10, 16, 28, 29
justice 186, 187
  access to 157–8, 160–61, 164, 171–2, 183, 185–6
  accreditation agencies 173–4
  bubbling up and filtering down 70, 85, 99, 106, 107, 115, 162, 187–95
  citizen participation in 163
  corporatized 180
  of the courts 157, 167–8, 170, 175, 188
  culture of 175, 181, 187
  deterrent 91, 158, 163
  healing and 163, 168
  incapacitative 91, 158, 163, 169–70
  of the law 70, 107, 162, 178, 187, 189
  metagovernance of 157–96
  occurrence in many rooms 160, 174, 194
  of the people 70, 107, 162, 178, 187
  private 80–84, 175
  procedural 52, 92, 176
  provision of 179
  responsive 75–9
  restorative 52, 58, 60, 75–9, 91, 158, 165
  state justice 194
  tripartite 75–9
justice plans 158, 171–2, 174, 178, 182–3, 188

Kapczynski, Amy 120
Kashoggi, Adnan 56
Keating, Charles 35

Keynes, J.M. 5, 11, 16, 27
Kilcullen, David 29
Klein, Rudolf 9
Kleinbard, Ed 51, 55, 80
Klepper, S. 51–2
knowledge economy xii, 4, 60, 109–39
Korea 6
KPMG 50

La Porta, R. 41
labour rights 74
labour standards 72, 73–4, 78, 83, 95
Lacey, Nicola 195
law
  competition law 131
  invincibility of 93–4, 99, 103
  principle-based 181
  quantity of 160–61
  rule-based 181
  rule complexity of 187
  tax law 160, 161, 166, 180
  whole of law hypothesis 165–7
law enforcement 40–41, 61, 71, 78–9, 92
  lessons about private enforcement reform 69–70
  private 45, 48–9, 53–4, 69–70, 64–86, 160
Lazer, D. 1
learning 78, 149, 155
  culture of 63, 137, 150
  triple-loop 149–50
Leeson, Nick 43
legal aid, access to 159, 173, 174, 177, 183, 188
legal opinions on tax shelters 50, 54
legal system, transformation of 170–74, 182–5
Levi-Faur, David viii–x, xi, xii, 1, 7, 9–11, 16, 26, 28, 29
liberal economy 14–15, 27
Lincoln, Abraham 66, 81
Lissack, Michael R. 71
listening 154, 155
litigation, private 64–6
Lloyd-George, David 15
Lloyd's of London 18, 23, 27
Lockheed 56

Macaulay, S. 180
Macquarie Bank 39

Index

Madison, James 162
Makkai, Toni 147
management creativity 183
managerial revolution 36
Mandela, Nelson 193
Margaret Thatcher Foundation 7
Marine Stewardship Council 96
market economies 3
markets 27
  amoral 198–9
  green 8
  and innovation 155
  market failure 28
  sophistication and innovation in 43, 50
  markets in vice 50–57, 58, 61, 197, 199, 206
  flipping 52–7
  intellectual property rights 121, 138
  markets in virtue 50–57, 58, 68, 84, 197, 206
  and continuous improvement 150–52
  intellectual property 114
  private 84
Massachusetts Bay Company 17
Maurer, S. 119
McCorkle, L. Virginia 195
McKnight Foundation 139
Means, G. 36, 40
mediation 169, 185
Menem, Carlos 5
mergers and acquisition 19
Merril Lynch 34, 51, 53, 69
Merton, Robert 141
metagovernance 11, 150–52, 157–96, 205, 207
metaregulation 11, 43, 59, 151, 157, 182, 184
  and access to justice 184, 186–9
Metropolitan Police (London) 13, 27
Michaels, Tom 120
Microsoft 2, 112, 131, 197
Milkin, Michael 9, 43
monitoring 3, 151
monopolies 2, 12, 109–10, 127–37
Monopolies Act 1948 (UK) 19
Montesquieu, C. de 13, 26
Moody's 23, 25, 39
Moran, M. 30
multinational corporations 52, 198

Munger, F. 174
Myriad Diagnostics 130

Nagin, D. 51–2
National Association of State Long-Term Care Ombudsman Programs (US) 191
National Citizens' Coalition for Nursing Home Reform (US) 148–9, 191
National Health and Medical Research Council (Australia) 124
National Institutes of Health (US) 124
National Nursing Home Residents' Day (US) 191
National Practice Guidelines on Restorative Justice in Schools (UK) 191–2
Natural Resources Defense Council (US) 73
Neglected Diseases License 120
Neocleous, M. 13
neoliberalism 1–31, 28, 142
Netherlands, litigation in 183
networked economy 2
networked governance 1–4, 138, 158, 179, 204, 207
  and qui tam suits 68, 83
  and regulatory ritualism 148–50
networks 148, 200
New Jersey Society for the Prevention of Cruelty to Animals 73
New York State Bar Association 54
New Zealand 6, 11, 102, 103
Nicol, Dianne 109–39
Nielsen, J. 118, 127, 130
Nike 95
nodal governance 205
  de-escalatory 106
  principles of 99–100, 105–6
  and the pyramid of networked escalation 97–100
  and responsive regulation 87–108
non-governmental organizations 2, 29, 64, 81, 138, 199, 200
  and alternative dispute resolution 177–8
  developing countries 84
  funding for 178, 179, 188
  as private prosecutors 73–5

and regulation 32, 40, 151, 184
   and regulatory ritualism 148–9
   whistle-blower protection 68–9
non-state actors 137, 138
Nonet, P. 162
Novartis 122, 131
nuclear industry 22–3
nursing homes, regulation of 205
   in Britain 9, 96, 134
   exit conferences 190
   ritualism and 141, 143–5, 146–7,
      148–9

occupational health and safety 75–6,
   78, 153
OECD 23
Oklahoma Ombudsman (US) 190–91
ombudsmen 26, 190–91
One-Tel 34–5
Open Source Initiative 123
open-source licensing of patents 121
open-source software 2, 112–13, 152
Osborne, D. 9
Oslander, Joseph 146
over-regulation 43

Paine, Thomas 162
Papua New Guinea 80, 81, 82, 83
paradox of discretion 144
paradox of reliability 144
Paris Club 17
Parker, Christine 149, 181, 190
   justice 70, 170, 175, 178–9, 182–3,
      184
   justice plans 158, 171–3
   metaregulation 43, 151, 161, 188
Partnoy, Frank 38, 40, 44
Pasquino, P. 30
patent licenses 113–14
patent pooling 114, 118, 119, 122–3,
   124
patents 127, 129, 134–6, 198
   blocking techniques 129
Paternoster, R. 93
Paulson Report 44
Pay As You Earn tax 24
Peel, Robert 13, 27
Peng, L. 36
persuasion 93
Pettit, P. 201, 202, 204

pharmaceutical companies 198
Philippines 80
PIPRA 121, 133, 139
Pokrywka, H.S. 146
Polanyi, K. 13
police 12–14, 27, 97–8
   community policing 100–103,
      104
police economy 4, 11, 12–14, 27
politics
   nodal social democratic 199–201
   participatory 204
Potrykus, Ingo 119, 122, 126
power
   abuse of 26, 137
   arbitrary exercise of 201
   imbalances of 174–5, 178, 179,
      185–6
   institutional 157
   organizational 187
   soft 2
Power, Michael 140–41
praise 153–4
Pranis, Kay 154
price fixing 71–2
PricewaterhouseCoopers 47
prisons 20–21, 173
privatization 5, 7, 8–11, 20–21, 87, 140,
   179, 185
professional associations 54
Progressivism 33–4
provider state 24, 27, 140
publicity, adverse 95; *see also*
   reputation
publicization of the private 7, 8
punctuated equilibria 32
punishment 92, 93, 94, 164
pyramids 58, 78, 87, 89, 90, 115, 137
   capacity-building 123
   collaboration-strengthening 115–26,
      129, 152
   education and persuasion in 129
   enforcement pyramid 76, 84, 154,
      163–4, 170
   monopoly-regulating 123
   of networked escalation 96–7,
      97–100
   partnering and 98–9
   strengths-based 96, 115, 126, 137,
      154

Qantas 39
qui tam suits 64–86, 206
　abuse of 68
　financial incentive for whistle-
　　blowers 68
　history of 66–73
　and labor standards 83
　networked governance quality of 68
　NGOs and 73–5, 151, 177–8
　private litigation and 64–6

Racketeer Influenced and Corrupt
　　Organizations statute (US) 64–5
Rai, A. 119
rail companies, regulation of 14, 15, 33
ratings agencies 23, 25, 29, 39, 57
rational actors 88, 90, 169
rational choice 92
Reagan, Ronald 5, 8–9
reconciliation 63, 189
Reebok 95
reframing 107–8
regulated state 25–6
regulation vii, ix, 4, 14, 63, 141, 145
　accountability of 186
　and big business 16–18
　and boom and bust cycles 33–5
　capture and 134, 177, 206
　collaborative 59
　conversational 59, 76
　demand for 21–2
　non-state 27
　private 22–3, 39, 40, 160, 171
　and private litigation 64–6
　public 40
　ratcheting up 20, 62
　responsive 50
　rushed reform of 41–4
　scandal and 32
　state 22–3
　street-level bureaucrats and 134, 142, 149
regulatory agencies vii–viii, 9–10, 26, 32, 198
regulatory capitalism viii, xi, 1–31, 11, 109–39, 197–207
　advantages of 206
　and alternative dispute resolution 185
　and corporatization 23–4
　cyclical nature of challenges to 32–63, 206
　democratically experimental 206–7
　financial complexity of 64
　justice and 179
　and privatized enforcement 64–86
　and ritualism 140–42
　and rural communities 73
regulatory innovation, cycles of 62
Regulatory Institutions Network xi
regulatory pyramid, see pyramids
regulatory reform 62
regulatory society 11
regulatory state viii, xi, 11, 24
relationships, human 165–6, 167, 169–70
republicanism 18, 85, 91–2, 164, 189, 199, 204
reputation 59, 62, 70, 95, 97, 129–30
Reputex Ratings Committee 57, 184
research and development 111
responsibility 76–7
Responsible Care 22, 94–5, 96
responsive justice 75–9
responsive regulation 50, 84, 129, 158, 173, 185, 205
　and alternative dispute resolution 174–7
　core ideas of 88–94
　nodal governance critique of 87–108
　presumption in favour of the lowest level of force 99
　and restorative justice 163–5
　virtues of 129, 136
restorative justice 52, 58, 60, 75–9, 88–94, 165
　access to 183
　and alternative dispute resolution 174–7, 178
　bottom-up programmes 182
　bubbling up and filtering down 189–91, 193
　conferences 77
　in criminal cases 77–8, 166
　dialogue 99
　government funding for 173–4
　problems with 188
　and responsive regulation 163–5
　right to 170
　in schools 191, 193

social movement for 204
  and tort, contract, labour or
    competition law 166
  as a win-win institution 167–9
Restrictive Trade Practices Act 1956
  (UK) 19
Rhodes, R.A.W. 1
Ribstein, Larry 35
rights
  culture of 193
  human 20, 26, 174, 178
  indigenous 177
  legal 164, 175
  welfare 177
Rio Tinto 81
risk management 23
risk-taking 37–8
ritualism, regulatory 43, 140–56, 206
  continuous improvement ritualism 151
  documentation ritualism 145–7
  participatory ritualism 148
  politics of 148
  random sampling ritualism 147
  rituals of comfort 140–41, 142, 146, 147, 148, 154, 155
  rule ritualism 142–3, 148
  scientific and technological 147
  transcending 147–50, 152–4
  typology of 141
  varieties of 142–7
Robb, John 2
Roche, Declan 190, 194
Rockefeller Foundation 121, 122, 139
Rodrik, Dani 28, 154
Roell, A. 36
root-cause analysis 41, 137
Royal Society for the Prevention of Cruelty to Animals 73
Rudd, Kevin 11
rule of law 7, 10, 187
rule ritualism 148
rural communities 30, 71–2
Russia 7, 10

Sabel, C. 2, 3, 28
Sachs, Jeffrey 28, 154
Sali, A. 119
Sandoz 131

Sarbanes–Oxley corporate law reform (US) 34–5, 44
SARS virus, vaccine for 122–3
scandal, and regulation 32, 46
Schnelle, J.F. 145–6
Scholz, John 58–9
schools, restorative justice in 191, 193–4
Science Commons 120
Scott, Colin 195
securities 17, 33
Securities and Exchange Commission (US) 69, 71
securitization 16, 18, 28, 30, 64, 197
security, privatization of 21, 185
self-regulation 15, 34, 50, 96, 198
  enforced 87
  regulated 43, 59, 61, 94, 151, 157
Selznick, Philip 157, 162–3
separation of powers 25–6, 85
shame 58
shareholders 36
Shearing, Clifford 30, 101–2, 202–3, 204
  citizens and denizens 202–4
  police 97–8
  principles of nodal governance 99–100, 104
Sherman Act (US) 18–19
Silver Haired Legislature (US) 191
Sima Qian 200–201
Simmons, R.F. 146
Simpson, S. 93
Sims, Theodore 80
Singapore 6
Slaughter, Anne-Marie 83
Smith, Adam 13, 15, 110
Smith Barney 71
social movements 184, 204
Société Général de Surveillance 29
Solomon Islands 80, 81, 82, 108
Sorensen, D. 202
Soskice, D. 28
South Africa, Truth and Reconciliation Commission 163
South Sea Company 44
sovereignty 201–2
Soviet economy 3, 5
Sparrow 106, 152
Spitzer, Elliot 34, 35, 51

Stallman, Richard 125
standards 56–7, 123, 142–4
Standards and Poors 23, 25, 57
Standards Australia 56, 182
states 3, 29, 171
  capacity of 27, 82, 84
  and intellectual property 132
  laissez-faire 15
  limits of state regulation 138
  nightwatchman state 11
  provider state 4, 15–16, 24, 27, 171
  regulated 25–6
  regulatory viii, xi, 11, 24, 87
  state failure 28, 81
  welfare state 5, 11, 15, 27, 200
Stigler, G.J. 79
Stiglitz, Joseph 6, 8, 28, 154
stock exchanges 17–18, 29, 39
stock market bubbles 33
stock market fraud 45
stock options 36–7
Stoker, Gerry 158
storytelling 166, 189, 191, 192
Strang, Heather 168, 187
Swiss Federal Institute of Technology 122
Swiss Federal Office for Education and Science 122
Synaptic Leap 120
Syngenta 122
system capacity problem 92, 94

Taiwan 26
Tanzi, Vito 48
tax advisers 51, 52, 55, 58, 206
tax, and regulatory capitalism 23–4
tax auditing, private 82
Tax Integrity Continuous Improvement Review (Australia) 56–7
tax law 160, 166, 180
tax planning, aggressive 42–3, 44–50, 51, 52
  in Australia 43, 46–8, 55–6, 60
  book-tax disclosure 55, 60
  corporate certification of continuous improvement in tax integrity 56
  education of investors 55–6, 60
  integration of private and public markets for advice 55
  legal opinions 47, 50, 54
  promoter penalties 52–3, 58
  shelter disclosure 55, 60
  strict liability 54–5
  targeting clients of 'A' list promoters 53–4, 59
tax professionals 52
tax shelters, *see* tax planning, aggressive
tear gas 101, 103–4
technology transfer 113, 138
telecommunications, regulation of 25
termites of globalization 48–9
Thailand 26, 80
Thatcher, Margaret 5, 9
3M Corporation 192
three-pronged investment 19, 28
Timor Leste 21
  East Timor Commission 192–3
  Guarda Nacional Republicana, Portugal 100
  New Zealand military peace-keepers 100, 102
  peace-keeping in 100–104
  United Nations police in 107
Tomlins, C.L. 12
Torfing, J. 202
Trade Practices Act 1974 (Australia) 195
trade unions 73–4, 75
traders 37
tragedy of the anti-commons 110–12, 127, 137
tragedy of the commons 110, 137
transfer pricing 52, 181, 182
Transfer Pricing Record Review and Improvement Project (Australia) 52, 56
transparency 7, 55, 57, 205
Tridgell, Andrew 125
triple bottom line 8
TRIPS Agreement 111, 130, 132
trust 94, 155, 167, 185
trusts 18–20
Truth and Reconciliation Commissions 63, 189, 192

Union Carbide 22, 83

United Nations
  Conference on Trade and
    Development 19–20, 138
  Educational, Scientific and Cultural
    Organization 125, 126
  police in Timor Leste 107
United New Netherland Company 18
United States
  Advanced Pricing Agreements 181
  American Disabilities Act 64
  business culture 16
  Business Review Letters 132
  capital markets regulation 40
  Citizens for Better Care 190
  Civil Rights Act 1964 64
  Consumer Product Safety Act 64
  Consumer Product Safety
    Commission 70
  corporate capitalism 18–20
  corporate tax collection 182
  Department of Justice 68, 132
  Electronic Communications Privacy
    Act 64
  False Claims Act 64–6, 67, 70–71,
    73, 79, 82
  Federal Aviation Administration
    83–4
  Federal Bureau of Investigation
    38
  Federal Trade Commission 16, 34,
    70
  Food and Drug Administration 16,
    34, 70
  free trade agreements 111, 132,
    133
  gerontological establishment 143
  intellectual property regulation 111,
    133
  Internal Revenue Service 38, 71
  Interstate Commerce Commission
    16
  law enforcement 40
  market power of 133, 136
  markets in virtue 84
  National Association of State Long-
    Term Care Ombudsman
    Programs 191
  National Citizens' Coalition for
    Nursing Home Reform 148–9,
    191

  National Institutes of Health 124
  National Nursing Home Residents'
    Day 191
  Natural Resources Defense Council
    73
  New Deal 16, 34, 40, 88, 199
  Oklahoma Ombudsman 190–91
  over- and under-regulation 44
  Patents and Trademarks Office
    135
  privatization 8–9
  Racketeer Influenced and Corrupt
    Organizations statute 64–5
  Sarbanes–Oxley corporate law
    reform 34–5, 44
  savings and loans industry 34,
    35
  Securities and Exchange
    Commission 69, 71
  securities regulation 33
  Senate Finance Committee 79
  Sherman Act 18–19
  Silver Haired Legislature 191
  state power over individuals 10
  trade officials 132
  Untie the Elderly Campaign
    148
Universal Postal Union 15
University of California 121
Untie the Elderly Campaign (US)
  148

values 91, 179, 186
Vanuatu 28
vice 51, 62; see also markets in vice
virtue 61, 62, 63; see also markets in
  virtue
virtuous circles
  of accountability 68–9
  between capitalism and regulation
    41
Vogel, S.K. 11

Wall Street 34, 63, 69
warfare 2
'Washington consensus' 6, 8, 10
Weber, Max 157, 160
webs of control 58–61, 201
welfare state 5, 11, 15, 200
welfare, state spending on 27

whistle-blowing 56, 67–8, 71, 82, 85, 131
Wiess, L. 26
Wolfensohn, James 6
Wood, Jennifer 101–2, 107
  citizens and denizens 202–4
  police 97–8
  principles of nodal governance 99–100, 104
World Bank 3, 25, 26

World Food Prize Symposium 119
World Health Organization 23
World Trade Organization 25, 83, 111, 133
WorldCom 33, 34, 79

Young, Iris 192

Zeneca 122
Zilberman, D. 121